THE MATRIX OF MODERNISM

Sanford Schwartz

THE MATRIX OF MODERNISM

POUND, ELIOT, AND EARLY TWENTIETH-CENTURY THOUGHT

PRINCETON UNIVERSITY PRESS
PRINCETON, NEW JERSEY

Copyright © 1985 by Princeton University Press

Published by Princeton University Press, 41 William Street,
Princeton, New Jersey 08540
In the United Kingdom: Princeton University Press,
Guildford, Surrey

All Rights Reserved

Library of Congress Cataloging in Publication Data will be
found on the last printed page of this book

ISBN 0-691-06651-5

Publication of this book has been aided by a grant from
the Paul Mellon Fund of Princeton University Press

This book has been composed in Linotron Caledonia

Clothbound editions of Princeton University Press books
are printed on acid-free paper, and binding materials are
chosen for strength and durability

Printed in the United States of America by Princeton University Press
Princeton, New Jersey

DESIGNED BY KAREN STEFANELLI

To Marion

CONTENTS

ACKNOWLEDGMENTS

I have benefited from the counsel of many colleagues without whose criticism and encouragement it would have been difficult to complete this project. My advisors at Princeton, A. Walton Litz, Hans Aarsleff, and Richard Rorty, helped to turn an unwieldy mass of ideas into a manageable thesis. A. Walton Litz continued to oversee the painful transformation from dissertation into book, and I speak not only for myself but for many others in expressing the deepest gratitude for his enduring support. My wife, K. Marion Schwartz, in the course of many patient readings and as many lively debates, offered valuable suggestions at virtually every stage of composition. I owe a special debt to Mark Schwehn, who helped me to rethink the major ideas of this book, and to Lisa Ruddick, who helped to bring it into final form. I am also grateful to Wayne Booth, Robert Langbaum, Lawrence Lipking, Jeffrey Makos, Janel Mueller, Michael Murrin, and Daniel Whitmore, whose suggestions for revision became part of this book. My thanks to the staff of Princeton University Press, especially to Marjorie Sherwood and Marilyn Campbell, whose gracious and steady care guided the manuscript into print.

My research was assisted by a grant from the American Council of Learned Societies, which made it possible to work at the Houghton Library during the summer of 1978. I wish to thank Mrs. Valerie Eliot and Mr. David Williams for permission to examine some unpublished materials.

Excerpts from the following works are reprinted by permission of the publishers and Literary Estates of Ezra Pound and T. S. Eliot.

Reprinted by permission of Harcourt Brace Jovanovich, Inc. and Faber & Faber Ltd.: T. S. Eliot, *Collected Poems, 1909-1962*, copyright © 1963, 1964 by T. S. Eliot.

Reprinted by permission of Farrar, Straus & Giroux and Faber & Faber Ltd.: T. S. Eliot, *Knowledge and Experience in the Philosophy of F. H. Bradley*, copyright 1964 by T. S. Eliot.

Reprinted by permission of Methuen & Co.: T. S. Eliot, *The Sacred Wood*, copyright 1960 by T. S. Eliot.

Reprinted by permission of New Directions Publishing Corporation and Faber & Faber Ltd.: Ezra Pound, *The Cantos*, copyright 1934 by Ezra Pound; *Collected Early Poems* (Michael John King ed.), copyright © 1976 by the Trustees of the Ezra Pound Literary Property Trust; *Personae: The Collected Shorter Poems*, copyright 1926 by Ezra Pound; *ABC of Reading*, copyright 1934 by Ezra Pound; *The Literary Essays of Ezra Pound* (T. S. Eliot ed.), copyright 1935, by Ezra Pound; *Gaudier-Brzeska*, copyright © 1970 by Ezra Pound; *Selected Letters of Ezra Pound, 1907-1941* (D. D. Paige ed.), copyright 1950 by Ezra Pound; *Selected Prose, 1909-1965* (W. Cookson ed.), copyright © 1973 by the Estate of Ezra Pound.

Reprinted by permission of New Directions Publishing Corporation and Peter Owen Ltd.: Ezra Pound, *Guide to Kulchur*, copyright © 1970 by Ezra Pound, all rights reserved; *The Spirit of Romance*, copyright © 1968 by Ezra Pound, all rights reserved.

THE MATRIX OF MODERNISM

INTRODUCTION

The aim of this book is to explore the affiliations between
Modernist poetics and contemporaneous developments in
philosophy. That there are such affiliations is beyond dispute.
The names of many philosophers—Bergson, James, Bradley,
and Nietzsche among others—appear frequently in studies of
the Modernist movement. But literary historians have for the
most part adopted an atomistic approach to the subject: they
generally confine themselves to individual influences or affinities, examining, for instance, the impact of Bradley on T. S.
Eliot or that of Santayana on Wallace Stevens. These studies
are often quite valuable, but they focus too narrowly on a
poet's debt to one philosopher and overlook his debts or affinities to others. More importantly, they violate our awareness that philosopher and poet alike are participating in developments that involve many of their contemporaries,
developments that may be difficult to define but are nonetheless "in the air." In this book I will propose an alternative to
the atomistic approach. Without ignoring specific influences
and affinities, I will construct a matrix that brings together a
significant number of philosophers and poets, and articulates
the relationships among them. This matrix will also provide a
new perspective on Modernism itself. It will reveal that the
stylistic features of Modernist verse—abrupt juxtaposition,
irony, paradox, and the like—were not merely accidents of
the history of taste; nor were the critical emphases on impersonality, the unified sensibility, and the autonomy of the literary text merely isolated or arbitrary phenomena. Modernist
poetics (along with its New Critical offspring) is part of a ma-

jor intellectual development that produced significant changes in philosophy, the arts, and other fields as well. This study, then, will situate an important literary movement in its intellectual context—not merely to provide new readings of familiar poems but to discover why we came to read the way we did.

It is never an easy task to examine the relationship between literature and other disciplines, but the cross-disciplinary study of modern culture is especially difficult. In the first place, we are not sufficiently detached from the object of investigation. We live in an age shaped by the very figures we are studying, and we have such a formidable array of facts before us that we often fail to see the forest for the trees. Secondly, the last century has witnessed massive intellectual changes that have necessitated the development of highly specialized disciplines. As a result of the increasing complexity of the subject matter, the closer we come to modernity the harder it is to gain more than a fragmentary grasp of intellectual life. Nevertheless, we can identify at least certain elements that transcend individual disciplines, and these elements suggest that it is possible to bring modern philosophy, poetics, and the human sciences into the same arena.

One element that I will emphasize is the tendency to pose a sharp opposition between conscious "surfaces" and unconscious "depths," between ordinary experience and a hidden realm of mental life of which we are generally unaware. This is, of course, the age of Freud and Jung, but the development of psychoanalysis is symptomatic of a larger intellectual phenomenon. In the human sciences, philosophy, and the arts we find the shared assumption that consciousness is not fully transparent to itself. It is regulated by mechanisms that define reality as we ordinarily know it.

This opposition between surface and depth takes several different forms. In the human sciences—psychoanalysis, linguistics, and ethnology—it appears as the distinction between ordinary consciousness and the unconscious systems that condition it. At the turn of the century, the human sciences were undergoing a global shift from the developmental (or "before-and-after") paradigms of the nineteenth century to the structural (or "surface-and-depth") paradigms of the twentieth. This turn from genetic to structural modes of explanation is evident in certain transitional works that display both sets of paradigms. For instance, Frazer's *Golden Bough* (1890-1915) retains a typically nineteenth-century evolutionary schema portraying human culture as a progression through successive Ages of Magic, Religion, and Science. But in the course of tracing this process, Frazer hints that beneath the surface differences there is a universal system of rituals that informs all cultures, including the ostensibly rational society of the West. Similarly, Freud's *Totem and Taboo* (1913) traces social evolution from the primal horde to modern civilization, but posits an enduring substratum of unconscious desires, which remains an inescapable (although progressively better repressed) dimension of human nature. Together, these books manifest the change from nineteenth-century theories of progressive development, which inevitably place Western society at the vanguard of civilization, to theories that stress the common foundations of all cultures, past and present, Western and non-Western, in an unchanging system of ritual behavior and psychic structure. Frazer and Freud illustrate only one aspect of a major intellectual transformation. In seemingly independent developments, the disciplines devoted to the study of the psyche, the sign, and society were reorganizing around the opposition between the world of ordinary awareness and the hidden structures that condition it.

In philosophy, the same tendency appears as an opposition between conceptual abstraction and immediate experience, or, more generally, between the instrumental conventions that shape ordinary life and the original flux of concrete sensations. This opposition is remarkably widespread at the turn of the century: Bergson's "real duration," James's "stream of consciousness," Bradley's "immediate experience" or "feeling," and Nietzsche's "chaos of sensations" all refer to a realm beneath the forms that organize daily existence. This notion of immediate experience distinguishes philosophy from the human sciences: the philosophers associate "depths" not with a determinate system of causes but with a flux of sensations irreducible to rational formulation. The difference may be gleaned from a comparison between Freud and Bergson. Both men argue that waking consciousness is ordinarily regulated by mechanisms that screen us from deeper mental processes. But whereas Freud posits an underlying system of forces that determines conscious experience, Bergson posits a deeper consciousness which is free from the mechanisms that ordinarily condition experience. In other words, the pioneers of modern psychoanalysis, linguistics, and ethnology identified unconscious "depths" with systems of hidden desires, linguistic codes, or cultural norms that shape our conscious existence. Philosophers such as Bergson, by contrast, identified these "depths" with the free flow of immediate experience that is the source of our individuality and our capacity for creative action.

The opposition between abstraction and sensation is also a prominent feature of Modernist poetics. Pound and Eliot, like the philosophers, assume that instrumental conventions displace us from immediate experience. Pound incessantly attacks our propensity to substitute conceptual abstractions for concrete sensations, and makes the precise rendering of immediate experience a cornerstone of his poetic program. Eliot also claims that poetry restores us to "the deeper, unnamed feelings which form the substratum of our being."[1] And New Critics such as Ransom and Tate argue that poetry leads us from the abstract discourses of everyday life to the essential reality that is revealed in immediate experience. Different critics develop variations on this theme, but the same opposition between abstraction and sensation, rational formulation and direct intuition, plays a central role in the works of virtually every figure associated with Modernist and New Critical poetics.

If philosophers and poets shared certain assumptions about abstraction and experience, they also proposed similar solutions to their problems. In certain instances they argue that we may escape the narrow circle of convention by attending carefully to the stream of immediate experience. In others, they claim that we must constantly create new abstractions, or new conventions, to liberate us from the old. Among the philosophers, Bergson proposes the first course, Nietzsche the second. But we find suggestions of a third course as well—the use of constructs that integrate abstraction and sensation, thereby achieving the unity of conceptual form without sacrificing the variety of sensory particulars. Pound, Eliot, and their successors adopt all of these positions at different times, but the last is especially significant. It sheds light on Pound's use of the ideogram as well as Eliot's attempt to create "new wholes" by amalgamating elements from disparate realms of experience. Like the philosophers, the architects of the Modernist tradition explored the dialectic of form and flux, and were attracted to constructs that unify concrete particulars without suppressing the differences between them. Philosophers and poets were thus addressing the same issues in much the same terms, and this coalescence of assumptions and interests makes it possible to construct a framework that unites them.

We should not forget that the opposition between abstraction and experience did not emerge suddenly at the turn of the century; its origins lie in the cultural revolution that occurred a century earlier. Bergson, James, Bradley, and Nietzsche are heavily indebted to their nineteenth-century forebears, and their innovations are virtually incomprehensible without the groundwork laid by Kant and Hegel many years before. Much the same is true of poetry, where we have become increasingly aware of the continuities between Romanticism and Modernism. Yet it would be a mistake to minimize the novelty of intellectual developments at the turn of the century. The human sciences certainly witnessed a major transformation during this period. In philosophy, figures such as Bergson, James, Bradley, and Nietzsche, for all their debts to the past, offered innovative responses to problems that Kant and Hegel did not have to face. Others, such as Husserl and Meinong on the Continent and Moore and Russell in England, exposed and decisively transformed the psychological orientation that dominated nineteenth-century philosophy. Significant changes also occurred in poetry: though most of us would acknowledge the continuities between Romanticism and Modernism, few of us would actually confuse a Romantic and a Modernist poem. Pound and Eliot each developed techniques that revolutionized English verse, and we will see that many of their critical precepts, even if they were used to support excessive claims to innovation, were part of a major intellectual turn from the nineteenth to the twentieth century. Hence, it would be wrong to insist solely on the continuities or on the discontinuities between Romanticism and Modernism. Admittedly, the drift of this study is toward the latter, simply by virtue of the fact that it examines not the literary antecedents of Modernism but its ties to contemporaneous developments in other disciplines. It is not my purpose, however, to challenge the work of literary historians who have disclosed important links between nineteenth- and twentieth-century poetics. My aim is rather to offer another perspective that may reveal previously neglected aspects of Modernism and clarify those that have been misunderstood. Such a perspective may not only enhance our understanding of Modernism itself but also help us to identify its relationship to Romanticism.

This study also touches on the relations between Modernist/New Critical poetics and the Continental poetics that is quickly replacing it. In the course of this book it will become apparent that the Anglo-American tradition is tied more closely than is ordinarily assumed to Nietzsche, Saussure, and other sources of contemporary critical theory. We will see, for instance, that Modernist views of abstraction and experience proceed from the same "inversion of Platonism" that occupied Bergson and Nietzsche in the late nineteenth century and motivates post-structuralist critics today. There is in fact a close correlation between the Modernist fascination with "functional" (as opposed to "ornamental") metaphor and Nietzsche's exploration of the fluid boundary between concept and figure, literal and metaphorical language. We will also see that there are ties between Modernist discussions of immediate experience and certain aspects of the phenomenological movement. Indeed, the expression "objective correlative" appears in Husserl's *Logische Untersuchungen* [Logical Investigations] (1900), and Eliot's early philosophical papers indicate that the poet knew exactly what he was doing when he lifted the term from Husserl. Modernism and New Criticism are thus related to the same early twentieth-century developments in philosophy and the human sciences that claim our attention today, and by placing Pound and Eliot next to figures such as Nietzsche and Husserl, we may once again see the modernity of Modernism.

■

A note on method. This book presents a matrix that brings together various authors and examines the relationships between them. Such a matrix allows us to identify both the elements that unite the group as a whole and those that distinguish each individual from the others. This procedure releases us from the limitations of a study confined to individual influences or affinities. It makes it possible, for instance, to compare individuals who have no direct ties to one another but exhibit similar patterns of thought. It can also illuminate specific features of a writer's work that influence cannot explain. No one doubts the influence of Bergson on Hulme. But Hulme's thought departs from Bergson's in certain crucial ways, and if we shift from Bergson to the larger framework in which Bergson participates, we can make better sense of Hulme's approach to art.

The procedure I am using to unite diverse individuals should not be regarded as an attempt to uncover the *Zeitgeist* or "deep structure" of a particular historical period. Indeed, in the messy world of historical events it would be difficult to determine when a period with precisely this structure originally appeared and when it came to an end. We may go so far as to say that in its pure form such a period never existed at all. Many intellectuals who flourished between the 1870s and the 1930s—the terminal points of this study—fall outside this structure altogether. They display patterns of thought that intellectual historians generally assign either to an earlier or to a later generation. Even the figures with whom we are concerned fail to conform to type in every detail. We should, therefore, be thinking less of a "deep structure" that *underlies* the surface manifestations of a particular era and more of a "model" that *overlies* a complex array of historical phenomena that defy exhaustive codification. From such a model·we can learn much, but not everything, about individual philosophers and poets. Hence this study, like Pound's ideogram and Eliot's "new wholes," will struggle to maintain the tension between the unifying form and its constituent particulars, the abstract model that bestows coherence and the distinctive qualities of each individual it brings into relation.

I will focus on two principal architects of the Modernist movement—Ezra Pound and T. S. Eliot—along with several critics who influenced them or were influenced by them— Remy de Gourmont, T. E. Hulme, I. A. Richards, and the New Critics. But it should be remembered that the principal axis of this study—the tension between abstraction and experience—is crucial to other twentieth-century poets as well. It is the central theme of Stevens's poetry, and it informs the work of Yeats, William Carlos Williams, and others. With certain adjustments this study could have included these poets, and it was in part the decision to sacrifice breadth of coverage for depth of exploration that led to their exclusion. More importantly, the figures I have selected form a group that dominated Anglo-American poetics for many years. All of them addressed the opposition between abstraction and sensation by appealing to techniques that exhibit "the swift perception of relations": abrupt juxtaposition of seemingly unrelated particulars; metaphor that integrates elements from disparate realms of experience; ambiguity that creates surprising relations between various meanings of a single expression; paradox, which reconciles apparent opposites; and irony, which reveals underlying differences between things superficially similar. In short, I will focus on the figures who espoused the poetic techniques and critical principles that rose to dominance in the first half of this century. Since that time the prevailing view of Modernism has been revised in a way that gives Yeats and Stevens a more prominent place in the canon, and future developments may do the same for Williams or others. The fact that my emphasis falls on Pound and Eliot should not be taken as a plea for an older view of Modernism or an attempt to revive an earlier canon. My aim is by no means to restore this older view but rather to offer a new perspective upon it.

CHAPTER I

"This Invented World": Abstraction and Experience at the Turn of the Century

Knowledge as Representation

At the turn of the century, many philosophers believed that they were forging a fundamentally new theory of knowledge. Announcing a major "inversion of Platonism" in Western philosophy, they claimed that reality lies in the immediate flux of sensory appearances and not in a rational order beyond it. Our conceptual systems, they argued, are not copies of eternal forms underlying the sensory flux; they are instrumental constructs that overlie an experiential stream irreducible to rational formulation. Despite the extraordinary progress of natural science in this era, philosophers (as well as certain scientists) denied that our knowledge reflects the essential structure of the external world. Indeed, the shifting attitude toward science—once the preserve of incontrovertible fact—provided the most conspicuous sign that a major change was taking place.

The new attitude toward science was a sharp break with that of the previous generation. During the third quarter of the nineteenth century, scientists believed that they would soon possess an exhaustive description of the physical universe. Building on the secure principles of Newtonian mechanics, physicists could rightfully boast of the spectacular advances they had made in thermodynamics, atomic chemistry, and electromagnetism in a single generation. Perhaps the supreme achievement was James Clerk Maxwell's field theory, which brought electricity, magnetism, and light into a unified framework and dramatized the remarkable power of modern physics to integrate an expanding range of natural phenomena. Most scientists believed that only a few minor problems blocked the way toward a definitive account of the physical world. Only a handful challenged the assumption that the laws of mechanics would eventually explain all physical processes.

The very success of the natural sciences, however, raised questions about the certainty of scientific knowledge. Well before relativity and quantum mechanics undermined the foundations of classical physics, philosophers and scientists were beginning to doubt that there is a one-to-one correspondence between scientific formulation and the external world. Paradoxically, the extraordinary pace of scientific development in the late nineteenth century actually fueled these suspicions. In 1904, William James articulated the epistemological problem succinctly:

"God geometrizes," it used to be said; and it was believed that Euclid's elements literally reproduced his geometrizing. There is an eternal and unchangeable 'reason'; and its voice was supposed to reverberate in *Barbara* and *Celarent* [mnemonic terms for the valid syllogisms of traditional logic]. So also of the 'laws of nature,' physical and chemical, so of natural history classifications—all were supposed to be exact and exclusive duplicates of pre-human archetypes buried in the structure of things, to which the spark of divinity hidden in our intellect enables us to penetrate. The anatomy of the world is logical, and its logic is that of a university professor, it was thought. Up to about 1850 almost everyone believed that sciences expressed truths that were exact copies of a definite code of non-human realities. But the enormously rapid multiplication of theories in these latter days has well-nigh upset the notion of any one of them being a more literally objective kind of thing than another. There are so many geometries, so many logics, so many physical and chemical hypotheses, so many classifications, each one of them good for so much and yet not good for everything, that the notion that even the truest formula may be a human device and not a literal transcript has dawned upon us.[1]

James drastically foreshortens the history of Western philosophy, omitting a long tradition of skepticism and nominalism. More mysteriously, he fails to mention Kant, who had fundamentally altered philosophical speculation on the nature of knowledge. Yet James believed that his generation was confronting problems that had no precedent, and that these problems arose from the spectacular rate of scientific and technical development that had profoundly transformed the Western world in the century since Kant.

The reaction to Kant reveals how the situation had changed. For example, in *Introduction à la métaphysique* (1903) Bergson agrees with Kant that the intellect legislates the forms of possible knowledge, but criticizes him for perpetuating the traditional search for a universal system of knowledge.[2] In Bergson's view, Kant merely shifts the foundation for this system from external reality itself to the structure of the human mind. While proving that absolute knowledge of *things* is impossible, Kant upheld that Euclidean geometry and Newtonian mechanics provide the necessary *relations* through which the intellect orders spatial and temporal experience. He simply replaced the static world of metaphysical essences with the equally static forms of a comprehensive science. Since he antedated the crucial developments in mathematics and physics that shook the authority of Euclid and Newton, Kant stopped short of the radical reevaluation of knowledge undertaken by his successors a century later.[a]

[a] This criticism notwithstanding, many turn-of-the-century philosophers realized the historical significance of Kant and hailed him as their most im-

The problem of geometry provides a concise illustration of this reevaluation of knowledge. For over two millennia almost everyone assumed that Euclid's *Elements* formalized once and for all the structure of physical space. The Euclidean system was considered a showcase example of logical rigor unlocking the door to physical reality. Mathematicians were never quite content with the last of Euclid's five postulates, but Euclid's authority remained unshaken. It was not until the 1830s that N. I. Lobachevsky and Farkas Bolyai, working independently, produced a successful alternative to Euclid's fifth postulate and thereby developed the first system of non-Euclidean geometry.[b] At first the appearance of non-Euclidean geometry aroused interest solely among mathematicians. But in the late nineteenth century, philosophers and scientists became increasingly concerned about the correspondence between conceptual system and external reality, and at that point the epistemological problem raised by non-Euclidean geometries began to attract a good deal of attention: How can there be more than one coherent system for organizing physical space?

At the turn of the century, the mathematician Henri Poincaré proposed a solution to the problem of geometry. In *La Science et l'hypothèse* (1902), Poincaré claims that Euclidean geometry is neither a transcript of the forms of external space, as traditionally assumed, nor is it a necessary a priori form through which the mind orders spatial experience, as it was for Kant; instead, Poincaré argues that Euclidean geom-

portant precursor. The cry of "Back to Kant" during the 1860s contributed to the defeat of mid-century positivism and the rise of the instrumental theory of knowledge in late nineteenth-century Germany. Several neo-Kantians, including Hans Vaihinger and Ernst Cassirer, espoused theories of knowledge closely related to those of Bergson and James.

[b] Euclid's fifth postulate states that if a straight line crosses two other straight lines so that the sum of the two interior angles on one side of it is less than two right angles, then the two straight lines, if extended far enough, cross on that same side. Early nineteenth-century mathematicians realized that there could be a formally consistent system of geometry that replaces the fifth postulate with a postulate contrary to it.

etry is one useful "convention" for organizing spatial relations. We should stop asking which geometrical system represents the actual order of the physical world. The question is simply meaningless:

> In other words, *the axioms of geometry . . . are only definitions in disguise*. What, then, are we to think of the question: Is Euclidean geometry true? It has no meaning. We might as well ask if the metric system is true, and if the old weights and measures are false; if Cartesian co-ordinates are true and polar co-ordinates false. One geometry cannot be more true than another; it can only be more convenient.[3] ʹ

The Euclidean system is the simplest and the most convenient for everyday needs; it works well at the scale of ordinary experience. But we should remember that we employ Euclidean geometry not for its inherent truth but for its greater utility in our daily affairs. If we depart from the usual scale of human experience, we will find that non-Euclidean geometries are more convenient:

> Experiment no doubt teaches us that the sum of the angles of a triangle is equal to two right angles, but this is because the triangles we deal with are too small. According to Lobatschewsky, the difference is proportional to the area of the triangle, and will not this become sensible when we operate on much larger triangles, and when our measurements become more accurate?[4]

When Poincaré wrote these words, non-Euclidean geometries were still the concern of mathematicians rather than physicists; they were intriguing constructs with no application to the physical world. But only a few years later Einstein began to "operate on much larger triangles" and applied non-Euclidean geometry to the magnitudes of interstellar space. By the 1920s both Euclidean geometry and Newtonian mechanics had lost their unquestioned authority. They still reigned over the world of ordinary experience, but at the cosmic and the molecular scale they no longer held sway. The world had to adjust to definitions of time and space that were unimaginable just one generation before.

Poincaré's "conventionalism" was no isolated phenomenon at the turn of the century. Many philosophers and scientists were arguing that rational constructs like Euclidean geometry were neither representations of external reality nor forms through which the mind necessarily organizes experience. Instead, they maintained that intellectual formulations are simply practical instruments for arranging the sensory flux in a convenient manner. Conceptual abstractions are in a sense the tools through which we establish intelligible order in the world around us. These concepts serve many of our existing needs, but in the future we may devise more efficacious tools and discard the ones we now use. Turning to Darwin for their model, some philosophers maintained that cognitive functions are bodily functions—practical mechanisms for transacting with the environment. The rational intellect is not a disinterested, contemplative faculty, but a complex bodily instrument for attaining practical ends. Our scientific systems arise not from dispassionate inquiry into the order of things, but from the needs, interests, and values of the inquirer. Once again, James makes the point graphically:

What now is a *conception*? It is a *teleological instrument*. It is a partial aspect of a thing which *for our purpose* we regard as its essential aspect, as the representative of the entire thing. In comparison with this aspect, whatever other properties and qualities the thing may have, are unimportant accidents which we may without blame ignore. But the essence, the ground of conception, varies with the end we have in view. A substance like oil has as many different essences as it has uses to different individuals. One man conceives it as a combustible, another as a lubricator, another as a food; the chemist thinks of it as hydro-carbon; the furniture-maker as a darkener of wood; the speculator as a commodity whose market price to-day is this and to-morrow that. The soap-boiler, the physicist, the clothes-scourer severally ascribe to it other essences in relation to their needs.[5]

There is no essential form behind the stream of sensory appearances; there are as many "essences" as there are points of view through which to order experience. What our rational constructs reveal about the world is relative to the nature of our involvement with it.

At the turn of the century, philosophers from distinct and often competing traditions converged on this instrumental theory of knowledge. A short list of the most celebrated figures of the period would include the following: the "pragmatists" James, John Dewey, and F.C.S. Schiller; the "empirio-critics" Ernst Mach and Richard Avenarius; certain neo-Kantians, such as Hans Vaihinger, author of *Die Philosophie des 'Als-Ob'* [*The Philosophy of 'As-If'*] (1911), and with certain qualifications Ernst Cassirer; the foremost representative of Anglo-American Idealism, F. H. Bradley, though again with certain qualifications; the "conventionalists" Poincaré, Édouard Le Roy, and Pierre Duhem; Bergson, with his roots in the "voluntarist" tradition of French philosophy; and finally Nietzsche, at once the child of the German tradition and its most trenchant critic. Not all philosophers supported this view, and developments well under way by the first decade of the century were already beginning to challenge it. There were also serious disagreements among those who did uphold the instrumental theory: William James and F. H. Bradley considered themselves members of rival camps; so did Ernst Mach and Ernst Cassirer. Nevertheless, the family resemblances among these philosophers are unmistakable. All of them acknowledge the instrumental efficacy of scientific constructs while denying that any one of them represents the essential order of external reality.

Philosophers of the period were eager to expose what Nietzsche called the "anthropomorphic error"—the error of identifying the practical constructs of the intellect with reality itself. For these philosophers, Euclidean geometry was only one manifestation of a habit that had plagued Western thought throughout its history. For example, in *Substanzbegriff und Funktionsbegriff* [*Substance and Function*] (1910), Ernst Cassirer examines the traditional logic that led philosophers and scientists to assume that concepts mirror eternal essences underlying sensory impressions. Cassirer maintains that the history of science is littered with misguided efforts to hypostatize new mathematical "functions" into "substances" for which we have no direct evidence. We constantly forget that these hypothetical substances, such as the "aether" and the "atom," are not realities to be explored in themselves; they are rather "instruments produced by thought for the purpose of comprehending the confusion of phenomena as an ordered and measurable whole."[6] Cassirer argues that scientists ought to abandon the search for hidden substances and remain content with purely mathematical relations. *Substance and Function* is in many ways typical of the period: while not every philosopher sought to eliminate substances from physical theory, many questioned the existence of entities like the "aether" and the "atom."[c] These philosophers were determined to expose the Western syndrome of equating scientific constructs with reality itself, the syndrome that Whitehead later named the "Fallacy of Misplaced Concreteness."[7]

In order to expose the "anthropomorphic error," philosophers posited a sharp opposition between conceptual abstraction and the flux of concrete sensations. Reality, they claim, lies in the preconceptual flow of appearances, which is irreducible to rational formulation, and our concepts, far from representing a reality beyond the sensory stream, are merely instrumental devices for organizing it. Bergson's "real duration," James's "stream of consciousness," Bradley's "immedi-

---

[c] New developments in physics, however, were about to leave them behind: while the "aether" went the way of "phlogiston" and other occult substances, the "atom" was suddenly finding strong experimental confirmation.

ate experience," and Nietzsche's "chaos of sensations"—all of these expressions designate the original presentation of reality beneath the instrumental conventions we use to order it. Philosophers varied considerably in their description of the sensory flux, but they agreed on the essential points. All of them employed the stream of sensations as a counterpoise to the abstract systems that organize reality, and they regarded it as a kind of repository for aspects of experience that we habitually ignore. The opposition between abstraction and sensation is one of the most prominent features of turn-of-the-century thought, and it will play a central role in our study of Modernist poetics.

The new attitude toward the sciences is symptomatic of a widespread tendency at the turn of the century. Many intellectuals shared the belief that instrumental conventions determine not only conceptual knowledge but every aspect of conscious life. Bergson maintains that the intellect is only one of several mechanisms—psychic, linguistic, and social—that impose instrumental grids upon experience. These mechanisms define reality as we ordinarily know it; they isolate those elements from the sensory flux that serve our practical interests and screen us from the rest. As a result, we inhabit a world that is suited to our everyday needs, but we are detached from the original stream of sensations. Bergson's opposition between instrumental conventions and immediate experience is one expression of a pervasive intellectual phenomenon, and in the pages that follow I will explore this phenomenon both in his works and in those of his major contemporaries.

Bergson, James, Bradley, and Nietzsche

Many philosophers at the turn of the century regarded conceptual abstractions as instrumental forms that we impose upon the flux of sensations. But while they employ a similar distinction between abstraction and sensation, there are considerable differences between them. Bergson identifies the sensory flux with a deeper consciousness to which we may regain access. Nietzsche, on the other hand, treats the stream of appearances not as a form of consciousness but as a blank mass of fleeting impressions—a kind of sensory tabula rasa— upon which we project the fictional constructs that order our lives. In order to take account of these variations, I will first juxtapose several views of abstraction and experience and then identify systematically the relationships between them. We will emerge with a matrix that elucidates both the similarities uniting these philosophers and the differences dividing them, and this matrix will guide us in turn through subsequent chapters.[d]

I

Beginning with his first book, *Essai sur les données immédiates de la conscience* [translated as *Time and Free Will*] (1889), Bergson distinguishes between the surface consciousness of everyday life and the deeper consciousness of immediate experience. He demonstrates that the intellect works with other instrumental mechanisms—psychic, linguistic, and social—to organize reality in a convenient and efficient manner. These mechanisms, however, facilitate practical existence by suppressing an important dimension of mental life: the brain censors experiences that are irrelevant to daily existence; language does not so much express our thoughts as arrange them for us; and to a greater degree than we realize, social conventions determine the way we act, think, and feel. A contemporary of Nietzsche and Freud, Bergson claims that ordinary consciousness is not transparent to itself; we pass our days unaware of the mechanisms that condition our experience, and are detached from a fundamental part of ourselves.

---

[d] Individual sections will be devoted to Bergson, Bradley, and Nietzsche successively. James will be introduced in each section to bring out points of similarity and difference among the group as a whole.

Bergson forcefully argues that the pressures of practical life deflect us from our own immediate experience:

> Every day I perceive the same houses, and as I know that they are the same objects, I always call them by the same name and I also fancy that they always look the same to me. But if I recur, at the end of a sufficiently long period, to the impression which I experienced during the first few years, I am surprised at the remarkable, inexplicable, and indeed inexpressible change which has taken place. It seems that these objects, continually perceived by me and constantly impressing themselves on my mind, have ended by borrowing from me something of my own conscious existence; like myself they have lived, and like myself they have grown old. . . . Yet this difference escapes the attention of most of us; we shall hardly perceive it, unless we are warned of it and then carefully look into ourselves. The reason is that our outer and, so to speak, social life is more practically important to us than our inner and individual existence. We instinctively tend to solidify our impressions in order to express them in language. Hence we confuse the feeling itself, which is in a perpetual state of becoming, with its permanent external object, and especially with the word which expresses this object.[8]

If we "carefully look into ourselves," we discover that the same object appears differently with changing moods and contexts. What we perceive is inseparable from how we perceive it. Things are permeated with emotions, facts with values, the objects of present sensation with the coloring of all that we have experienced in the past. But we usually attend to the selfsame object rather than its ever-changing appearances, and therefore lose sight of an important dimension of experience.

Bergson is not denying the existence of external objects apart from our perception of them. He is asserting that our habitual attention to the selfsame object deceives us into thinking that our experience of the object remains the same as well. Careful attention to our experience reveals that our psychic states are constantly changing, and that the same state will never repeat itself exactly. The same object, seen for the second time, is altered in consciousness by the very fact that it was perceived once before. Bergson refers to this dynamic temporality of our psychic experience as "real duration" (*durée réelle*):

> Now, if duration is what we say, deep-seated psychic states are radically heterogeneous to each other, and it is impossible that any two of them should be quite alike, since they are two different moments of a life-story. While the external object does not bear the mark of the time that has elapsed and thus, in spite of the difference of time, the physicist can again encounter identical elementary conditions, duration is something real for the consciousness which preserves the trace of it, and we cannot here speak of identical conditions, because the same moment does not occur twice. (*Time and Free Will*, pp. 199-200)

The external object is part of the material world; it is determined and extended in space. Our psychic experience, on the contrary, transcends the world of inanimate matter; it is free and develops over time. There is a profound difference between the "mechanistic" laws governing physical objects and the "vital" processes of the human psyche.

Why does Bergson insist on this distinction between the external object and its changing appearances, or more generally, between the physical and the psychical worlds? We must remember that Bergson came of age at a time when the natural sciences enjoyed an enormous prestige: the apostles of scientism, far less restrained than scientists themselves, did not hesitate to reduce the whole of reality, including human nature, to a system of determinate laws. Bergson, like others of his generation, resisted this militant scientism and attacked the various doctrines that reduce consciousness to a mere mechanism: the materialist view, which treats the mind as an epiphenomenon of the brain's physiological activity, and maintains, in the words of one proselyte, that the brain secretes thought just as the liver secretes bile; the psycho-physical method, which establishes quantitative laws correlating variations in external stimuli with variations in sensory response; and the associationist school, which uses the laws of mechanics to describe the life of the mind. The last of these doctrines had been around since the eighteenth century, and Bergson was by no means the first to attack it. But despite the efforts of Coleridge and others, associationism had never been laid to rest, and it came to the fore once again in the mid-nineteenth century. Bergson and William James revived the struggle against associationism, and their critiques of this doctrine reveal their reasons for distinguishing between the physical object and its changing appearances.[9]

The associationists, Bergson argues, begin with the erroneous assumption that the same object makes an identical impression each time it appears. They imagine that a particular house always has the same appearance, or salt the same taste, and dispose of any differences in presentation as merely secondary, subjective associations. But Bergson contends that these seemingly trivial differences make all the difference in the world. A rose is a rose, but its scent is never the same:

> I smell a rose and immediately confused recollections of childhood come back to my memory. In truth, these recollections have not been called up by the perfume of the rose: I breathe them in with the very scent; it means all that to me. To others it will smell differently.—It is always the same scent, you will say, but associated with different ideas.—I am quite willing that you should express yourself in this way; but do not forget that you have first removed the personal element from the different impressions which the rose makes on each one of us; you have retained only the objective aspect, that part of

the scent of the rose which is public property.
. . . (*Time and Free Will*, pp. 161-62)

Here Bergson exposes the tactics of his adversaries, who claim that there is a uniform rose-scent to which each of us adds a "personal element." He shows that the associationists arrive at the notion of a uniform rose-scent by subtracting the "personal element" from each sniff of the rose and retaining only "the objective aspect, that part of the scent of the rose which is public property." In other words, the associationists take the recurrent element in every presentation of an object—the object itself—and treat that recurrent element as if it made a simple, direct impression each time it appears. Bergson, by contrast, maintains that there is no reason to treat the personal element as an accidental addition to the original impression; the personal element is an integral part of the total experience. True, for practical purposes we may speak of a rose-scent that is the same for everyone. But in "real duration" the consciousness of an object is suffused with the inner life of a particular individual.

Bergson also objects to the associationist description of experience as a collection of discrete "ideas," or "atoms," which preserve direct impressions of external objects. The associationists believe that we begin with these elementary bits of thought and then combine them through various associative laws, primarily those of similarity and contiguity, to form more complex ideas. Bergson counters by claiming that "atomism" seriously misrepresents the nature of psychic experience, and leads to false conclusions about human nature itself. If we assume that the mind simply registers external things, we begin to think of the psychic world as a mirror reflection of the physical world. The associationists have transferred a model originally designed for physics to the study of consciousness, and they end up believing that human thought is governed by laws as determinate as those that govern inanimate things. As a result of these errors, they not only present a distorted image of experience but also lend support to the view that free will is little more than an anti-quated illusion.

Both Bergson and James replace this mechanical picture of distinct "atoms" with an organic description of consciousness as a continuous and unbroken flow of experience. Bergson describes successive moments of "real duration" as "permeating" or "interpenetrating" one another in a seamless temporal unity. James employs the now famous image of the "stream of consciousness":

> Consciousness, then, does not appear to itself chopped up in bits. Such words as 'chain' or 'train' do not describe it fitly as it presents itself in the first instance. It is nothing jointed; it flows. A 'river' or a 'stream' are the metaphors by which it is most naturally described. *In talking of it hereafter, let us call it the stream of thought, of consciousness, or of subjective life.*[10]

Today the distinction between the "chain" and the "stream" of consciousness would arouse little interest. But in the nineteenth century it was central to the great debate between determinism and free will. Bergson and James, like the Romantics before them, employ organic metaphors to rescue human nature from the spectre of scientific determinism. The organic "stream" of thought places psychic experience beyond the reach of mechanistic explanation.

Bergson acknowledges that the associationists are right in one respect—their doctrine accurately describes the superficial consciousness of everyday life. Since we are usually interested in the physical object rather than its changing appearances, we ignore the "personal element" of experience in real duration. Instead of attending to our deeper psychic states, which are perpetually changing in time, we apprehend a world of discrete and stable objects laid out before us in space. Furthermore, as a result of this habitual neglect of real duration, we become less like "vital" beings who are free and constantly developing, and more like "mechanical" entities that are determined and remain perpetually the same. We think and act in a practical but highly predictable manner:

The greater part of the time we live outside ourselves, hardly perceiving anything of ourselves but our own ghost, a colourless shadow which pure duration projects into homogeneous space. Hence our life unfolds in space rather than in time; we live for the external world rather than for ourselves; we speak rather than think; we "are acted" rather than act ourselves. (*Time and Free Will*, pp. 231-32)

In our daily routines we fail to act as free agents. Our thoughts operate according to laws as calculable as those that govern external things. But beneath the level of ordinary awareness there is the life of deeper consciousness that we (like the associationists) generally overlook. And it is here, in this dynamic temporal flux, that we are liberated from the habits of everyday life and restored to our own humanity. In Bergson's words, "to act freely is to recover possession of oneself, and to get back into pure duration."[e]

After *Time and Free Will* Bergson continued to develop the distinction between surface consciousness and real duration. His principal strategy was to demonstrate how the instrumen-

---

[e] Bergson's opposition between the "mechanistic" structure of everyday life and the "vital" process of real duration is one manifestation of late nineteenth-century "life philosophy" [*Lebensphilosophie*]. This movement arose in response to the mid-century habit of studying human phenomena in the same way that we study physical phenomena. Bergson, Dilthey, and Nietzsche independently asserted that the expressions of "life" cannot be reduced to mechanistic forms of explanation. Dilthey maintains that the methods of the natural sciences [*Naturswissenschaften*] must be separated from those of the human sciences [*Geisteswissenschaften*]. Like Bergson, he argues that we must replace "explanatory" psychology, which is modeled on the natural sciences, with a "descriptive" psychology that captures the "lived experience" [*Erlebnis*] of human beings. Late nineteenth-century *Lebensphilosophie* anticipates twentieth-century existentialism both in its reaction to positivism and in its aspiration to identify that which is distinctively and authentically human.

tal nature of various organic functions—the physiological mechanisms of the brain, the cognitive operations of the intellect, and the communicative devices of language—displace us from immediate experience. In *Matière et mémoire* [*Matter and Memory*] (1896), for example, he shows that the brain is not so much a storehouse of memories as a mechanism for censoring, or masking, memory and allowing "only what is practically useful to emerge through the mask."[11] It is only when we suspend the practical orientation that the mask is removed and we are restored to our deeper memories.

Bergson also views the intellect as a practical mechanism that censors immediate experience. The intellect is an instrumental rather than a speculative faculty, and its purpose is to replace the stream of sensations with a network of stable and useful concepts. Contrary to traditional beliefs, the intellect is designed not to find a preexisting reality behind the sensory flux but to project a useful grid upon it: "We do not aim generally at knowledge for the sake of knowledge, but in order to take sides, to draw profit—in short, to satisfy an interest. . . . All knowledge, properly so called, is then oriented in a certain direction, or taken from a certain point of view."[12] Hence the intellect, like the brain, is not a distinterested coordinator of experience but a mechanism that selectively takes account of certain experiences and discards the rest. It serves our practical interests, but only at the expense of real duration.

Language is another mechanism for arranging practical existence. Words like concepts are designed to facilitate practical transactions but only at the expense of immediate experience. They do not so much express our thoughts as condition them. Most of us fail to realize the extent to which language shapes the very way we register impressions:

> This influence of language on sensation is deeper than is usually thought. Not only does language make us believe in the unchangeableness of our sensations, but it will sometimes deceive us as to the nature of the sensation

felt. . . . In short, the word with well-defined outlines, the rough and ready word, which stores up the stable, common, and consequently impersonal element in the impressions of mankind, overwhelms or at least covers over the delicate and fugitive impressions of our individual consciousness. (*Time and Free Will*, pp. 131-32)

As an instrument for ordering practical existence, language compels us to express an infinite variety of sensations with a limited number of tokens, and the repeated use of the "rough and ready word" diminishes our sensitivity to fleeting states of consciousness.

The instrumental mechanisms of the brain, intellect, and language regulate conscious experience, but Bergson maintains that it is still possible to recover real duration. There are moments in our lives when we suspend our practical orientation and place in abeyance the mechanisms that ordinarily condition our existence. It is in these moments that we are made aware of the deeper psychic states that usually escape our attention. Such experiences often occur in dreams, but in waking life they are far less frequent, and we must depend upon the philosopher, and especially upon the artist, to restore us to our essential selves.

Bergson calls on philosophers to reverse their traditional role and develop not the analytical intellect but the power of direct "intuition." Philosophers should be guiding us not from immediate experience to conceptual abstractions but from conceptual abstractions back to immediate experience. Although the analytical intellect provides useful maps that facilitate practical life, intuition leads us to reality itself. Reversing the habitual function of the mind, intuition develops "fluid concepts, capable of following reality in all its sinuosities and of adopting the very movement of the inward life of things."[13] The philosopher can lead us, Bergson claims, from relative to absolute knowledge, from the world of everyday appearances to a more fundamental reality. And true to his "inversion of Platonism," he identifies this reality not with a transcendent domain of eternal forms but with the immanent flux of real duration.

As early as his first book, Bergson considered art a principal means of recovering immediate experience:

> Now, if some bold novelist, tearing aside the cleverly woven curtain of our conventional ego, shows us under this appearance of logic a fundamental absurdity, under this juxtaposition of simple states an infinite permeation of a thousand different impressions which have already ceased to exist the instant they are named, we commend him for having known us better than we knew ourselves. (*Time and Free Will*, p. 133)

Anticipating the stream-of-consciousness novel, Bergson envisions a mode of writing that reveals the flow of experience beneath the surface of everyday awareness. Of course, the novelist must use language, a medium designed for practical transactions, and therefore cannot communicate the deeper life of consciousness directly. But through his capacity to use words more skillfully than others, the artist may lead us back to real duration: "Encouraged by him, we have put aside for an instant the veil which we interposed between our consciousness and ourselves. He has brought us back into our own presence" (*Time and Free Will*, p. 134).

Bergson's ideas about art, intuition, and experience enjoyed an enormous vogue in the early twentieth century. They were especially popular during the half-decade before the outbreak of World War I—the formative years of the Modernist movement in England.[f] In 1909 T. E. Hulme be-

---

[f] Bergson's international reputation was based largely on *L'Évolution créatrice* (1907), where he extended "vitalism" from the domain of mental life to the processes of nature itself. His postulate of a spontaneous creative impetus, the *élan vital*, which raises organic life to ever higher forms of development, dispelled the threatening implications of Darwinism: it incorporated the theory of biological evolution into a cosmology that reaffirmed the spiritual aspirations of humankind. However, popular enthusiasm for this vision of progressive development disintegrated rapidly as the First World War

gan to use Bergson's aesthetics to justify Imagist poetry, maintaining that images restore us to immediate experience. Hulme's lectures were attended by Ezra Pound, who commented favorably upon them, and certain critics detect Bergsonian elements in Pound's early works. T. S. Eliot attended Bergson's own lectures in 1910-11, and passages from "Rhapsody on a Windy Night" and other poems from that period reveal the imprint of Bergson's philosophy. Furthermore, all of these writers stress the opposition between intellectual abstraction and concrete sensation; they share Bergson's belief that art is a principal means of lifting the veil of conventions interposed between us and our immediate experience.

It would be a mistake, however, to identify Modernism too closely with Bergson's theory of art or attribute too much to his influence. Other philosophers of this period also stress the opposition between abstraction and experience, and in some cases their influence on particular poets is greater than Bergson's. T. S. Eliot, as we shall see, owes far more to Bradley's formulation of this distinction than to Bergson's. Even T. E. Hulme supplemented Bergson with Nietzsche, and his approach to art seems strangely un-Bergsonian until we see how he amalgamates these two philosophers. Hence, we should not consider Bergson in isolation from other philosophers; rather we should view him as one participant in a development that includes other philosophers as well.

II

Few of us today are familiar with the works of F. H. Bradley. Once the most respected philosopher in Great Britain, he fared badly at the hands of G. E. Moore and Bertrand Russell, and the triumph of the new philosophy guaranteed the eclipse of his reputation. Those who are acquainted with Bradley think of him more as a figure of the nineteenth cen-

---

dragged on, and Bergson's philosophy would never again command the attention it did before 1914.

tury rather than the twentieth, and rarely associate him with the views of Bergson, James, or Nietzsche. Even in his own time he appeared to represent a more traditional cast of mind than those who were transforming Western philosophy. Indeed, for many years he quarreled with William James and the newfangled pragmatism he espoused. Yet in certain respects Bradley is closely related to his innovative contemporaries. With certain qualifications, he upholds an instrumental theory of knowledge, and the opposition between abstraction and experience is central to his thought. We should, therefore, consider the common ground he shares with others as well as the distinctive features of his own philosophy.

Bradley's "immediate experience" has much in common with Bergson's "real duration" and James's "stream of consciousness." Like its counterparts, "immediate experience" points to the original and undivided "whole of feeling" beneath the level of common awareness. Bradley also joins Bergson and James in attacking the associationists for describing experience as a bundle of discrete atoms. He claims that if we put aside our theories and turn to experience itself, we find not a collection of separate impressions but "a continuous mass of presentation in which the separation of a single element from all context is never observed."[14] Beyond these points of agreement, however, there are certain differences between Bradley and his contemporaries. Bergson and James identify the stream of sensations by distinguishing the self-same object from its changing appearances. Thus they *presuppose* the external object in the very effort to show that consciousness is not a mere reflection of that object. Bradley, on the other hand, thinks of immediate experience as the original whole from which we subsequently derive the very distinction between consciousness and its objects. In immediate experience the internal "I" and the external "world" are still one; we can speak neither of conscious subjects nor of physical objects since the two have not yet been distinguished. Immediate experience is not a form of consciousness but the undifferentiated totality that we inevitably divide into the categories which organize our existence.[g]

In his metaphysical treatise, *Appearance and Reality* (1893), Bradley argues that immediate experience is the foundation of all our knowledge, but that it is "most imperfect and unstable, and its inconsistencies lead us at once to transcend it. . . . we hardly possess it as more than that which we are in the act of losing."[15] As a result of this instability, we find ourselves conscious subjects in a world of objects, minds attempting to comprehend an external reality. Unfortunately, the intellect is not equal to the task; it must use concepts and procedures that misrepresent the reality it is supposed to explain. In the first section of *Appearance and Reality*, Bradley demonstrates that the fundamental concepts of philosophy, science, and common sense—causation, space and time, primary and secondary qualities, even the self and the physical object—cannot withstand logical analysis and must be relegated to the wreckage of mere "appearances." Such concepts are "a makeshift, a device, a mere practical compromise, most necessary, but in the end most indefensible" (*Appearance and Reality*, p. 28). Once we depart from immediate experience, the rational intellect can provide only convenient fictions. We are compelled to distort reality in our efforts to explain it.

In contrast to the fragmented world of appearances, Bradley presents his notion of the Absolute, which synthesizes immediate experience and conceptual thought into an inclusive whole: "There somehow, we do not know how, what we think is perceived. Everything there is merged and reabsorbed in an experience intuitive, at once and in itself, of both ideas and facts" (*Appearance and Reality*, p. 246). Brad-

---

[g] In his later writings, James moves a step closer to Bradley by claiming that the sensory flux precedes the division of experience into subjective and objective worlds: "The instant field of the present is at all times what I call the 'pure' experience. It is only virtually or potentially either object or subject as yet" (*Essays in Radical Empiricism* [Cambridge, Mass.: Harvard University Press, 1976], p. 13).

ley maintains that the Absolute is not some higher reality beyond the world of experience. The Absolute—and on this point his opponents refused to take him seriously—is experience, the undivided whole of immediate experience raised to a level that includes but transcends the fragmentary formulations of the intellect:

> And we found that this Absolute is experience, because that is really what we mean when we predicate or speak of anything. It is not one-sided experience, as mere volition or mere thought; but it is a whole superior to and embracing all incomplete forms of life. This whole must be immediate like feeling, but not, like feeling, immediate at a level below distinction and relation. The Absolute is immediate as holding and transcending these differences. (*Appearance and Reality*, p. 213)

The Absolute is radically immanent: "The Absolute *is* its appearances, it really is all and every one of them" (*Appearance and Reality*, p. 431). For Bradley, it is the totality that reveals to us the limits of any and all of our useful but ultimately fictitious concepts.

Other philosophers considered the Absolute an embarrassing relic of the past. It especially piqued William James, who debated Bradley in the journal *Mind* for nearly a decade. James accuses Bradley of measuring the instrumental truths of the intellect—the only truths we have—by the standard of an archaic rationalism that deems them mere "fictions" or "convenient mythologies." James argues that concepts are true insofar as they guide us successfully through the sensory flux: "True ideas are those that we can assimilate, validate, corroborate and verify. False ideas are those that we cannot."[16] The only criterion we have for measuring the truth of our concepts is whether or not they actually "work."

Bradley, for his part, agrees that concepts are essentially useful instruments, and that "any idea which in any way 'works,' has in some sense truth."[17] But he refuses to go the full distance with James by equating truth with instrumental efficacy. Philosophy, he claims, is an activity pursued for theoretical rather than practical satisfaction: the rational cannot be reduced to the instrumental, the logical to the psychological. In the quest for truth philosophers are concerned less with the utility than with the logical consistency of concepts, even if that pursuit leads them to recognize the limits of the rational intellect itself.

Despite the intensity of their debate, Bradley and James were not as far apart as they imagined, and many philosophers of the next generation treated their famous confrontation as a family quarrel. There are certainly areas of profound disagreement: James contends that successful concepts disclose *real* relations in the sensory flux; Bradley insists that all relations are *ideal*, that is to say, imposed upon experience by the mind. Whereas James stresses the unlimited prospects for discovering new and more fruitful conceptual schemas, Bradley dwells more on the limitations of any one schema. These differences are fundamental, and we should not minimize their significance. But from a certain vantage point the differences are largely a matter of emphasis. Both James and Bradley agree that conceptual formulations are essentially practical instruments that in some sense misrepresent reality as it originally appears in immediate experience.

Thus Bradley's thought was far less antiquated than James led his contemporaries to believe. Writing in the language of his own philosophical tradition, he adopted a view of knowledge and experience that was very similar to those of other turn-of-the-century philosophers. His retention of the Absolute notwithstanding, Bradley belongs in the company of Bergson, James, Nietzsche, and other philosophers who were challenging traditional assumptions about mind and reality.

Unlike Bergson, James, and Nietzsche, Bradley never became an international celebrity; he was a philosopher read mostly by other philosophers. Nonetheless, he occupies a special place among the philosophers affiliated with Modernist poetics. Bradley was the subject of T. S. Eliot's doctoral dissertation, and his influence on Eliot's thought was profound. Unfortunately, the nature of this influence has been misunderstood and its extent underestimated. As we shall see, Bradley's philosophy—or more precisely, Eliot's approach to Bradley's philosophy—illuminates the key terms and arguments of Eliot's early criticism. It is true that Eliot makes certain assumptions about abstraction and experience that are simply the common fare of the period. But Bradley's thought has its own distinctive character, and his account of the relationship between abstraction and experience sheds considerable light on Eliot's essays.

III

Unlike Bradley, Nietzsche continued to attract attention after his death and still does so today. Indeed, his writings have been so influential in recent years that the "New Nietzsche" is hailed as one of the great prophets of contemporary thought. Yet in our singular fascination with this philosopher we often forget that he was also a man of his age. Like Bergson, James, and Bradley, Nietzsche employs the distinction between the conventions of ordinary life and the flux of sensations. He, too, espouses the instrumental theory of knowledge so typical of the period. To be sure, the differences between Nietzsche and his contemporaries are often quite striking, and in certain respects he is a unique and prophetic figure. Nevertheless, the similarities are equally compelling, and they suggest that we may regard his work as another variant of a common philosophical tendency.

Nietzsche describes the sensory flux as a "chaos of sensations." Like "real duration," "stream of consciousness," and "immediate experience," the "chaos of sensations" serves as a counterpoise to the conventions that organize everyday life. It points to a reality beneath the surface forms of ordinary consciousness. Unlike Bergson and James, however, Nietzsche refuses to identify the sensory flux with a psychic realm to which we must regain access; for him the flux is simply an indifferent mass of fleeting impressions, "the formless unformulable world of the chaos of sensations."[18] While Bergson and James equate the stream of appearances with a deeper consciousness, Nietzsche denies that we ever have access to unmediated sensations and contends that consciousness is always "arranged, simplified, schematized, interpreted through and through" (*The Will to Power*, pp. 263-64). Bradley makes the same criticism of Bergson and James, but his "immediate experience" is also a far cry from Nietzsche's "chaos of sensations." Bradley in fact uses the notion of immediate experience to support his vision of the Absolute: immediate experience presents reality as the original undivided whole to be recovered at a higher level. For Nietzsche, this preoccupation with the unity of immediate experience is merely a vestige of metaphysical thinking. Insofar as we find unity in the chaotic stream of sensations, it is we who have introduced it.

The differences between Nietzsche's "chaos of sensations" and Bergson's "real duration" are especially striking. At first glance they appear remarkably similar: both Bergson and Nietzsche emphasize Becoming over Being, the irrational stream of "life" over timeless rational essences. They also posit a similar dichotomy between the static abstractions of the intellect and the dynamic flux of sensations. But real duration and the chaos of sensations are not the same, and the differences between them are magnified when we consider the cosmologies to which they gave rise. Whereas Bergson's real duration evolved into the cosmic *élan vital*, which raises "life" to progressively higher forms of development, Nietzsche's chaos of sensations became a cosmic "sea of forces flowing and rushing together, eternally changing, eternally flooding back" (*The Will to Power*, p. 550) with no progressive development or coherent purpose. Here the seemingly inconsequential differences grow into a stark contrast: Bergson is attempting to establish a new foundation for Western metaphysics; Nietzsche, on the other hand, is struggling to overcome metaphysical thinking entirely.

From Nietzsche's perspective, Bergson's inversion of Platonism is a thinly veiled expression of Platonism itself. The metaphysician's homeland has merely transferred its locale from the transcendent world of eternal Forms to the imma-nent surge of the *élan vital*. Having discredited the tradi-tional assumption that there is an unchanging reality reflected in the structures of the rational intellect, Bergson relocates metaphysical reality in the irrational stream of "life," which is accessible through direct intuition. The *élan vital* is simply an ingenious way of perpetuating the traditional aims of West-ern metaphysics. Nietzsche, for his part, also celebrates the ceaseless flux of "life," but he strives to eradicate all traces of metaphysical thinking from his vision of cosmic Becoming. For him "life" manifests itself in the perpetual expressions of "will to power" that bring forth new forms of organizing, in-terpreting, and mastering reality. At first the expression "will to power" seems no different from any other metaphysical notion: it reduces all of reality to a single governing principle. But soon we realize that Nietzsche is using this notion to undermine metaphysics itself. Will to power is the produc-tion of forms that express no underlying unity, the perpetual creation of new modes of life that manifest no universal prin-ciple, the ceaseless play of differences without ultimate iden-tity. And in response to this undirected cosmic flux with no first cause and no final goal, Nietzsche calls for the bold affir-mation of life, the proud assertion of our power to lay down new values, new interpretations, new forms that create and sustain a self-authenticating existence.

Nietzsche maintains that the Platonic (and Judaeo-Chris-tian) ethos of the West is "a special case of will to power." Platonism is an expression of will to power that maintains dominion paradoxically by denying will to power. It demands that we renounce our own creative impulses and conform to a transcendent reality which is the source of eternal Truth, Goodness, and Beauty. This manifestation of life negates life's creative capacities: it suppresses the inventive powers of the mind by instituting the notion of eternal Truth to which the mind conforms; it combats the spontaneous assertion of new values by demanding fidelity to an immutable Good; and it stifles the production of new (and potentially subversive) illusions by subordinating the creative imagination to a transcendent source of Beauty. In sum, Platonism is an ingenious strategy for helping humankind to "forget" that it creates the forms that bring order and value to existence.

In Nietzsche's view, Platonism had entered a time of crisis during the nineteenth century, a crisis precipitated by the triumph of the natural sciences. Like many positivists, Nietzsche was pleased that the scientific attitude was purging Western thought of its metaphysical illusions. Nevertheless, he considered the rise of positivism both a blessing and a curse, a means of deliverance from Platonism and, paradoxically, the most pernicious manifestation of Platonism itself. He recognized that for all its salutary effects the scientific outlook still manifested the Platonic "will to truth," and with devastating moral consequences. Although it discredited the vision of a spiritual homeland beyond the realm of sensory appearances, it replaced this higher world with a mechanistic cosmos utterly indifferent to traditional moral and spiritual sentiments. Identifying its own constructs with reality itself, modern science left Western man stranded in a universe devoid of any source of transcendent value. Its destruction of traditional metaphysics deprived the Platonic ethos of whatever life-enhancing power it once possessed, and thereby produced a fundamental crisis of values.

Nietzsche responds to the crisis of Platonism by declaring that the scientific account of the universe is as fictitious as any other. We have been led to believe that "truth" lies in the correspondence between concepts and reality, "error" in the failure of this correspondence. But Nietzsche claims that the very distinction between truth and error is a Platonic ruse, a ruse perpetuated by modern science:

> The aberration of philosophy is that, instead of seeing in logic and the categories of reason means toward the adjustment of the world for utilitarian ends (basically,

toward an expedient *falsification*), one believed one possessed in them the criterion of truth and *reality*. . . . one
believed one possessed a criterion of reality in the forms
of reason—while in fact one possessed them in order to
become master of reality, in order to misunderstand
reality in a shrewd manner. (*The Will to Power*, pp.
314-15)

Our conceptual abstractions do not mirror a preexisting reality; we invent the concepts through which we order reality.
Therefore, we have nothing to fear from the mechanistic explanations of modern science: scientific truths are merely expedient errors, and truth itself a special case of error.

The triumph of natural science also provides us with a new
opportunity. By challenging our belief in a transcendent
source of value, it allows us to see that we ourselves are the
sole source of Truth, Goodness, and Beauty. Reality has no
preexisting form; it is a blank slate upon which we impress
our own forms: "Whatever has *value* in our world now does
not have value in itself, according to its nature—nature is
always value-less, but has been *given* value at some time, as
a present—and it was *we* who gave and bestowed it. Only we
have created the world *that concerns man!*" Nietzsche hails
the new man who has the courage to be "*value-creating*." He
celebrates the spontaneous power "that forms, simplifies,
shapes, invents" and welcomes those "*genuine philosophers*"
who realize that "their 'knowing' is *creating*, their creating is
a legislation, their will to truth is—*will to power*."[19]

Nietzsche's response to the crisis of Western values invites
comparison to that of his contemporary, William James. During the 1860s, James suffered through a personal crisis of
scientism. He endured a long and sometimes suicidal depression, which he attributed to despair over life in a determin-
istic universe. If free will, moral responsibility, and divine
agency were all illusions, and reality reducible to a system of
determinate laws, there was little purpose to one's own existence. But in 1870 James made an important discovery.

Reading the works of Charles Renouvier, one of Bergson's predecessors, he realized that choosing to believe in free will may actually produce liberating consequences. The wish may be father to the fact:

> I think that yesterday was a crisis in my life. I finished the first part of Renouvier's second "Essais" and see no reason why his definition of Free Will—"the sustaining of a thought *because I choose to* when I might have other thoughts"—need be the definition of an illusion. At any rate, I will assume for the present—until next year—that it is no illusion. My first act of free will shall be to believe in free will. . . . Hitherto, when I have felt like taking a free initiative, like daring to act originally, without carefully waiting for contemplation of the external world to determine all for me, suicide seemed the most manly form to put my daring into; now, I will go a step further with my will, not only act with it, but believe as well; believe in my individual reality and creative power. My belief, to be sure, *can't* be optimistic—but I will posit life (the real, the good) in the self-governing *resistance* of the ego to the world. Life shall [be built in] doing and suffering and creating.[20]

Undoubtedly, these intellectual quandaries were not the only source of James's psychic difficulties, and his discovery of Renouvier did not liberate him entirely from the tendency to depression. But we should not underestimate the importance of this occasion. Out of the intellectual struggles of the 1860s James began to realize that we are free to act on postulates that support our moral and spiritual sentiments.

James's view of free will and the existence of God must be distinguished both from Nietzsche's view and from the notion that we should believe in "vital lies."[21] Often accused of encouraging others to believe things they know are false, James countered by discriminating between the "meaning" and the "truth" of a proposition:

Reducing, by the pragmatic test, the meaning of each of these concepts [God, freedom, and design] to its positive experienceable operation, I showed them all to mean the same thing, viz., the presence of 'promise' in the world. 'God or no God?' means 'promise or no promise?' It seems to me that the alternative is objective enough, being a question as to whether the cosmos has one character or another, even tho our own provisional answer be made on subjective grounds. Nevertheless christian and non-christian critics alike accuse me of summoning people to say 'God exists,' *even when he doesn't exist,* because forsooth in my philosophy the 'truth' of the saying doesn't really mean that he exists in any shape whatever, but only that to say so feels good.[22]

The *meaning* of the proposition "God exists" may be defined by its "positive experienceable operation": " 'God or no God?' means 'promise or no promise?' " If the choice were ours, virtually all of us would prefer to believe that there is hope and purpose in the world. However, the *truth* of the proposition "God exists" does not depend on whether or not we want it to be true: God either exists or he does not, "the alternative is objective enough." The complication is that we cannot determine "whether the cosmos has one character or another." The proposition "God exists" belongs to a class of statements that can be neither verified nor falsified. Since there is no way of determining truth in this matter, James advises us to act on the more desirable proposition: we have little to lose by proceeding on the assumption that there is "promise" in the world, and even in this life we have a great deal to gain.

To be sure, James does not always maintain such a clear distinction between the meaning and the truth of a proposition. On occasion he asserts that certain propositions require affirmation as a condition of verification: "The belief creates its verification. The thought becomes literally father to the fact, as the wish was father to the thought."[23] In other words, there are times when we must believe that something is true in order to see that it is. But James never asks us to assent to a demonstrably fictitious proposition simply on the grounds that it is desirable to believe it. There is thus a fundamental difference between the "will to believe" and belief in a "vital lie."

James's approach to free will and God should also be distinguished from Nietzsche's. James wagers that the more desirable of two equally possible and mutually exclusive hypotheses—free will or no free will—is true. He hopes that his subjective preference is right, but remains haunted by the possibility that he is mistaken. Nietzsche, on the other hand, discards the question of truth and error entirely; for him both alternatives are fictions, and James has simply chosen to believe a life-enhancing rather than a life-denying illusion. Both men argue that subjective interests should determine the values that guide our lives. But James is far less radical than Nietzsche; he wants to justify traditional beliefs that Nietzsche wishes to discredit, and holds to the distinction between truth and error that Nietzsche tries to deconstruct.

James and Nietzsche diverge in other ways as well. James argues that our concepts are true to the extent that they guide us successfully through the sensory flux. Nietzsche contends that even efficacious concepts are merely expedient lies, useful fictions, that we project upon the otherwise formless mass of sensations. This distinction may seem trivial at first—a matter of whether to ascribe the label of "truth" or "fiction" to the same conceptual instruments. More is at stake, however, than a mere quibble over words. James contends that true concepts disclose real relations, that is to say, structures within reality itself. While conceptual systems are human *inventions*, these inventions may lead to the *discovery* of new dimensions of the real. Nietzsche, for his part, warns us not to equate these inventions with an order external to ourselves. Intellectual constructs tell us far more about the interests and values of their creators than they tell us about reality itself. Dismissing the traditional search for a truth

guaranteed by a preexisting reality, Nietzsche declares that
we are radically free to shape our world, to create the forms
that bring order and meaning to existence.

Nietzsche's writings made a profound impact on early
twentieth-century intellectuals. His ideas were hotly debated
and found their way into the works of many artists of the
period. For our purposes, Nietzsche's significance lies primarily in his approach to conceptual and figurative language.
As we shall see, Nietzsche articulates the relationship between abstraction and sensation in a way that assigns a pivotal
position to poetic metaphor (see Chapter II). In his view,
metaphor performs the function of abstraction without leading us into the anthropomorphic error: it holds together conceptual form and sensory flux, establishing relations between
concrete particulars without erasing the differences between
them. Nietzsche's view of metaphor was adopted by Remy de
Gourmont and T. E. Hulme, who transmitted it (or domes-
ticated versions of it) to Pound, Eliot, and others. But aside
from any influence it exerted, Nietzsche's examination of the
fluid boundary between conceptual and figurative language
helps us to understand why metaphor—"the swift perception
of relations"—came to play such a prominent role in Modernist and New Critical poetics.

IV

In this section I have juxtaposed several related views of abstraction and experience, and explored some of the similarities and differences among them. It is possible, however, to
go a step further and consider these similarities and differences more methodically. I will proceed by comparing in turn
the various approaches to 1) conceptual abstraction, 2) immediate experience, and 3) the relationship between abstraction and experience. In each instance we can arrange the
views of individual philosophers by establishing a spectrum
that defines the range of possible views. In this way we can

turn a mere collection of philosophical positions into a matrix that displays systematically the relationships between them.

Abstraction.   All of these philosophers agree that concepts are essentially practical instruments for ordering the sensory flux. Yet they differ on the epistemological status of concepts. James occupies one end of the spectrum, claiming that abstractions are true to the degree that they are useful guides through the sensory flux. While no conceptual system embraces all of reality, any one system may disclose actual relations within reality itself. Nietzsche stands at the other end of the spectrum, contending that intellectual abstractions are merely fictions projected upon the chaotic mass of sensations. Between these two extremes, Bergson and Bradley (along with Poincaré, Mach, and Cassirer) assume intermediate positions. Bradley, for example, considers every abstraction at once a "partial truth" and a "convenient fiction," the choice between truth and fiction being a matter of relative emphasis.

Sensation.   Along this axis there are at least two significant lines of comparison. We can observe the relative values assigned to the realm of concrete sensations, and the relative degree to which a philosopher emphasizes the subjective or the objective aspect of this realm. On the question of values, Bergson stands at one extreme, Nietzsche at the other. Bergson attaches utmost importance to "real duration," which he considers the repository of our deepest thoughts and feelings. Nietzsche, on the other hand, attaches no value whatever to the "chaos of sensations": our authentic selfhood lies in our capacity to project significant forms upon a blank mass of impressions. James and Bradley take up intermediate stances between these two positions. James, for instance, claims to agree with Bergson, but his "stream of consciousness" merely flirts with the vitalism that eventually turned real duration into a cosmic principle. He often seems to be concerned less with the sensory flux itself than with the constructs we use to order it.

The second line of comparison—the degree of emphasis given to the subjective or objective side of experience—is more complex, and it requires the introduction of several philosophers not considered thus far. Here Bergson and the early James occupy one end of the spectrum, emphasizing the personal and subjective nature of the sensory stream. Bradley, Nietzsche, and the later James assume a somewhat different position, arguing that the sensory flux precedes the distinction between subject and object, and that the point at which we mark the boundary between them is a matter for transient practical interests to decide. But there is a third position as well, and it is occupied by philosophers who approach immediate experience in terms of the objects to which consciousness is directed. In *Principles of Psychology*, James identifies this position with the Austrian philosopher, Franz Brentano, and to Brentano's name we should add those of his two illustrious students, Alexius von Meinong and Edmund Husserl.[24] Brentano propounded the view that "direction upon an object" is the distinctive feature of mental (as opposed to physical) phenomena. Mental acts are always "intentional," or as Husserl puts it, "consciousness is consciousness *of* something." By virtue of the intentionality of mental life, the philosopher can examine the various objects of consciousness and submit the entire stream of experience to systematic investigation. Thus, as we compare individual views of immediate experience, we can establish a spectrum that runs from Bergson and the early James at one end to Brentano and his students at the other. Although all of these philosophers agree that immediate experience transcends the conventional division of reality into subjective and objective domains, their individual emphases vary considerably.

This second line of comparison is especially relevant to Modernist poetics. In Chapter II we shall see that Pound and Eliot frequently appeal to immediate experience, but that neither of them holds to a single manner of describing it. At times they assume Bergson's stance and stress the personal and subjective side of experience; at other times they adopt

Husserl's position and stress its impersonal and objective side. As a result of this apparent inconsistency, Pound and Eliot have been accused of wobbling erratically between two antithetical positions, the one supporting an overt commitment to Classical impersonality and objectivity, the other revealing a covert allegiance to the Romantic aesthetics of personal emotion and subjective expression. I will argue, however, that these seemingly antithetical formulations are not contradictory but complementary descriptions of the same experiential domain. Pound and Eliot shift back and forth between the alternatives offered by Bergson and Husserl depending upon the particular argument they wish to make. Hence, if we identify immediate experience not with the view of a particular philosopher but with the spectrum that defines the range of possible views, we will begin to see certain aspects of Pound and Eliot in a new light, and revise some prevailing misconceptions of their work.

Relation between abstraction and experience. These philosophers offer distinctive responses to the "anthropomorphic error," and once again it is possible to arrange their positions systematically. At one end are those who emphasize the recovery of immediate experience; at the other, those who stress the invention of forms that project new order upon experience. Here Bergson and Nietzsche assume the extreme positions. Whereas Bergson claims that we can delve beneath all conventions and regain access to real duration, Nietzsche maintains that we overcome existing conventions not by recovering a realm of pristine experience but rather by positing new and more productive conventions. Bradley and James occupy the middle ground. James admires Bergson and dislikes Nietzsche, but adopts a stance that mediates between them. He focuses on the interplay between abstraction and experience, arguing that the creation of new conceptual forms restores us to previously hidden dimensions of the sensory flux. In other words, James employs Nietzschean means to achieve Bergsonian ends: conceptual innovation leads to experiential revelation.

It is significant that these differences between Bergson, Nietzsche, and James also appear in their discussions of art. Whereas Bergson identifies art with the recovery of immediate experience, Nietzsche identifies it with the creation of new abstractions that impose shape and significance on experience. William James, in his occasional remarks on art, once again occupies the middle ground. Art for James is at once invention and discovery, the production of a system of relations and the revelation of immediate experience. The new work of art, like a new concept, abstracts us from the sensory stream but only to isolate a particular pattern within it.[h] Thus each philosopher's view of art varies with his approach to abstraction and experience: art may be associated with the recovery of immediate experience, the invention of new abstractions, or with the interaction between the two.

Pound and Eliot may also be situated on this spectrum. But unlike the philosophers, they range freely among all three of these approaches to art, shifting their emphasis from one to the other as the occasion demands. In certain instances, they assume Bergson's stance and identify art with the recovery of immediate experience; in other instances, they adopt Nietzsche's position and associate it with the creation of new abstractions or conventions. And occasionally they take James's middle path and envision art as a form of mediation between the abstract and the concrete, between

[h] According to James, poetic creation and philosophical conception "have the same function. They are, if I may use a simile, so many spots, or blazes,—blazes made by the axe of the human intellect on the trees of the otherwise trackless forest of human experience. . . . We can now use the forest, wend across it with companions, and enjoy its quality. It is no longer a place merely to get lost in and never return. The poet's words and the philosopher's phrases thus are helps of the most genuine sort, giving to all of us hereafter the freedom of the trails they made. Though they create nothing, yet for this marking and fixing function of theirs we bless their names and keep them on our lips . . ." ("Philosophical Conceptions and Practical Results," in *Collected Essays and Reviews*, pp. 408-409).

the unifying power of the concept and the diversity of sensory particulars it relates. For Pound and Eliot, the distinctive positions of Bergson, Nietzsche, and James are not mutually exclusive but rather complementary options. Their position should be identified not with the viewpoint of a particular philosopher but with the spectrum that embraces multiple views.

Our matrix, then, displays various lines of comparison between different philosophers. It allows us to pass from the mere accumulation of individual viewpoints to a structure that arranges these views in systematic order. To be sure, there is an element of artifice in this structure: I have established coordinates that make possible certain kinds of comparison to the exclusion of others. Nonetheless, this matrix clarifies certain relationships among the philosophers of this period, and it suggests a framework for approaching the group as a whole. In subsequent chapters we will be able to use not only the views of individual philosophers but also the structure that binds them together. While figures such as Bergson and Bradley will remain central to this study, the larger structure will illuminate various elements of Modernist poetics and lead us through its many tangles.

CHAPTER II

Elements of
the New Poetics

The same configuration that unites turn-of-the-century philosophers also unites the principal poets of the Modernist
movement. Pound and Eliot, like the philosophers, assume
that instrumental conventions shape our thoughts and feelings in everyday life. They also envision similar means of
overcoming the anthropomorphic error—the direct recovery
of immediate experience and the invention of new forms that
reorder experience. The present chapter will be devoted to
this dialectic of form and flux in Modernist poetics. I will
begin with the case of T. E. Hulme, who outlines the essential shape of the new movement. Roughly stated, Hulme synthesizes Bergson's emphasis on the recovery of immediate
experience with Nietzsche's emphasis on the creation of new
forms—both metaphors and "models"—that disclose relations
we have hitherto failed to discern. From Hulme I will turn
to Pound and Eliot, and discuss in succession their approach
to immediate experience, poetic metaphor, and the models
of nonrepresentational art, touching on some of the critical
issues raised by each of these elements of the new poetics.
The section on immediate experience clarifies the Modernist
commitment to poetic impersonality and thus addresses the
perennial debate over the relationship between Romanticism
and Modernism. The following section, which explains the
pervasive concern with radical juxtaposition, metaphor, and

paradox, reveals that there is a significant link between Nietzsche and the Modernists, and by extension, between post-structuralist criticism, so heavily influenced by Nietzsche, and the Anglo-American tradition. Finally, the section on nonrepresentational art, which explores the relationship between artistic and critical developments in the early twentieth century, deals with the controversies produced by the rise of the formalist strain in criticism. Taken together, these investigations of immediate experience, metaphors, and models show that the individual articles of the Modernist creed—the emphases on the impersonality of the artist, the "swift perception of relations," and the autonomy of the text—are more closely related than we generally believe. They reveal that Modernist (and New Critical) poetics should be regarded not as a loose collection of critical precepts but as a coherent and highly integrated program.

Bergson, Hulme, and the Image

When he began writing for the *New Age* in 1909, T. E. Hulme was already exploring the affiliations between early twentieth-century philosophy and contemporaneous developments in the arts. Only in his mid-twenties, Hulme had quickly established himself among the London avant-garde, which was about to bring English poetry, painting, and sculpture into the twentieth century. During his brief career, which ended on the battlefield in 1917, Hulme published only a handful of short poems and a few dozen brief pieces on philosophy, art, and politics. But his gift for conversation drew many artists and intellectuals to his Tuesday evening salon, and turned him into a minor celebrity. It is difficult to assess Hulme's contribution to the artistic ferment of prewar London; he kept company with major artists but was not one himself. During the Thirties and Forties, Hulme was considered a major influence on the Modernist movement. He was praised by Eliot and often quoted by the New Critics. More recently, scholars have questioned this view, pointing out that the posthumous appearance of *Speculations* (1924), which received widespread acclaim, led to the exaggeration of Hulme's influence during his lifetime.[1] The vicissitudes of Hulme's reputation, however, need not concern us here. His interest for us lies not in his influence but in his effort to find a thread that binds together early twentieth-century philosophy, Imagist poetry, and the abstract art of the Cubists and Vorticists.[a]

I

Hulme's reflections on poetry depend heavily on Bergson's theory of art. Hulme met Bergson on several occasions, and considered him the most significant representative of the new philosophy sweeping Europe in the early twentieth century. Between 1909 and 1912, he composed about a dozen articles explaining and defending Bergson's philosophy. His own translation of *Introduction à la métaphysique* appeared in 1913, and two additional essays on Bergson were published in *Speculations*. Nevertheless, we should not identify Bergson and Hulme too closely. On certain issues Hulme could be quite critical of Bergson, and he had little enthusiasm for the cosmological vision of *L'Évolution créatrice*. More strikingly, his description of Bergson's philosophy is to a certain extent a misreading of the original. In the process of explicating Bergson, Hulme often sounds as if he is discussing James or Nietzsche. And when he considers Bergson's theory of art, he presents a peculiar amalgamation of Bergsonian and non-Bergsonian elements. In order to understand these deviations from Bergson, we must situate Hulme in the larger matrix of which Bergson was merely a part.

Bergson's aesthetics provided Hulme with a starting point for his own approach to art. Hulme adopts Bergson's distinc-

[a] I will pass over Hulme's well-known critique of Romanticism and focus on some less celebrated but no less important aspects of his work.

(꒐ꗳꗳ)

tion between abstraction and sensation, and asserts that the
artist must restore us to immediate experience. But he uses
Bergson in a very un-Bergsonian manner. Bergson maintains
that the artist cuts through a network of static abstractions to
the transient stream of consciousness in real duration.
Hulme, on the other hand, seems less interested in recovering real duration than in rendering the objects of perception
as precisely as possible. In everyday life "we never ever perceive the real shape and individuality of objects. . . . We tend
to see not *the* table but only *a* table" (S, 159).[b] For Hulme,
it is the task of the artist to overcome this habit of perceiving
"stock types" and reveal the "individuality of objects."

Hulme agrees with Bergson that the experience of each
individual is different, but once again the emphasis falls on
the exact presentation of the objects of perception: "The great
aim is accurate, precise and definite description. . . . each
man sees a little differently, and to get out clearly and exactly
what he does see, he must have a terrific struggle with language" (S, 132). The artist recovers not the individual's
unique stream of consciousness, but a publicly identifiable
element of experience that others have simply failed to notice: ". . . an individual way of looking at things . . . does not
mean something which is peculiar to an individual, for in that
case it would be quite valueless. It means that a certain in-

[b] The following abbreviations are used in this chapter. Hulme: FS—*Further Speculations,* ed. Sam Hynes (Lincoln: University of Nebraska Press,
1962); and S—*Speculations: Essays on Humanism and the Philosophy of Art,*
ed. Herbert Read (London: Kegan Paul, 1936). Pound: LE—*Literary Essays
of Ezra Pound,* ed. T. S. Eliot (New York: New Directions, 1968); P—*Personæ: The Collected Shorter Poems of Ezra Pound* (New York: New Directions, 1971); SP—*Selected Prose, 1909-1965,* ed. William Cookson (New
York: New Directions, 1975); SR—*The Spirit of Romance* (New York: New
Directions, 1968); and CWC—Ernest Fenollosa, *The Chinese Written Character as a Medium for Poetry,* ed. Ezra Pound (1936; rpt. San Francisco:
City Lights Books, 1968). Eliot: CP—*Collected Poems, 1909-1962* (New York:
Harcourt Brace, 1963); SE—*Selected Essays* (New York: Harcourt Brace,
1964); and SW—*The Sacred Wood: Essays on Poetry and Criticism* (London:
Methuen, 1960).

dividual artist was able . . . to pick out one element which is really in all of us, but which before he had disentangled it, we were unable to perceive" (S, 150). Here Hulme disregards the essential features of real duration. While Bergson wishes to restore the subjective flux of experience, Hulme wants to present an objective element that all of us can apprehend.

In his misreading of Bergson's duration, Hulme displays a subtle shift in attitude, a shift that we also find in Pound and Eliot. In a certain respect, Hulme is turning from Bergson to Husserl, from the subjective to the objective side of experience. Similarly, Pound identifies concrete experience with objects of perception, and argues that the poet should express his individual feelings by presenting exactly what he sees. Eliot also demands fidelity to the object; he contrasts the Romantic poet, who expresses his inner life by creating a vague and dreamlike atmosphere, to the Classical poet, who transmutes his emotions into their "objective correlative." Although today we may object to this distinction between Romantic and Classic, we will later see that together with Hulme and Pound Eliot is participating in a shift from subject to object that marks one of the differences between nineteenth- and twentieth-century thought.

II

Like his approach to experience, Hulme's approach to poetic language begins with Bergson and then veers off in another direction. Hulme initially follows Bergson by asserting that language imposes an instrumental grid upon the flux of sensations. He also reiterates Bergson's claim that our words usually express "never the exact thing but a compromise—that which is common to you, me and everybody" (S, 132). But beyond this point Hulme diverges from his mentor. As he describes the artist's effort to recapture immediate experience, he begins to lay out a conception of poetic language quite foreign to Bergson's philosophy.

In his discussions of art, Hulme distinguishes between two

kinds of language—the "counter" language of ordinary (and metaphysical) discourse and the "visual" language of poetry. In everyday life we employ abstract "counters" that are designed for quick communication. These counters allow us to avoid the laborious process of describing each individual object in detail. We can speak, for instance, of a "table" without attending to the unique features that distinguish the object before us from others of its kind, and most of us are content to pass our days at this level of convenient abstraction. Poets, however, wish to reveal the individuality of objects, and in the process they lead us back to concrete experience. Poetry for Hulme "is not a counter language, but a visual concrete one. It is a compromise for a language of intuition which would hand over sensations bodily" (S, 134).

At first glance, Hulme's distinction between two kinds of language seems faithful to Bergson's aesthetics. Both men claim that the artist cuts through the abstractions of ordinary language and recovers immediate experience. But when Bergson discusses literary language, he emphasizes not precise visual images but the movement of verbal sequences as we experience them in time. Like many nineteenth-century intellectuals, he prizes language that approximates the purely expressive character of music. The writer transmits the deeper life of consciousness through discourse in which individual words melt into the flow of the whole:

> The words may then have been well chosen, they will not convey the whole of what we wish to make them say if we do not succeed by the rhythm, by the punctuation, by the relative lengths of the sentences and parts of the sentences, by a particular dancing of the sentence, in making the reader's mind, continually guided by a series of nascent movements, describe a curve of thought and feeling analogous to that we ourselves describe. . . . the words, taken individually, no longer count: there is nothing left but the flow of meaning [*le sens mouvant*] which runs through the words, nothing but two minds which,

without intermediary, seem to vibrate directly in unison with one another.[2]

In short, Bergson evokes the presence of real duration by appealing to temporal rather than spatial forms, musical sequence rather than visual image.[c]

Hulme, by contrast, has no interest in restoring the temporal flow of real duration. The visual language of poetry "endeavours to *arrest* you, and to make you continuously see a physical thing, to prevent you *gliding* through an abstract process" (italics mine; S, 134). Associating abstraction with movement and sensation with fixity, Hulme stands Bergson on his head by granting priority to the spatial over the temporal. Indeed, Hulme seems far more attracted to stasis rather than motion, form rather than flux:

It is as if the surface of our mind was a *sea in a continual state of motion*, that there were so many waves on it, their existence was so transient, and they interfered so much with each other, that one was unable to perceive them. The artist *by making a fixed model of one of these transient waves* enables you to isolate it out and to perceive it in yourself.   (italics mine; S, 150-51)

---

[c] Bergson does not entirely neglect the use of images. In *Introduction à la métaphysique*, which Hulme translated, he argues that images are closer than concepts to immediate experience: "Now the image has at least this advantage, that it keeps us in the concrete. No image can replace the intuition of duration, but many diverse images, borrowed from very different orders of things, may, by the convergence of their action, direct consciousness to the precise point where there is a certain intuition to be seized. By choosing images as dissimilar as possible, we shall prevent any one of them from usurping the place of the intuition it is intended to call up, since it would then be driven away at once by its rivals" (pp. 27-28). Viewed in isolation, this passage has certain ties to Hulme's treatment of images. The connection is a remote one, however. Bergson is concerned primarily with the juxtaposition of diverse images in order to guarantee that no one of them usurps "the place of the intuition it is intended to call up." For the most part, he appeals to musical sequence rather than visual image.

Instead of recovering the transient stream of consciousness, Hulme's artist makes a "fixed model" of one element in the confusing flood of sensations. Like Bergson, Hulme wishes to restore immediate experience, but his artistic instincts are in certain respects opposed to the spirit of Bergsonism.

The distinction between visual and counter language probably owes less to Bergson than to Nietzsche (and perhaps to Remy de Gourmont).[3] Bergson maintains that language by its very nature removes us from immediate experience. Hulme, however, has a somewhat different view. Introducing a historical dimension to his view of language, he claims that the abstract counters of ordinary discourse were originally concrete visual metaphors. In a review of R. B. Haldane's *The Pathway to Reality*, Hulme states that even the most refined metaphysical abstractions "were born out of humble metaphors":

> Conceive the body of metaphysical notions as a river; in the hills it springs from the earth, and can be seen to do so. But far down stream, on the mudflats where Haldane sits counting his beads with marvelous rapidity, the river seems to be eternal. Metaphysical ideas are treated as sacrosanct, and no one imagines that they were born out of humble metaphors, as the river was of earth. (FS, 11)

Following the lead of philologists who traced the etymology of abstract terms to acts of concrete perception, Nietzsche, Gourmont, and Hulme agree that "abstract words are merely codified dead metaphors" (FS, 11). According to Gourmont, "Language is full of clichés, which originally were bold images, happy discoveries of metaphorical power. All abstract words are the figuration of a material act: pondering is weighing [*penser, c'est peser*]."[4] Ordinary (and metaphysical) language is nothing more than a tissue of forgotten figures, or, in Hulme's words, "the museum where the dead metaphors of the poets are preserved" (S, 152).

Hulme, like Nietzsche and Gourmont, dissolves the traditional distinction between "literal" and "figurative" language, claiming that the former is a special case of the latter. Fresh visual metaphors "soon run their course and die" (S, 151), attenuating into the counters of ordinary language. Such counters embody the associations most useful to our practical affairs, and they guide us effectively through everyday life. But as we grow accustomed to them, we forget that they are merely "dead metaphors," and begin to equate them with reality itself. New metaphors are needed to remind us that these counters are only convenient abstractions and to restore our awareness of immediate experience. Hulme maintains, therefore, that the figurative language of poetry is not a superfluous embellishment of the literal language of fact. In his celebrated dictum, new metaphors (or what he calls "images") are "not mere decoration, but the very essence of an intuitive language" (S, 135).

Hulme provides a simple illustration of the visual language of images:

> If I say the hill is *clothed* with trees your mind simply runs past the word "clothed," it is not pulled up in any way to visualise it. You have no distinct image of the trees covering the hill as garments clothe the body. But if the trees had made a distinct impression on you when you saw them . . . you would probably not rest satisfied until you had got hold of some metaphor which did pull up the reader and make him visualise the thing. If there was only a narrow line of trees circling the hill near the top, you might say that it was *ruffed* with trees. I do not put this forward as a happy metaphor: I am only trying to get at the feeling which prompts this kind of expression. (S, 151)

A fresh metaphor such as "ruffed" establishes a new relation between previously unconnected particulars, and enables us to see one in terms of the other. A simile or a direct juxtaposition of two distinct particulars performs the same function: it reveals a new association and thereby conveys a heightened visual impression of the object. Hulme's own haiku images offer further illustration:

The flounced edge of skirt, recoiling like waves off a cliff.

*　　*　　*

The lark crawls on the cloud
Like a flea on a white body.
(FS, 217-18)

Each of these haikus first identifies the object of perception and then intensifies the visual impression by juxtaposing the object to another. Such juxtapositions establish a "visual chord" (FS, 73) that transmits the artist's perception of an object precisely as it is seen.

Hulme realizes that the visual impact of a metaphor depends upon its novelty. The once vivid metaphors in expressions like a *coat* of paint or the *hood* (Br. *bonnet*) of a car no longer stir the senses. "The visual effect of a metaphor . . . soon dies" (S, 151), and the visual language of one generation becomes the counter language of subsequent generations:

> [Poetry] chooses fresh epithets and fresh metaphors, not so much because they are new, and we are tired of the old, but because the old cease to convey a physical thing and become abstract counters. A poet says a ship 'coursed the seas' to get a physical image, instead of the counter word 'sailed.' Visual meanings can only be transferred by the new bowl of metaphor; prose is an old pot that lets them leak out.　(S, 134-35)

Many of his contemporaries would have objected to certain aspects of this passage. Hulme hastily equates prose with the counters of ordinary language, and arbitrarily restricts the production of new visual metaphors to poetry. He also reduces metaphor to little more than a means of communicating vivid sensory impressions. Nonetheless, Hulme reveals the pivotal position of metaphor in Modernist poetics. Pound, Eliot, and the New Critics may not have agreed with Hulme on every detail, but they too placed metaphor—"the swift perception of relations"—at the center of their poetic program.[d] Thus Hulme's remark—"Images in verse are not mere decoration, but the very essence of an intuitive language"— anticipates an entire generation of Anglo-American critics for whom the illuminating juxtaposition, metaphor, or paradox is the primary means of awakening us to neglected aspects of experience.

III

Hulme's approach to the "models" of nonrepresentational art is parallel to his approach to metaphors. If a poetic image fixes a single relation in the sensory flux, a work of abstract art in its totality contains a system of relations, or a "model," which reveals a new way of organizing experience.[e] In defense of the Cubists and Vorticists, Hulme posits a distinction between "formulae" and "abstractions," which is very similar to his distinction between visual and counter language: ". . . the new movement does not use *formulae*, but *abstractions*, quite a different thing. Both are 'unlike nature,' but while the one is unlike, owing to a lack of vitality in the art, resulting in dead conventions, the other is unlike, of deliberate intent, and is very far from being dead" (FS, 121). Formulae are like the counters of ordinary language—conventions that suppress immediate experience. Abstractions, on the other hand, are like the visual metaphors of poetry—forms that arise out of fresh observation: "There must be just as much contact with nature in an abstract art as in a realistic one. . . . In Picasso,

---

[d] It was common among Modernists and New Critics, as it is today, to use metaphor as a generic term for any device that establishes a new relation.

[e] Many philosophers, most notably Max Black, have shown the similarities between metaphors and models. According to Black, both metaphors and models "bring about a wedding of disparate subjects" and "help us to notice what otherwise would be overlooked . . . in short, to *see new connections*" (*Models and Metaphors: Studies in Language and Philosophy* [Ithaca: Cornell University Press, 1962], p. 237).

for example, there is much greater research into nature, as far as the relation of planes is concerned, than in any realist painting; he has isolated and emphasised relations previously not emphasised" (FS, 128). When Wyndham Lewis paints a human arm that looks like a mechanical lever, he is departing from the ordinary appearance of the limb in order to highlight its structural properties. Such an abstraction is a poetic image writ large: the poetic juxtaposition, simile, or metaphor establishes a new relation between two particulars; an abstract painting establishes a new system of relations, or a new "world," that reorganizes visual experience. Like non-Euclidean geometries, which ignore the spatial relations of the everyday world, the abstractions of Lewis and Picasso depart from conventional reality in order to reveal "relations previously not emphasised." Thus artistic abstractions actually restore us to concrete experience by illuminating aspects of the sensory flux we have previously failed to observe.

Hulme also considers a new artistic abstraction akin to a new conceptual abstraction. Both the artist and the scientist construct forms that disclose new associations: "Thought is the joining together of new analogies, and so inspiration is a matter of an accidentally seen analogy or unlooked-for resemblance" (FS, 84). At this point, Hulme has abandoned Bergson entirely. For Bergson, the concept and the artwork are radically different: the first organizes the surface level of homogeneous space into useful categories; the second penetrates beneath the veil of abstractions to the depths of heterogeneous duration. Hulme, on the other hand, takes the position of Nietzsche and James. He argues that the scientist and the artist alike provide relational constructs, or models, through which to reorder the perceptual field. The new abstractions of science and art remove us from the sensory flux but only to reveal new aspects of it.

Pound and Eliot were also intrigued with abstract art. Like Hulme, they believed that modern poetry and modern painting were closely related. The poet's "new bowl of metaphor" serves the same function as the painter's "models": it disrupts habitual forms of thought and feeling, and projects new forms for organizing experience. Pound and Eliot also discerned the link between artistic and conceptual innovation: the artist, like the scientist, presents new relational schemes to restructure conventional reality. Hulme is therefore not alone in his attempt to integrate early twentieth-century poetry, painting, and philosophy. His approach to these phenomena has its own peculiar twists and turns, but it employs the same assumptions about abstraction and experience that play a central role in the works of Pound, Eliot, and their successors.

IV

In sum, Hulme provides us with one attempt to situate art within the epistemic field articulated by Bergson, James, Bradley, and Nietzsche. At the risk of reducing him to his sources, we can say that Hulme combines Bergson's emphasis on the recovery of immediate experience with Nietzsche's emphasis on the production of new metaphors or models. Using this dialectic of form and flux, Hulme lays out the essential shape of Modernist poetics. Pound and Eliot are far more complex than Hulme, but they assume the same relationship between abstraction and experience that Hulme presents in bold relief. Hulme also shows us that Modernist views of immediate experience, poetic metaphor, and artistic abstraction are all interrelated aspects of a single program, and in the following sections, we will consider in succession each of these elements of the new poetics.

Personality, Impersonality, and the Poetry of Experience

Pound and Eliot, like Hulme, regard poetry as the presentation of immediate experience. But neither of them seems to possess a consistent view of experience. They seem unable to decide whether it is subjective or objective, or whether the artist's rendering of experience is a form of personal expression or impersonal observation. In this section I will examine the ambiguities of the Modernist appeal to immediate experience. Employing the spectrum established in the previous chapter, I will attempt to clarify some of the apparent inconsistencies and correct certain misconceptions regarding personality and impersonality in Modernist poetics.

In Chapter I we compared several accounts of immediate experience, and saw that each philosopher assumes a distinct position along a spectrum that runs from the subjective at one end to the objective at the other. Bergson and the early James stress the personal and subjective dimension of experience, the dimension that is lost in everyday life when we focus exclusively on external objects. Meinong and Husserl, on the other hand, attend to the objects of consciousness. Every mental act, they claim, is directed to an object; consciousness is consciousness *of* something. A third group, which includes Bradley, Nietzsche, and the later James, falls neither on one side nor the other. It maintains that there is no fixed division between subject and object; transient practical interests determine the boundary between *my* experience and the experienced *world*, internal sensation and external object. Immediate experience may therefore be defined as personal and subjective, impersonal and objective, or as something between the two.

Pound and Eliot also appeal to immediate experience, but unlike the philosophers, neither of them holds to one point on the spectrum. At times they describe experience as personal and subjective, at other times, as impersonal and objective. This shift from one alternative to the other indicates neither confusion nor self-contradiction: Pound and Eliot employ two distinct but complementary formulations of the dichotomy between abstraction and sensation, each of which offers a different perspective on immediate experience. Once we recognize this pattern in their works, we may clear up some of the confusion surrounding the terms "personality" and "impersonality" in twentieth-century poetics.

I

Bergson's aesthetic theory helps us to get our bearings. Although he identifies art with the expression of the personal and subjective dimension of consciousness, Bergson also reveals how art may be considered impersonal and objective. Artists are able to penetrate further into the depths of consciousness precisely because they are more detached from the practical interests that "tend to limit the field of vision."[5] Adopting a dispassionate and in a sense impersonal attitude, they are free from the instrumental mechanisms that shape ordinary experience.

Implicit in Bergson's aesthetics are two complementary ways of deploying the terms "personal" and "impersonal." We may say that artists are free from the "impersonal" conventions that organize practical life, and consequently they are more in touch with the "personal" dimension of experience we usually ignore. Bergson generally uses the terms "personal" and "impersonal" in this manner. But, alternatively, we may say that artists are free from the "personal" interests that shape everyday life and that their "impersonality" makes them more receptive to immediate experience. Eliot usually associates "personality" with the "practical and active" self, and stresses the impersonal stance that allows the artist to register impressions "which to the practical and active person would not seem to be experiences at all" (SW, 58). We have, then, two distinct but complementary oppositions: 1) impersonal abstractions/personal experience, and 2) conventional personality/impersonal detachment. Although a writer may lean toward one formulation or the other, he may without inconsistency shift back and forth between the two alternatives.

I. A. Richards provides a concise illustration of this shift from one position to the other. Richards maintains that artists are free from the practical interests that shape everyday experience, and as a result, they are receptive to a wider range of impressions than the ordinary person. Like Bergson and the Modernists, Richards formulates the opposition between abstraction and experience in two different ways. In certain places he compares the "extreme impersonality" of bad poetry to the "peculiar personal twist" we always find in the best.[6] Elsewhere, he seems to contradict this position, and claims that the artist is first and foremost detached and impersonal. But he is well aware that both formulations amount to the same thing: to say that artists are "impersonal" is simply another way of stating that they are more in touch with their "personal" experience:

> To respond, not through one narrow channel of interest, but simultaneously and coherently through many, is to be *disinterested* in the only sense of the word which concerns us here. A state of mind which is not disinterested is one which sees things only from one standpoint or under one aspect. At the same time since more of our personality is engaged the independence and individuality of other things becomes greater. . . . We see them apart from any one particular interest which they may have for us. . . . The less any one particular interest is indispensable, the more *detached* our attitude becomes. *And to say that we are impersonal is merely a curious way of saying that our personality is more completely involved.*[7]

Mutatis mutandis, Richards's programmatic assertion holds good for Pound and Eliot. Whether they emphasize the personality or the impersonality of the artist, all three share the essential distinction between abstraction and experience, and without inconsistency pass casually from one formulation of this distinction to the other.

II

In his early essays, Pound uses two distinct and seemingly antithetical vocabularies. In the first he advocates a Flaubertian impersonality and objectivity: "[Art] means constatation of fact. It presents. It does not comment."[8] Most of us allow the prevailing network of intellectual, moral, and social interests to organize our experience. But the serious artist possesses no "personal predilection for any particular fraction of the truth"; he is "open to all facts and to all impressions." Pound maintains that the artist has the same responsibility as the scientist to report exactly what he sees:

> The arts, literature, poesy, are a science, just as chemistry is a science. . . . Bad art is inaccurate art. It is art that makes false reports. . . . If an artist falsifies his report as to the nature of man, as to his own nature . . . or on any other matter in order that he may conform to the taste of his time, to the proprieties of a sovereign, to the conveniences of a preconceived code of ethics, then that artist lies. (LE, 42-44)

The English poets from the Elizabethans to the Victorians betrayed the true purpose of art. By succumbing to the conventions of their times, they transformed poetry into "the bear-garden of doctrinaires. . . . the 'vehicle' of opinion" (LE, 363). In response to his predecessors, Pound asserts that the artist, like the scientist, must remain an impartial observer: "[Art] is not a criticism of life, I mean it does not deal in opinion. It washes its hands of theories. It does not attempt to justify anybody's ways to anybody or anything else."[9]

In his other set of terms, Pound identifies art with personal expression. The source of poetry is "emotional energy" (LE, 52), which produces forms in the mind. According to Pound, Imagism is not mere description but emotionally charged presentation, and to forestall obvious misinterpretations of his ideas, he reminds the poet that "emotional force gives the image" (SP, 374). Art is above all the "expression of emotional values,"[10] and even the highly cognitive design of an abstract painting is an attempt to convey a special type of emotion.

Each of these vocabularies is misleading and must be qualified by the other. Although phrases like "expression of emotional values" and "constatation of fact" evoke opposite sides of a subject/object dualism, Pound was actually attempting to bridge the distinction between subjective and objective domains. For instance, the language of scientific objectivity leads us astray until we realize that Pound's artist is more akin to the phenomenologist than the natural scientist: "The arts give us a great percentage of the lasting and unassailable data regarding the nature of man, of immaterial man, of man considered as a thinking and sentient creature" (LE, 42). Merleau-Ponty's account of phenomenology as a descriptive psychology serves well as a Poundian manifesto: "All its efforts are concentrated upon re-achieving a direct and primitive contact with the world. . . . It tries to give a direct description of our experience as it is . . . being apparent in our desires, our evaluations and in the landscape we see, more clearly than in objective knowledge."[11] According to Pound, the serious artist records the changing modes of sentient experience; he attends to the subtle shifts in feeling and expression that prefigure a new sensibility. Insofar as his art is a science, it is the science of subjective life.

Pound's second vocabulary, which considers art the expression of personal feeling, also needs qualification. Poetry expresses subjective emotions, but these emotions are objectified in the very things we perceive. The poet expresses subjectivity by presenting the objects and configurations that appear before him in certain passionate states of mind: "Intense emotion causes pattern to arise in the mind—if the mind is strong enough" (SP, 374). Pound's famous haiku, "In a Station of the Metro," illustrates this process. Discussing the genesis of the poem, Pound states that he was moved by a succession of beautiful faces in the Paris Metro, and then attempted to render the experience artistically. In his own dualistic language, he tried to capture "the precise instant when a thing outward and objective transforms itself, or darts into a thing inward and subjective."[12] Dissatisfied by his ini-

tial efforts, he decided to convey the experience by presenting an imaginary object arising from the instant of rapture:

> The apparition of these faces in the crowd;
> Petals on a wet, black bough.
>
> (P, 109)

Pound learned from his study of classical and medieval poetry
that intense emotion may be presented through the imaginary object it induces. He praised ancient poetry in which
passionate identification with nature gives rise to visionary
images of the gods, and the natural landscape seems alive
with the presence of divine forms. Similarly, he admired the
Tuscan love poetry in which the sight of the beloved lady
causes "air to tremble with a bright clearenesse,"[13] and the
woman seems to radiate energy akin to magnetic "lines of
force" about her. Analytically, these visionary experiences are
projections of the subject's emotions onto the object; phe-
nomenologically, however, the visionary form is as real and
objective as the natural object that inspires the emotion, and
the two appear together at one instant in a vision of nature
transfigured. In this respect, subjective emotion is objectively observable, and it is the task of the poet to present the
"realities perceptible to the sense" (LE, 154) that appear under the pressure of intense emotion.

Thus Pound's seemingly antithetical vocabularies obscure a
coherent project aimed at the verbal transmission of immediate experience. At times he claims that the artist suspends
all "personal predilections" and presents dispassionately the
objects of perception. Yet, these are not objects of ordinary
perception, but those that appear in rare states of emotion.
At other times, Pound contends that the artist frees himself
from impersonal conventions and expresses personal emotions. Yet, he expresses these emotions not by telling us how
he feels, but by showing us the very things he perceives. The
artist finds "equations for the human emotions" (SR, 14),
equations that present clearly and precisely the objects correlative to special types of feeling. Whether the emphasis falls

on impersonal presentation or personal expression, Pound is referring to much the same thing.[f]

III

Eliot, like Pound, employs both forms of the personal/impersonal distinction. In his better known passages, he turns from the nineteenth-century emphasis on personal expression to a new "impersonal theory of poetry" (SW, 53). Eliot usually identifies "personality" either with the conventional self—the "practical and active person"—or with the aesthete, who loses contact with immediate experience in the course of cultivating a self-conscious persona. Unlike the ordinary person and the aesthete, the artist must be "detached from [him]self," able "to stand by and criticise coldly [his] own passions and vicissitudes."[14] Art arises not from the expression but from the suspension of personality. The poet must enter an impersonal state, a state in which the familiar division between subject and object dissolves and "feelings are at liberty to enter into new combinations" (SW, 54).

It is generally overlooked, however, that Eliot sometimes reverses his use of the terms personal and impersonal. In certain passages he talks about the impersonal conventions that obscure our personal feelings:

> . . . the ordinary processes of society which constitute education for the ordinary man . . . consist largely in the acquisition of *impersonal* ideas which obscure what we really are and feel, what we really want, and what really excites our interest. . . . Tennyson is a very fair example of a poet almost wholly encrusted with parasitic opinion,

[f] In Chapter III, we shall see that Pound attempts to recover not only his own immediate experience but also that of his poetic predecessors. The problem of personality and impersonality will thus become more complex. Through his efforts to "make new" forgotten modes of sentience, Pound produced a body of poetry that bridges the distinction between personal expression and impersonal mask, poetic innovation in the present and fidelity to voices of the past.

almost wholly merged into his environment. (italics mine; SW, 154)

This type of impersonality leads to a literary style in which words seem divorced from concrete sensation and personal emotion. Philip Massinger, for example, suffered from a "defect of personality," a defect typical of the man who has "looked at life through the eyes of his predecessors" (SW, 143). Massinger's plays exhibit an abstract and impersonal morality: ". . . when Massinger's ladies resist temptation they do not appear to undergo any important emotion; they merely know what is expected of them" (SW, 134). Massinger is the heir to a vigorous moral tradition, but his plays express "the disappearance of all the *personal* and *real emotions* which this morality supported" (italics mine; SW, 133-34). Massinger has feelings and emotions, but like Tennyson's, they are "overlaid with received ideas" (SW, 131).

We find, then, that Eliot employs two distinctions between personality and impersonality: first, the conventional "personality" (and the pose of the aesthete) versus the "impersonality" of the serious poet; second, the impersonal conventions that organize everyday experience versus the personal sensations and emotions we usually ignore. Although Eliot gave priority to the first of these distinctions, we should not for that reason overlook the second. Moreover, in a later chapter we will see that Eliot's shift between personal and impersonal sides of experience is part of a more fundamental strategy that proceeds from his doctoral dissertation on Bradley. In his thesis Eliot examines the arbitrary division of immediate experience into subjective and objective realms, and then attacks several disciplines that consider either of these realms in isolation from the other. In the case of psychology, which purports to be a science of subjective life, Eliot shows that consciousness cannot be detached from its objects. In the case of epistemology, which examines our knowledge of external reality, he shows that objects cannot be detached from the subjects who constitute them. The same pattern obtains in the literary essays: Eliot offsets excessive subjectivity by emphasizing objectivity and impersonal detachment, while he counteracts the opposite vice by reaffirming the value of personal sensations and emotions. This dialectical strategy will later help us to clarify and, in effect, to redefine the central terms of his literary criticism.

IV

For many years the terms "personality" and "impersonality" have been pressed into service either to defend or to attack the Modernist cause. The Modernists and New Critics used the idea of impersonality to emphasize the differences between Romantic and Modern poetry; the next generation of critics claimed that this self-professed commitment to impersonality was little more than a polemical ploy to mask the essential continuities between Romanticism and Modernism. The issue is an important one, but the very terms of the debate have led to the neglect of certain aspects of Modernism and to the distortion of others. Perhaps the time has come to disentangle terms such as "personality" and "impersonality" both from the self-representation of the Modernists and from the excesses of the revisionists.

From the Twenties to the Fifties, the Modernist movement was considered a radical departure from the Romantic ethos of the nineteenth century. During Eliot's long reign as critical arbiter of the English-speaking world, the modern poet was applauded for cultivating impersonality, objectivity, and detachment—in short, what were thought to be Classical rather than Romantic values. Expanding on Eliot's "impersonal theory of poetry," the New Critics shifted the focus of attention from the author to the work, from the "spontaneous overflow of powerful feelings" to the "verbal icon" itself. The artist was no longer "a man speaking to men" but a craftsman designing a complex artifact. Whether or not it misrepresented the Modernist movement, this emphasis on imperson-

ality allowed Eliot and the New Critics to drive a wedge between themselves and their predecessors.

However, as the hegemony of Eliot and the New Critics
declined in the late Fifties, a new generation of critics started
to challenge the prevailing view of Modernism. Beginning
with Frank Kermode's *Romantic Image* (1957) and Robert
Langbaum's *The Poetry of Experience* (1957), critics have
shown that many elements of the Modernist creed, such as
the superiority of the concrete image over the discursive intellect, have their origins in the nineteenth century. They
have also demonstrated that the Modernists are as concerned
with personal emotion and subjective expression as the Romantics themselves. By uncovering this previously hidden
side of Modernism and New Criticism, the revisionists were
able to dissolve the sharp opposition between nineteenth-
and twentieth-century poetics. They successfully pushed back
the great historical divide from 1910 to 1798, and reaffirmed
the priority of the Romantic tradition.[g]

Both the traditional and the revisionist views of Modernism
have their merits, and neither should be accepted or rejected
without qualification. Hulme, Pound, and Eliot were indeed
reacting to what they regarded as the excessive subjectivity
of the nineteenth century. This reaction appears in Hulme's
deviation from Bergson—his emphasis on the accurate presentation of perceived objects rather than the flux of subjective life. It also appears in Pound's desire to render the objects of perception dispassionately, and in Eliot's demand that
the artist transmute feeling into its "objective correlative."
But it can hardly be denied that the Modernists and their
New Critical successors exaggerated their break with the
nineteenth century. Overplaying their allegiance to imper-

---

[g] More militant revisionists such as Harold Bloom sought to decanonize
Pound and Eliot and replace them with Yeats and Stevens, the true heirs of
the Romantic heritage. Such critics heralded the new ethos of the Sixties by
rejecting the values of Eliot—"classicist in literature, royalist in politics, and
Anglo-Catholic in religion"—and reasserting the Romantic, radical, and Prot-
estant tradition in English literary history.

sonality and objectivity, they characterized the new poetry in a way that obscures its ties to the Romantic tradition.

The revisionists discerned this misrepresentation, demonstrating that Modernists and New Critics propagated an ideal of impersonality, objectivity, and Classical detachment which conceals a more complex reality. But certain revisionists proceed from this point to the conclusion that the Modernists simply belie their own poetic program. In their view, the Romantic elements of Modernism blatantly contradict its Classical precepts, and cast suspicion on the movement as a whole. Yet, if we adopt the point of view put forward in this chapter, a very different picture emerges. Far from contradicting themselves, Pound and Eliot articulate a coherent dialectical relationship between personal and impersonal aspects of poetry, a relationship familiar to students of turn-of-the-century philosophy. These poets shift between two complementary formulations, the first identifying poetry with impersonal presentation, the second with personal expression. To be sure, they themselves emphasized their commitment to the former, and it was the revisionists who called attention to the latter. Ultimately, however, the revisionists may have shown us not that the Modernist enterprise is self-contradictory, but that its substance is superior to its slogans.

Metaphor, Metaphysics, and the Language of Poetry

"Visual meanings can only be transferred by the new bowl of metaphor. . . . Images in verse are not mere decoration, but the very essence of an intuitive language." In one form or another, Hulme's dictum is reiterated by virtually every writer associated with Modernism and New Criticism. Pound frequently makes the same point by quoting Aristotle: "The apt use of metaphor, arising, as it does, from a swift perception of relations, is the hall-mark of genius" (SR, 158). We find similar remarks in Eliot, especially after he read Gourmont's *Le Problème du style*: "Metaphor is not something applied externally for the adornment of style, it is the life of style, of language."[15] A quarter of a century later, this fascination with the swift perception of relations was still very much alive, and it became the central focus of New Critics such as Cleanth Brooks. In varying degrees writers of every generation are attracted to metaphor, but for the poet-critics of the early twentieth century it became the very essence of poetry itself.

The swift perception of relations includes not only metaphor but any technique that displays a new relation, or what Pound calls a "comparison":

> I use the term "comparison" to include metaphor, simile (which is a more leisurely expression of a kindred variety of thought), and the "language beyond metaphor," that is, the more compressed or elliptical expression of metaphorical perception, such as antithesis suggested or implied in verbs and adjectives. . . . It is in the swift forms of comparison . . . that Dante sets much of his beauty. Thus: "dove il sol tace," ("where the sun is silent,") or, "l'aura morta," ("the dead air"). In this last the comparison fades imperceptibly into emotional suggestion. (SR, 158-59)

"Comparison" thus extends beyond metaphor itself to the entire panoply of Modernist and New Critical techniques: the abrupt juxtaposition of seemingly unrelated particulars; ambiguity, which establishes surprising relations between the various meanings of a single expression; paradox, which unifies apparent opposites; and irony, which reveals underlying differences between things superficially similar. Eliot discovered these techniques in John Donne and his contemporaries, and as the Modernist movement gained recognition, the lyric and dramatic poets of the early seventeenth century, especially Donne himself, enjoyed an astonishing revival.

It is possible to treat this fascination with "new and sudden combinations" (SW, 128) as merely an accident of literary history. Yet the works of Hulme and others suggest that this

phenomenon was closely tied to contemporaneous developments in philosophy. Hulme, for example, derived his view
of metaphor from Nietzsche, who taught him that the terms
of so-called "literal" language are merely dead metaphors,
and that new metaphors awaken us to previously neglected
aspects of experience. As we shall see, metaphor (or the swift
perception of relations) occupies a pivotal position in both the
philosophy and the poetics of the period. For Nietzsche and
the Modernists alike, metaphor is a construct that mediates
between conceptual abstraction and concrete sensation, a
form that unifies sensory particulars without losing sight of
the differences between them.

In this section, four views of metaphor will be juxtaposed—
those of Nietzsche, Remy de Gourmont, Pound, and Eliot.
These writers are united both by shared assumptions and by
a chain of specific influences. The bond between Nietzsche
and the Modernists is especially significant: it reveals not only
the affiliations between philosophy and poetry in the early
twentieth century, but also the affiliations between Anglo-
American Modernism and contemporary post-structuralism,
which has been inspired by Nietzsche's approach to metaphor.

I

Nietzsche's most celebrated analysis of metaphor appears in
an early essay, "Über Wahrheit und Lüge im aussermora-
lischen Sinne" ["On Truth and Lies in a Nonmoral Sense"]
(1873). In this piece, which has become a kind of post-structuralist manifesto, Nietzsche dissolves the traditional division
between "truth" and "fiction," conceptual abstraction and figurative invention. He argues that no concept represents a
reality beyond the flux of sensations. Even the most elementary concept is a human construct—a fiction—produced to
serve particular needs, interests, and values. Taking the
seemingly innocent example of the term "leaf," he shows that
no generic leaf inheres in nature; the term is produced by

isolating the common element in a variety of concrete particulars and then "forgetting" the differences between them:

> Every concept arises from the equation of unequal
> things. Just as it is certain that one leaf is never totally
> the same as another, so it is certain that the concept
> "leaf" is formed by arbitrarily discarding these individual
> differences and by forgetting the distinguishing aspects.
> This awakens the idea that, in addition to the leaves,
> there exists in nature the "leaf": the original model ac-
> cording to which all the leaves were perhaps woven,
> sketched, measured, colored, curled, and painted—but
> by incompetent hands, so that no specimen has turned
> out to be a correct, trustworthy, and faithful likeness of
> the original model. . . . We obtain the concept, as we do
> the form, by overlooking what is individual and actual;
> whereas nature is acquainted with no forms and no con-
> cepts, and likewise with no species, but only with an X
> which remains inaccessible and undefinable for us.[16]

Nietzsche is not denying that "leaf" is an immensely useful
concept. He is exposing the Platonic habit of identifying the
abstraction with a reality underlying the sensory particulars
it relates. We perceive a relationship between distinct particulars, and then assume that the name which expresses the
relationship mirrors a reality beyond those particular things.
In general, the Platonic tradition assigns priority to abstraction over sensation, unity over multiplicity, identity over difference. In response to this traditional hierarchy, Nietzsche
calls for a fundamental subversion of Platonism, a conquest of
the metaphysical ruse through which useful fictions are con-
verted into eternal essences. We must begin to see that our
concepts are anthropomorphic projections upon the chaos of
sensations: "If I make up the definition of a mammal, and
then, after inspecting a camel, declare 'look, a mammal,' I
have indeed brought a truth to light in this way, but it is . . .
a thoroughly anthropomorphic truth which contains not a sin-

gle point which would be 'true in itself' or really and universally valid apart from man."[17] For Nietzsche, there is no rational order beyond the flux of concrete particulars. Our conceptual forms are only human inventions; our "truths" are the "fictions" we value most.

If truth is a special case of fiction, then a concept is a special case of figuration. A term such as "leaf" is essentially a metaphor—the imaginative apprehension of a relationship between distinct particulars. Our concepts are the figures we use to organize the otherwise chaotic flux of sensations. Conceptual abstractions differ from metaphors in only one crucial respect: we "forget" that they are metaphors and take them as transcripts of reality itself. Thus our concepts are "dead" figures, our truths forgotten fictions:

> What then is truth? A movable host of metaphors, metonymies, and anthropomorphisms: in short, a sum of human relations which have been poetically and rhetorically intensified, transferred, and embellished, and which, after long usage, seem to a people to be fixed, canonical, and binding. Truths are illusions which we have forgotten are illusions; they are metaphors that have become worn out and have been drained of sensuous force, coins which have lost their embossing and are now considered as metal and no longer as coins. . . . [Mankind] forgets that the original perceptual metaphors are metaphors and takes them to be the things themselves.[18]

This act of "forgetting" is no innocent lapse of memory; we do not so much forget as suppress the source of our concepts. It is a principal strategy of Platonism to draw a fundamental distinction between concept and figure, and then to grant ontological priority to the first over the second. By identifying a set of privileged metaphors with reality itself and consigning all others to mere fancy, Platonism suppresses the spontaneous power of the imagination to organize reality in a new way.[h] Nietzsche questions this opposition between concept and figure, along with similar oppositions that uphold Western metaphysics—philosophy/poetry, logic/rhetoric, reason/ imagination, truth/fiction. He searches for the motives that led to the institution of these distinctions and at the same time attempts to dissolve them. Overturning the Platonic hierarchy that privileges concept over figure, Nietzsche claims that abstractions are merely forgotten metaphors, the traditionally superior term a special case of the subordinate term.

Near the end of his essay, Nietzsche identifies human creativity with the power to produce new metaphors. Platonism attempts to stifle this power, but it resurfaces in the form of artistic invention:

The drive toward the formation of metaphors is the fundamental human drive, which one cannot for a single instant dispense with in thought, for one would thereby dispense with man himself. This drive is not truly vanquished and scarcely subdued by the fact that a regular and rigid new world is constructed as its prison from its own ephemeral products, the concepts. It seeks a new realm and another channel for its activity, and it finds this in *myth* and in *art* generally. This drive continually confuses the conceptual categories and cells by bringing forward new transferences, metaphors, and metonymies. It continually manifests an ardent desire to refashion the world which presents itself to waking man, so that it will be as colorful, irregular, lacking in results and coher-

[h] "Only by forgetting this primitive world of metaphor can one live with any repose, security, and consistency: only by means of the petrification and coagulation of a mass of images which originally streamed from the primal faculty of human imagination like a fiery liquid . . . only by forgetting that he himself is an *artistically creating* subject, does man live with any repose, security, and consistency" (*Philosophy and Truth: Selections from Nietzsche's Notebooks of the Early 1870's*, p. 86). Here Nietzsche anticipates his later notion that Platonism expresses the will to power of an inferior species. Platonism provides "repose, security, and consistency" by controlling the natural impulse to produce new metaphors.

ence, charming, and eternally new as the world of
dreams.[19]

Both conceptual knowledge and artistic invention arise out of
the same "drive toward the formation of metaphors." The
metaphysician denies that his concepts are simply metaphors,
and equates them with reality itself. The artist, on the other
hand, has no pretensions to "truth." His new metaphors
openly display their fictional status, and his works manifest
our suppressed desire to destroy our conceptual "prison" and
to "refashion the world." By inventing new figures, valua-
tions, and points of view, the artist disrupts the prevailing
system of concepts, and projects new possibilities for organizing experience.

Nietzsche's blurring of the line between concept and figure, cognition and imagination, is quite familiar to students
of contemporary criticism. Those who have read Derrida and
de Man realize that Nietzsche is the inspiration behind current efforts to explore the relationship between logic and
rhetoric, literal and metaphorical language.[20] But Nietzsche
was not an isolated case at the turn of the century. Both his
fellow philosophers and a company of poets were moving in
much the same direction. Nor was Nietzsche's own view of
metaphor entirely neglected in the early twentieth century.
T. E. Hulme, as we have seen, introduced a version of
Nietzsche's ideas into the Modernist vortex. And similar
ideas were also conveyed by Remy de Gourmont, who exerted a profound influence on Pound and Eliot during the
1910s.

II

When Remy de Gourmont died in 1915, Ezra Pound an-
nounced to the readers of *Poetry* magazine that "the world's
light is darkened." His eulogy echoed the sentiments of many
younger poets: "Remy de Gourmont is irreplaceable. . . . I
think that every young man in London whose work is worth

considering at all, has felt that in Paris existed this gracious presence, this final and kindly tribunal where all work would stand on its merits. One had this sense of absolute fairness—no prestige, no overemphasis, could work upon it" (SP, 420). By 1915, most of Pound's circle had come to admire Gourmont as a poet, novelist, critic, and editor of the *Mercure de France*. A few years later, T. S. Eliot would join this group of admirers: in *The Sacred Wood*, Gourmont is the only figure besides Aristotle whom Eliot considers "the perfect critic."[21] We should not be misled by Gourmont's relative obscurity today; in the second decade of this century, he was a major presence in French letters, and had a considerable impact on Anglo-American Modernism.

Gourmont's most influential work of criticism, *Le Problème du style* (1902), combines Nietzsche and other sources to give metaphor the central position it would occupy in Modernist poetics. Although he was indebted to Nietzsche, Gourmont pursued an unusually wide range of intellectual interests, and all of these inform his literary criticism. He was a serious student of psychology and biology, two of the most innovative fields in late nineteenth-century France. He also wrote numerous philosophical and philological pieces, and in 1899 published a full-length study of the French language, *Esthétique de la langue française*. *Le Problème du style* incorporates many of these diverse enthusiasms, and therefore should be considered not merely a popularization of Nietzsche but a largely independent statement on the significance of metaphor, a statement that was itself remarkably influential.

Gourmont's literary criticism is based primarily on a theory of mind that had been flourishing since the publication of Taine's *De l'intelligence* (1870). Like many French psychologists of the period, Gourmont associates consciousness with the physiological process through which the nervous system integrates sensory impressions. Since no two organisms are physiologically identical, it requires only a minor departure from Taine to conclude that every person perceives the world somewhat differently. Appropriating Schopenhauer's dictum, "the world is my representation," Gourmont espouses a philosophical idealism that emphasizes the individual's unique sensibility:

> Idealism is definitely founded on the very materiality of thought, considered as a physiological product. . . . [If] knowledge of the world is the work of a humble physiological product, thought, a product which varies in quality, in modality, from man to man, from species to species, then the world can be considered as unknowable, since each brain or each nervous system draws from its vision and its contact a different image, or one which, if it was at first the same for all, is profoundly modified in its final representation by the intervention of individual judgment. . . . Idealism means materialism, and conversely, materialism means idealism.[22]

The proposition that the external world is ultimately unknowable is of secondary importance to Gourmont. Of primary importance is the recognition that each person thinks and feels differently from every other.

In *L'Idéalisme* (1893), Gourmont argues that Symbolism is the aesthetic counterpart to philosophical idealism. Both encourge the free development of individual sensibility:

> Idealism signifies free and personal development of the intellectual individual in the intellectual sphere; Symbolism may be (and even must be) considered by us as the free and personal development of the aesthetic individual in the aesthetic sphere, and the symbols which he imagines or interprets will be imagined or interpreted according to the special conception of the world morphologically possible to each symbolizing brain.[23]

For most of the 1890s, Gourmont used his idealism in support of the elusive verbal magic of Symbolist poetry. He believed that the individual's flow of thought is best conveyed in language which eschews exact denotation and thereby liberates

words from their usual meanings: ". . . the words that I adore
and collect as jewels are those whose sense is closed to me,
or almost closed, the imprecise word, the enchanted syllables
. . . flowers never seen, fleeting fairies that haunt only nurs-
ery songs."[24] In the late 1890s, however, Gourmont's tastes
began to change. Although he maintained his allegiance to
idealism, he began to advocate a new means of expressing
individual sensibility. Turning sharply from the dreamy opac-
ity of Symbolist poetry, he developed a conception of style
based on the creation of striking visual metaphors.

Gourmont's interest in metaphor arose in part from his research on the history of the French language, which culmi-
nated in *Esthétique de la langue française.* Drawing on the
historical semantics of Arsène Darmesteter and Michel Bréal
(the father of modern semantics),[25] he observed how metaphors gradually lose their power to convey a discernible relation and become the colorless clichés of ordinary language:
"Every cliché is a coin thrown into circulation; a metaphor is
the first copy of this coin; it will return for resmelting, will
enter some collection of rare objects, or else it will be printed
by the millions and become so common that no one will ever
think of looking at the actual figure engraved upon it."[26] Pursuing this line of reasoning one step further, Gourmont asserts that the terms of "literal" language are merely forgotten
metaphors. In everyday speech and in metaphysical discussion, we "forget" that our concepts are essentially the figures
we value most, and that "to conceptualize," as Nietzsche puts
it, is merely to work with one's favorite metaphors.[i]

---

[i] The association between metaphor and metaphysics also appears in *Le
Jardin d'épicure* (1895), a novel by Anatole France. Here one of the protag-
onists, Polyphile, maintains that metaphor gives rise both to myth and to
metaphysics: while primitives turn metaphors into stories, Western man elevates them into "ideas." "Ideas," he claims, are nothing other than "white
mythology." Derrida's essay "La Mythologie blanche" opens with an account
of Polyphile's argument ("White Mythology: Metaphor in the Text of Philosophy," in *Margins of Philosophy,* trans. Alan Bass [Chicago: University of
Chicago Press, 1982], pp. 207-71).

In the last chapter of *Esthétique de la langue française*, Gourmont distinguishes between the "verbal" mind, which simply repeats the words it hears, and the "visual" mind, which forges new metaphors in order to make language express its immediate sensations:

> The ear is the favorite entryway; the Holy Spirit always enters through the ear; but in the form of words and sentences that are engraved in the brain just as they are pronounced, just as they have been heard; and they will emerge from it some day, identical in sound and perhaps bereft of signification. That which enters through the eye, on the contrary, can only emerge from the lips after an original effort of transposition; to tell what one has seen is to analyze an image, a complex and laborious operation; to tell what one has heard is to repeat sounds, perhaps like an echoing wall.[27]

In *Le Problème du style*, Gourmont expands this distinction into a contrast between the "emotive," "sentimental," or "ideo-emotive" mind, and the "visual," "plastic," or "sensorial" mind. The emotive mentality is abstract, the visual concrete. When the emotive mind hears a word, it responds primarily to the suggestive aura of the word itself:

> When the word *ocean* is mentioned, instead of a glaucous immensity, or a sandy beach or cliffs or any similar vision rising before them, they [the "emotives"] see— admirable simplification—the word itself written in space in printed letters, OCEAN. More advanced intellectually than the visuals, these privileged individuals are grouped at the negative pole of the magnet whose positive pole is occupied by the artists. A great step has been taken toward simplification; the world of things has been replaced by the world of signs.[28]

In the emotive mind, the word no longer conveys a visual impression. Instead, it produces a vague feeling that feeds on the sound of the word. But in the visual mind, the same word elicits a precise visual image; language and its object are one. Whereas the emotive sensibility dwells exclusively in "the world of signs," the visual sensibility maintains the connection between language and "the world of things." Gourmont maintains that true artists are visual rather than emotive—in other words, Imagist rather than Symbolist. The artist is in direct touch with his immediate experience, and discerns new and unusual associations that give rise to bold visual metaphors.

From an epistemological standpoint, these visual metaphors are simply pleasing fictions. Like Nietzsche, Gourmont considers every metaphor (and therefore every word) a lie: "The lie is the very basis of language and the absolute condition of its being. . . . every word contains a metaphor and every metaphor is a displacement of reality."[j] There are, however, two sorts of lies—the concealed lies of "literal" language and the open lies of art. The artist, who openly displays the metaphorical impulse that informs all discourse, "lies in a superior fashion."[29] Detached from any commitment to truth, he renders the free play of sensations as they form new and surprising conjunctions in his mind:

> There are no ideas so remote, no images so incongruous, that an easy freedom of association cannot join them at least for the moment. Victor Hugo, seeing a cable wrapped in rags at a point where it bore on a sharp edge, saw at the same moment the knees of tragic actresses which are padded against the dramatic falls of the fifth act; and two such disparate things—a cable anchored on a rock and the knees of an actress—are evoked, as we read, in a parallelism that intrigues us because the knees

[j] For Nietzsche, "genius in lying" gives rise not only to metaphor but to every discourse through which we order the sensory flux: "Metaphysics, morality, religion, science . . . merit consideration only as various forms of lies. . . . products of [man's] will to art, to lie, to flight from 'truth,' to *negation* of 'truth' " (*The Will to Power*, pp. 451-52). Here "truth" refers to the bare chaos of sensations, "lies" to the fictions that bestow order upon it.

and the rope are both "furred" . . . because, even while perceiving the logic of these comparisons, we perceive no less well their delicious absurdity.[30]

Such associations, in "their delicious absurdity," manifest the basic "drive toward the formation of metaphors" that gives rise to "figurative" and "literal" language alike. According to Gourmont, the artist dissolves our attachment to the "dead metaphors" of literal discourse, and liberates us from habitual patterns of thought. By challenging conventional associations and proposing new ones, he encourages in each of us the development of a free sensibility.

III

Nietzsche and Gourmont situate metaphor between conceptual abstraction and concrete sensation. A metaphor is both like and unlike a concept: while it identifies resemblances between distinct particulars, metaphor does not hypostatize the resemblance into an autonomous entity. It prevents us from detaching the generic "leaf" from the individual leaves. Whereas the concept creates identity by suppressing differences, metaphor establishes identity-within-difference; it mediates between the unifying idea and the things it relates.[k] This view of metaphor prepares us for the poetics of Ezra Pound. Though he differs from Nietzsche and Gourmont in

[k] In *The Rule of Metaphor*, Paul Ricoeur argues that metaphor creates a "tensional" relationship between conceptual abstraction and concrete sensation, identity and difference. Like a concept, a metaphor unifies previously unrelated particulars. But unlike the concept, metaphor reveals "the genus within the differences, and not elevated beyond differences": "A family resemblance first brings individuals together before the rule of a logical class dominates them. Metaphor, a figure of speech, presents in an *open* fashion, by means of a conflict *between* identity and difference, the process that, in a *covert* manner, generates semantic grids by fusion of differences *into* identity" (*The Rule of Metaphor: Multi-Disciplinary Studies of the Creation of Meaning in Language*, trans. Robert Czerny et al. [Toronto: University of Toronto Press, 1977], p. 198).

certain details, Pound constantly searches for "tensional" constructs that hold together abstraction and sensation, identity and difference, and these tensional constructs are central to his works.

Pound's interest in metaphor generally receives little attention. Many critics believe that he simply rejects metaphor in favor of the ideogram. To a certain extent these critics are right: Pound repeatedly attacks certain uses of metaphor, and few metaphors (in the narrow sense of the term) are to be found in his poetry. This viewpoint, however, suffers from several difficulties. First, Pound discriminates between "ornamental" and precise "interpretive" metaphors, and while he dismisses the former, he attaches the utmost significance to the latter. Second, it is a mistake to distinguish sharply between metaphor and ideogram. Like a metaphor, an ideogram unites previously unrelated elements and establishes identity-in-difference. For Pound, the ideogram is closely related to the precise interpretive metaphor. Both are constructs that order experience without collapsing the distinction between the organizing form and the sensory field to which it gives shape. While the ideogram exhibits both the unifying concept and its constituent particulars, the precise interpretive metaphor displays both the "interpretive" pattern and the natural object it interprets. Both constructs establish a "tensional" relationship between form and flux, conceptual abstraction and concrete sensation. In this section we will first consider each of these constructs individually, and then identify the fundamental similarities between them.

Ideogram. The source of the "ideogrammic method" is well known. Around 1914 Pound read Ernest Fenollosa's tract, *The Chinese Written Character as a Medium for Poetry*, and immediately began to praise it as "a whole basis of aesthetic."[31] Fenollosa offered Pound an approach to conceptual and figurative language similar to Nietzsche's. Just as Nietzsche exposes the "anthropomorphic error"—the fallacy of identifying a conceptual abstraction with reality itself—Fenollosa attacks the Western "logic of classification"—the process through which we produce abstract concepts and grant them priority over the concrete particulars they connect. Using an example similar to Nietzsche's "leaf," Fenollosa shows how we reduce the multiplicity of particulars to conceptual unity:

> Let us consider a row of cherry trees. From each of these in turn we proceed to take an 'abstract,' as the phrase is, a certain common lump of qualities which we may express together by the name cherry or cherry-ness. Next we place in a second table several such characteristic concepts: cherry, rose, sunset, iron-rust, flamingo. From these we abstract some further common quality, dilutation or mediocrity, and label it 'red' or 'redness.' It is evident that this process of abstraction may be carried on indefinitely and with all sorts of material. We may go on for ever building pyramids of attenuated concept until we reach the apex 'being.'   (CWC, 26)

Like Nietzsche, Fenollosa unmasks the strategy through which Western metaphysics privileges unity over multiplicity, identity over difference, abstract form over concrete sensation. Both men challenge the belief that there is an eternal, unchanging Being behind the flux of Becoming.

Fenollosa saw the Chinese ideogram as an ideal way to overcome the "logic of classification." By presenting a picture of the elements it relates, the ideogram binds the abstract concept to its constituent elements. Pound illustrates:

> . . . when the Chinaman wanted to make a picture of something more complicated, or of a general idea, how did he go about it?
>
> He is to define red. How can he do it in a picture that isn't painted in red paint?
>
> He puts (or his ancestor put) together the abbreviated pictures of

ROSE	CHERRY
IRON RUST	FLAMINGO

That, you see, is very much the kind of thing a biologist does (in a very much more complicated way) when he gets together a few hundred or thousand slides, and picks out what is necessary for his general statement. Something that fits the case, that applies in all of the cases.[32]

Western phonetic script lacks this capacity to ground an abstraction in concrete particulars. Since it represents sound rather than sense, our script severs the term "red" from particular red things, and therefore makes us more prone to consider it an entity independent of the things it relates. The ideogram, by contrast, anchors the term in immediate experience: it performs the function of abstraction without allowing us to hypostatize the concept into an autonomous entity. We are able to *see* simultaneously the unifying form and its constituent particulars.

Fenollosa's ideogram has another advantage over phonetic script: it openly displays its etymology. In every language words continually change their meaning over time through a process of figurative extension and transformation. Hence, if we trace the etymology of any particular word, we may well find "metaphor . . . piled upon metaphor in quasi-geological strata" (CWC, 23). In the West we easily forget the origin and subsequent metamorphoses of the word: ". . . there is little or nothing in a phonetic word to exhibit the embryonic stages of its growth. It does not bear its metaphor on its face" (CWC, 25). But the Chinese ideogram shows us "the lines of metaphoric advance" through which the word has passed:

Its etymology is constantly visible. It retains the creative impulse and process, visible and at work. After thousands of years the lines of metaphoric advance are still shown, and in many cases actually retained in the meaning. Thus a word, instead of growing gradually poorer and poorer as with us, becomes richer and still more rich from age to age, almost consciously luminous. . . . Poetic language is always vibrant with fold on fold of overtones and with natural affinities, but in Chinese the visibility of the metaphor tends to raise this quality to its intensest power. (CWC, 25)[1]

Thus the ideogram establishes not only a synchronic but also a diachronic identity-in-difference. By exhibiting the successive stages of its formation, the ideogram reveals the work of metaphor in the formation of abstract concepts.

Fenollosa's ideogram provides an effective antidote to Nietzsche's "anthropomorphic error": by tying the concept to its constituent particulars, the ideogram keeps us from detaching the abstract form from concrete sensation—the "leaf" from individual leaves, or "redness" from particular red objects. And by displaying its own etymology, the ideogram prevents us from assuming an absolute distinction between concept and figure, metaphysical truth and metaphorical imagination: we are less prone to forget that our abstractions arise from the swift perception of relations. There is an important difference between Nietzsche and Fenollosa, however. Nietzsche maintains that metaphors are merely creative fictions that we project upon the chaos of sensations. Fenollosa, by contrast, claims that metaphor is the "revealer of nature" (CWC, 23). The metaphors buried in our concepts reflect not "arbitrary *subjective* processes" but "objective lines of relations in nature herself":

The whole delicate substance of speech is built upon substrata of metaphor. Abstract terms, pressed by etymology, reveal their ancient roots still embedded in di-

---

[1] Most Sinologists have little patience with such remarks. They argue that the Chinese are no more likely to see the etymology of a concept in an ideogram than we are likely to see cotton-wool padding in the term "bombast." Moreover, while certain Chinese characters visually depict their original meaning, it is hard to imagine an ideogram that reveals all of its successive meanings in "quasi-geological strata." Here as elsewhere Fenollosa was indulging in a flight of fancy. His ideogram was an idealized form—a form whose value lay not in its factual accuracy but in its power to incite the imagination of a major poet.

rect action. But the primitive metaphors do not spring from arbitrary *subjective* processes. They are possible only because they follow objective lines of relations in nature herself. Relations are more real and more important than the things which they relate. The forces which produce the branch-angles of an oak lay potent in the acorn. Similar lines of resistance, half-curbing the outpressing vitalities, govern the branching of rivers and of nations. Thus a nerve, a wire, a roadway, and a clearing-house are only varying channels which communication forces for itself. This is more than analogy, it is identity of structure. Nature furnishes her own clues. Had the world not been full of homologies, sympathies, and identities, thought would have been starved and language chained to the obvious. (CWC, 22)

Here Fenollosa stands diametrically opposed to Nietzsche's fictionalism. Language is not a network of ingenious lies, but the embodiment of nature's own processes. Our words were originally "embedded in direct action"; they traced the "entangled lines of forces as they pulse through things" (CWC, 12). And while these words have undergone numerous transformations, they continue to follow "relations in nature herself." Thus metaphor "is at once the substance of nature and of language" (CWC, 23).[m]

Pound deeply admired these aspects of Fenollosa's ideogram. He was drawn to constructs that hold together conceptual form and concrete sensation, unity and multiplicity. He was also intrigued by the idea that words are palimpsests that

[m] Fenollosa erects a new cosmology on the ruins of the one he has destroyed. The "logic of classification" produced the illusion of an unchanging reality behind the flux of appearances. But the metaphors buried in our concepts (and openly revealed by the ideogram) reawaken us to nature as it really is—a dynamic network of forces in perpetual transformation. Pound was attracted to Fenollosa's view of metaphor and to his vision of nature, but his position is not the same as Fenollosa's. For Pound, metaphor does not "explain" but "interprets" nature (see the section on "interpretative metaphor" below).

accumulate meanings "ply over ply." Fenollosa was not the first or the only proponent of this idea, but he reinforced Pound's belief that etymological exploration reveals "our forgotten mental processes" (CWC, 21). Pound considered the ideogram a means of restoring language to immediate experience. By tying the abstract to the concrete and the present to the past, the ideogram seems to guarantee the essential connection between language and reality.

In the *Cantos*, Pound employed the "ideogrammic method" to ground his argument in concrete historical particulars. Just as the ideogram signifies "redness" by juxtaposing rose, iron rust, cherry, and flamingo, Pound presents his ideas through the juxtaposition of diverse cultural fragments:

> Palace in smoky light
> Troy but a heap of smouldering boundary stones,
> ANAXIFORMINGES! Aurunculeia!
> Hear me. Cadmus of Golden Prows![33]

Here Pound connects four distinct elements: the burning of Troy, Pindar's second Olympian ode (ANAXIFOR-MINGES!), Catullus's Epithalamion (Aurunculeia!), and the founding of Thebes. Both the destruction of Troy and the creation of Thebes issue from acts of passion: Paris has run off with Helen, and Zeus has abducted the sister of Cadmus. The fragments from Pindar and Catullus are also concerned with passion—the successful sublimation of passion in rites and institutions that sustain a civilized society. Taken together, these fragments set the stage for a canto concerned with the expression and control of our ineradicable instincts, which give rise to the most creative as well as the most destructive acts of human nature. The element that unites these fragments represents a constant that manifests itself in different or even antithetical forms and ultimately directs the course of human affairs.[34]

Pound recognized that the ideogram conveys the impression of historical authenticity. It directs attention away from the poet's own voice and toward the historical documents themselves. But Pound also seemed to believe that he could actually secure objectivity by resolving abstractions into their constituent particulars, discursive statement into concrete image. The "ideogrammic method" would guarantee that the poet's "ideas" are moored in the "luminous details" (SP, 21) of history. It would also establish an essential bond between imagination and truth, presenting the imaginative apprehension of new relations without sacrificing historical veracity (or at least the impression of it). By employing this method, the poet could project form upon the past while maintaining fidelity to historical fact.[n]

Interpretive metaphor. Pound often distinguishes between "untrue, or ornamental, metaphor," and "true metaphor, that is interpretive metaphor, or image."[35] In an essay on Guido Cavalcanti, he opposes Petrarch's "fustian and ornament" to Guido's "precise interpretive metaphor" (LE, 162). Petrarch's metaphors are painted rhetoric; they are designed merely to embellish. But Guido's metaphors, like Dante's, express "definite sensations undergone" (LE, 162); they have the "precision" that comes from the attempt "to reproduce exactly the thing which has been clearly seen" (SR, 126). The "thing which has been clearly seen" is a visionary form—an image or pattern—that transfigures the world as it ordinarily appears. For example, in the presence of the beloved lady, Guido sees the air "tremble with a bright clearenesse." The poet, inspired by intense emotion, envisions a "radiant world . . . of moving energies 'mezzo oscuro rade,' 'risplende in se perpetuale effecto,' magnetisms that take form, that are seen, or that border the visible" (LE, 154). This "radiant world" is a precise interpretive metaphor. Neither a clever fiction nor a scientific fact, it is an exact rendering of the "realities perceptible to the sense" in a special state of mind.

[n] On the strengths and weaknesses of the ideogrammic method, see Chapter III.

Pound identifies the interpretive metaphor not only with Guido's "radiant world" but with a number of visionary forms, all of which superimpose an image or pattern upon the sensory field: the single-image haiku, which places one object upon another; the geometrical forms that the Vorticist projects upon experience; the "magic moment" of metamorphosis, which reveals a cosmic pattern of ceaseless transformations between seemingly discrete entities; and the visionary experience of gods inhabiting the landscape. The haiku offers a simple illustration of a precise interpretive metaphor. It is a form that avoids the ornamental use of metaphor and uses "the age-old language of exploration, the language of art":

> The Japanese have had the sense of exploration. They have understood the beauty of this sort of knowing. . . .

> "The fallen blossom flies back to its branch:
> A butterfly."

>   *   *   *

> "The footsteps of the cat upon the snow:
> (are like) plum-blossoms."

> The words "are like" would not occur in the original, but I add them for clarity.
> The "one image poem" is a form of super-position, that is to say, it is one idea set on top of another.[36]

Pound considers the haiku not merely a juxtaposition of two objects, but the super-position of an imagined object upon a natural one. Reflecting on his Metro poem, he states that his intense response to a natural scene—"The apparition of these faces in the crowd"—eventually produced the image of another object in his mind—"Petals on a wet, black bough." The image functions as a kind of lens through which to "interpret" the natural object. In the same way, the Vorticist painter projects an "interpretive" pattern upon the visual field; and the ancient poet, responding to the beauty of nature, projects visionary deities upon the external landscape.

According to Pound, the poet is "an organiser of form" (SP, 375), and his precise interpretive metaphor super-poses a particular form on the world around us.

Pound distinguishes the interpretive metaphor not only from the ornamental but also from the "explanatory" metaphor (SP, 374). Whereas interpretive metaphors "make us aware of certain possibilities," explanatory metaphors are a "lurch toward proof."[37] The poet who sees gods in the landscape is not "explaining" but "interpreting" the world about him. If he treats the gods as explanatory forces, he commits the anthropomorphic error of equating his own imaginative constructs with reality itself. For Pound, the gods are interpretive forms that *overlie* natural phenomena rather than explanatory agencies that *underlie* them. The precise interpretive metaphor stands, therefore, between ornamental and explanatory metaphor. Neither mere fancy nor scientific fact, it projects as experiential possibility rather than conceptual certainty a particular way of apprehending experience.°

Pound's view of metaphor stands between those of Nietzsche and Fenollosa. Nietzsche, at one extreme, considers metaphor an ingenious fiction that we impose upon the sensory flux. Fenollosa, at the other extreme, considers metaphor the "revealer of nature": the metaphors buried in our concepts "follow objective lines of relations in nature herself." Pound's interpretive metaphor, however, is neither fact nor fiction but a construct that bridges the distinction between them. It transcends fiction in that it discloses reality exactly as it appears in a special state of mind. Nevertheless, the interpretive metaphor stops short of "explaining" reality, since it is the "revealer of nature" not as it exists in itself but as it appears to a perceiving subject. Pound avoids both

---

° Pound's distinction between interpretive and explanatory metaphor resembles Wilhelm Dilthey's distinction between hermeneutic *Verstehen* (understanding) and scientific *Erklären* (explanation). According to Dilthey, the human sciences yield interpretations, the natural sciences yield explanations. There is no evidence that Dilthey influenced Pound, but the two men share a number of common concerns. See Chapter III.

Nietzsche's fictionalism and Fenollosa's realism: the interpretive metaphor enables us to view the world "as if" it possesses certain forms, but it projects these forms as experiential rather than factual, as "interpretation" rather than "explanation."

What is the relationship between the ideogram and the interpretive metaphor? At first glance, these two constructs seem quite different: whereas the ideogram *juxtaposes* two (or more) individual elements, the interpretive metaphor *super-poses* one element upon another. In the ideogram, each individual element interacts with the others to form a complex whole; in the interpretive metaphor, one element— the visionary image or pattern—functions as a lens through which to view the other element—the natural object. But in another respect these constructs are quite similar. Both the ideogram and the interpretive metaphor bestow form on the sensory flux: the ideogram projects conceptual unity on an array of concrete particulars; the interpretive metaphor projects an image or pattern on the world around us. Moreover, both constructs bestow order without collapsing the distinction between the organizing form and the sensory field to which it gives shape. The ideogram resists the dangers of abstraction by exhibiting both the unifying concept and its constituent particulars; the interpretive metaphor resists the dangers of "explanation" by displaying both the "interpretive" pattern and the natural object it interprets. The ideogram and the interpretive metaphor are therefore structurally identical: they establish the same tensional relationship between form and flux, a relationship which lies, as we shall see, at the very core of Pound's poetics.

IV

Eliot shares Pound's attraction to the swift perception of relations. He, too, maintains that the poet is distinguished by a capacity for integrating seemingly unrelated elements:

When a poet's mind is perfectly equipped for its work, it is constantly amalgamating disparate experience; the ordinary man's experience is chaotic, irregular, fragmentary. The latter falls in love, or reads Spinoza, and these two experiences have nothing to do with each other, or with the noise of the typewriter or the smell of cooking; in the mind of the poet these experiences are always forming new wholes. (SE, 247)[p]

Eliot is searching for poetry that holds together identity and difference. The superior poet creates "new wholes," or "new combinations" (SW, 54), which maintain a tensional relationship between conceptual unity and sensory multiplicity.

Eliot's "new wholes," however, are different from Pound's. Pound employs constructs like the ideogram, which ignores syntactical progression and presents its constituent elements in abrupt juxtaposition. Eliot, by contrast, praises and composes verse that generally follows the rules of syntax but creates "new and sudden combinations" (SW, 128) as it proceeds from one part of the sentence to the next:

One of the greatest distinctions of . . . Middleton, Webster, Tourneur—is a gift for combining, for fusing into a single phrase, two or more diverse impressions.

. . . in her strong toil of grace

of Shakespeare is such a fusion; the metaphor identifies itself with what suggests it; the resultant is one and is unique—

[p] Compare I. A. Richards: "The wheeling of the pigeons in Trafalgar Square may seem to have no relation to the colour of the water in the basins, or to the tones of a speaker's voice or to the drift of his remarks. A narrow field of stimulation is all that we can manage, and we overlook the rest. But the artist does not, and when he needs it, he has it at his disposal" (*Principles of Literary Criticism*, p. 185). Eliot and Richards have much in common: Eliot's emphasis on the unification of disparate particulars has its equivalent in Richards's claim that the artist resolves "a welter of disconnected impulses into a single ordered response" (ibid., p. 245).

Does the silkworm *expend* her *yellow labours*? . . .
Why does yon fellow *falsify highways*
And lays his life between the judge's lips
To *refine* such a one? keeps horse and men
To *beat their valours* for her?

Let the common sewer take it from distinction. . . .
Lust and forgetfulness have been amongst us. . . .

These lines of Tourneur and of Middleton exhibit that perpetual slight alteration of language, words perpetually juxtaposed in new and sudden combinations, meanings perpetually *eingeschachtelt* into meanings, which evidences a very high development of the senses, a development of the English language which we have perhaps never equalled.   (SW, 128-29)[q]

The same gift "for fusing . . . two or more diverse impressions" drew Eliot to the Metaphysical poets and to Jules Laforgue, who inspired his first successful poems. From his English and French masters Eliot learned the technique of "amalgamating disparate experience," and it became one of the most prominent features of his early verse.

Eliot's first major success, "The Love Song of J. Alfred Prufrock" (1910-11), displays this gift for dissolving the boundary between separate realms of experience:

Let us go then, you and I,
When the evening is spread out against the sky
Like a patient etherised upon a table;

[q] The passage from Tourneur exhibits not only the fusion of "diverse impressions" but also a "balance of contrasted emotion" (SW, 57). In "Tradition and the Individual Talent," Eliot states that these lines reveal "a combination of positive and negative emotions: an intensely strong attraction toward beauty and an equally intense fascination by the ugliness which is contrasted with it and which destroys it" (SW, 57). Compare Richards's description of tragedy as a form that synthesizes the antithetical emotions of pity and terror, the impulse to approach and the impulse to withdraw (*Principles of Literary Criticism*, pp. 245ff.).

> Let us go, through certain half-deserted streets,
> The muttering retreats
> Of restless nights in one-night cheap hotels
> And sawdust restaurants with oyster-shells:
> Streets that follow *like* a tedious argument
> Of insidious intent
> To lead you to an overwhelming question. . .
> Oh, do not ask, 'What is it?'
> Let us go and make our visit.
> > (italics mine; CP, 3)

similes of lines 3 and 8 unify seemingly discordant elements. The "patient etherised upon a table" at first seems to involve an incongruous shift from one mood to another. The simile undermines the atmosphere established by the opening couplet: the sense of movement and anticipation slows down with the word "etherised" and comes to an abrupt halt with the word "table" (followed by a semi-colon). Yet the fusion of opposing moods accurately expresses the ambivalence of the speaker: the opening lines present the first of many images that manifest the conflict between the desire to approach others and the need to withdraw into private revery.

The second simile—"Streets that follow like a tedious argument"—bridges the distinction between the physical and the mental. "Streets" flows so casually into "argument" that we nearly overlook the fact that we have passed from the external world into the world of discourse. Once again, the speaker seems to dissolve the boundary between separate realms of experience. The simile also establishes an ironic relationship between epic journey and introspective voyage. The poem began with an epigraph from Dante, and now the reference to an "argument" that leads to "an overwhelming question" contains hints of an epic invocation. But for this speaker the very approach to the "overwhelming question" produces a sharp recoil: "Oh, do not ask, 'What is it?' / Let us go and make our visit." As the speaker hastily retreats to the security of the commonplace, the final rhyme (What is it?—visit) seals the ironic bond between the metaphysical and the trivial, the epic past and the mundane present.

These similes are characteristic of the entire poem. Eliot repeatedly fuses disparate realms of experience. If the first stanza blurs the division between physical and mental worlds, the third blurs the distinction between animate and inanimate. The yellow fog becomes a dog (with catlike qualities), even though it soon lapses into a dormant state:

> The yellow fog that rubs its back upon the window-panes
> The yellow smoke that rubs its muzzle on the window-
>   panes,
> Licked its tongue into the corners of the evening,
> Lingered upon the pools that stand in drains,
> Let fall upon its back the soot that falls from chimneys,
> Slipped by the terrace, made a sudden leap,
> And seeing that it was a soft October night,
> Curled once about the house, and fell asleep.
>   (CP, 3)

Subsequent passages also establish surprising connections between apparent opposites—the heroic and the commonplace, spiritual struggle and social decorum:

> Should I, after tea and cakes and ices,
> Have the strength to force the moment to its crisis?
> But though I have wept and fasted, wept and prayed,
> Though I have seen my head (grown slightly bald) brought
>   in upon a platter,
> I am no prophet—and here's no great matter;
> I have seen the moment of my greatness flicker,
> And I have seen the eternal Footman hold my coat, and
>   snicker,
> And in short, I was afraid.
>   (CP, 5-6)

Both John the Baptist and Prufrock reject sexual involvement; but the one does so out of principle, the other out of weakness, and thus the speaker's fantasy of his head "brought in upon a platter" only reminds him of the contrast between the prophet's courage and his own timidity. Throughout the poem, Eliot creates ironic relationships such as this. He also sets up a peculiar "balance of contrasted emotion" (SW, 57): the poem is at once serious and humorous, and its persona both pitiful and ridiculous. Even the form of the poem defies easy categorization: Is this a real journey or an imagined one? Are we hearing a speaker address an auditor or overhearing the persona's stream of consciousness? In all these cases, Eliot confounds the distinctions that uphold conventional reality and weds elements from seemingly unrelated or opposing realms. He had learned the technique of "amalgamating disparate experience," and it would become the hallmark of his early poetry.

V

Nietzsche, Gourmont, Pound, Eliot (and to this group we may add T. E. Hulme) all celebrate the potentials of metaphor. Three of them—Nietzsche, Gourmont, and Hulme—form a coherent subgroup: they maintain that conceptual abstraction is merely a special case of metaphorical invention, and literal language a special case of figurative language. Pound and Eliot avoid this formulation, and to that extent depart from the others. Nevertheless, the family resemblances among the entire group are unmistakable. All situate metaphor between conceptual abstraction and concrete sensation, and all are concerned with constructs that posit relations between distinct particulars without losing sight of the differences between them.

It is no accident that a major philosopher and a group of poets hold similar views of metaphor and attach such importance to it. In a certain respect, philosophy and poetry at the turn of the century drew closer together as the traditional opposition between conceptual and imaginative processes began to dissolve. Philosophers were emphasizing the contribution of subjective interests and personal creativity to our knowledge of the external world. They were describing conceptual systems not as mirror reflections of reality but as useful inventions or ingenious fictions. Nietzsche is most explicit in this regard, treating intellectual abstraction as a species of imaginative invention. Poets, for their part, were elevating metaphor to a position previously reserved for concepts. Dismissing merely ornamental metaphor, they began to emphasize the power of interpretive or "functional" metaphor to reveal new ways of organizing experience. Like a new concept, the significant juxtaposition, metaphor, or paradox challenges conventional reality and discloses previously neglected aspects of experience. Thus the new fascination with metaphor was tied to the intellectual changes of the late nineteenth and early twentieth century. As the traditional boundary between concept and figure began to erode, metaphor began to enter philosophy and to assume new prominence in the arts.

The conjunction of Nietzsche and the Modernists should give us pause. Today, Nietzsche's view of metaphor is closely associated with post-structuralist criticism. The "New Nietzsche" is often considered the principal source of contemporary interest in the relationship between literal and figurative language. As a rule critics assume that there is little connection between this new development in Continental criticism and the Anglo-American tradition they have left behind. But Nietzsche's exploration of the fluid boundary between concept and metaphor is closely tied to the Modernist/ New Critical preoccupation with the swift perception of relations. Furthermore, the Modernists are connected to Nietzsche both by influence and by a shared approach to abstraction and experience. In returning to Nietzsche, then, we are unwittingly returning to Pound and Eliot. Certainly the differences between them are significant, and the differences between New Criticism and post-structuralism even greater. But in light of the undeniable kinship between Nietzsche and the Modernists, we ought to reconsider our existing assumptions about the relations between the Continental and the Anglo-American traditions.

Representation, Abstraction, and the Issue of Formalism

The early twentieth century witnessed major changes in painting, fiction, and the other arts previously associated with the representation of external reality. Painters began to violate traditional canons of representation by disrupting the continuity between the world on the canvas and the world of ordinary perception. In a similar fashion, novelists were abandoning the linear sequences, reliable narrators, and consistency of narrative mode through which nineteenth-century "realists" seemed to mirror the external world. Instead, they introduced techniques to heighten the discontinuity between the text and everyday reality: distortions of temporal order; limited or unreliable narrators, often with unusual points of view; and pastiches, parodies, and other rhetorical devices that make the modes of representation as prominent as the things they represent. Nineteenth-century novelists tend to use language as a transparent medium for rendering social reality. By contrast, modern novelists such as Joyce tend to foreground the signifying medium itself. In the later episodes of *Ulysses*, Joyce employs a dazzling array of modes, gleaned from a variety of popular and esoteric sources, which openly display the verbal artifice through which he portrays the life of modern Dublin. Painters and novelists alike were thus declaring their independence from mimetic constraints: the modern artist no longer *represents* a preexisting reality but *presents* a new set of relations, a "model," through which to order the world anew.[r]

[r] This description of the twentieth-century novel should not be confused with Roland Barthes's notion of the modern "writerly" or "absolutely plural"

Early twentieth-century poets were moving in the same direction. If painters were severing their ties with the everyday world, poets like Pound and Eliot were increasing the distance between the poem and ordinary life by disrupting accepted patterns of communication. They used abrupt juxtaposition, metaphor, and other techniques to break down conventional habits of thought and create new relations between previously unconnected aspects of experience. In other words, the poet's "new bowl of metaphor" is analogous to the painter's new "model"; both detach us from the familiar world and project new ways of organizing experience.[38] It is therefore no wonder that Pound identified poetic Imagism with the painting of Picasso and Wyndham Lewis; nor is it surprising that Eliot equated the process of "amalgamating disparate experience" into "new wholes" with the novelist's construction of a "new world." Both Pound and Eliot believed that they were doing for poetry what Picasso and Joyce were doing for the representational arts.

This development in the arts corresponds to contemporaneous developments in philosophy. Many philosophers of the period declared that conceptual knowledge does not *represent* a preexisting reality but *presents* a system of relations for projecting form upon reality. Cassirer maintains that a conceptual system does not "copy a fixed, given being," but posits a system of relations—a "plan for possible constructions of unity"—that bestows order on the sensory flux.[39] He would have had no trouble comprehending George Braques's artistic credo: "I do not believe in things, I believe in relationships." Early twentieth-century intellectuals readily dis-

---

novel. Unlike a text that presents an identifiable system of relations, Barthes's "absolutely plural text" is irreducible to one system of relations and suggests ever new ways of ordering its elements. Establishing a problematic relationship between signifier and signified, the writerly text is open to interpretations whose "number is never closed, based as it is on the infinity of language" (S/Z, trans. Richard Miller [New York: Hill and Wang, 1974], pp. 3-16). In the Conclusion I will return to this distinction between Modernist and post-structuralist views of the text.

cerned this correlation between philosophy and the arts. They believed that Western thought was undergoing a general crisis of representation, a global transformation of its assumptions about the forms we use to organize our experience.[5]

Changes in the arts are usually attended by changes in criticism, and such is the case in the early twentieth century. The appearance of paintings and poems removed from ordinary experience engendered critical theories that focused on the internal dynamics of the work itself. Nineteenth-century critics emphasized the continuity between the author and the text, and the continuity between the text and the external world. They treated lyric poetry as the expression of the author's subjective life, and the novel as an exposé of prevailing social conditions. Early twentieth-century critics, by contrast, often divorced the text from its author and from the social world it represents. For example, the appearance of Futurist poetry encouraged the Russian Formalists to examine the properties of the poetic "medium" rather than the poet's "message," the signifier rather than the signified. The Formalists adopted a similar approach to fiction: rejecting the habit of treating the novel as social commentary, they approached the text as an autonomous entity, studying the formal devices through which the writer "defamiliarizes" the world as we ordinarily know it. Twentieth-century critics thus developed a new sensitivity to the material properties of the verbal medium, the peculiarities of "literary" (as opposed to "ordinary") language, and the formal principles that govern literary genres. In the pages that follow I will examine this

---

[5] The epistemological shift from substances to relations also has its counterpart in modern linguistics. According to Saussure, *"language is a form and not a substance"* (Ferdinand de Saussure, *Course in General Linguistics,* trans. Wade Baskin [New York: McGraw-Hill, 1966], p. 122). Individual terms derive their meaning not from preexisting ideas but from their relations to other terms in the linguistic system. Each language is thus a relational grid that imposes order upon an otherwise "shapeless and indistinct mass" (ibid., p. 111).

new orientation to literature, proceeding from Pound and Eliot on nonrepresentational art to a brief discussion of the controversies surrounding the rise of critical formalism.

I

From the outset of his career, Pound campaigned against naive mimesis: "In every art I can think of we are dammed and clogged by the mimetic" (SP, 42). In his early essays he distinguishes between the "symptomatic" and the "donative" artist. Symptomatic writers are mimetic; they "reflect," "mirror," or "register" the everyday world: "In them we find a reflection of tendencies and modes of a time. They mirror obvious and apparent thought movements. They are what one might have expected in such and such a year and place. They register" (SP, 25). Donative artists, on the other hand, project new forms for ordering sensations. They have the capacity for "discerning that things hitherto deemed identical or similar are dissimilar; that things hitherto deemed dissimilar, mutually foreign, antagonistic, are similar and harmonic." Although the symptomatic author may be a good "seismograph," the donative author "can, within limits, not only record but create" (SP, 376).

Two forms of donative, or nonmimetic, art were especially attractive to Pound—ancient mythological art and twentieth-century abstract art. He discusses the first of these in "Psychology and Troubadours" (1912), where he distinguishes between the mimetic consciousness, which reflects "sundry patches of the macrocosmos," and the "germinal" consciousness, which projects visionary forms upon experience and thereby transfigures the everyday world:

. . . the consciousness of some seems to rest, or to have its center more properly, in what the Greek psychologists called the *phantastikon*. Their minds are, that is, circumvolved about them like soap-bubbles reflecting sundry patches of the macrocosmos. And with certain others their consciousness is "germinal." Their thoughts are in them as the thought of the tree is in the seed, or in the grass, or the grain, or the blossom. And these minds are the more poetic, and they affect mind about them, and transmute it as the seed the earth. And this latter sort of mind is close on the vital universe; and the strength of the Greek beauty rests in this, that it is ever at the interpretation of this vital universe, by its signs of gods and godly attendants and oreads.   (SR, 92-93)

These germinal minds produced an art unfettered by mimetic constraints. Inspired by the beauty of the world around them, they expressed their feelings not by reproducing nature as it ordinarily appears but by creating visionary forms that "interpret" it. Revealing how nature appears in a particular state of intense emotion, their art provides a model for organizing, or interpreting, the "vital universe" around us.

Pound also welcomed the resurgence of nonmimetic art in the early twentieth century. He saw that artists were once again producing visionary forms that aspire to transfigure rather than copy the natural world. In defense of this new art, Pound distinguishes between the "receiving" mind, which reflects ordinary reality, and the "conceiving" mind, which imposes new forms upon it:

> There are two opposed ways of thinking of a man: firstly, you may think of him as that toward which perception moves, as the toy of circumstance, as the plastic substance *receiving* impressions; secondly, you may think of him as directing a certain fluid force against circumstance, as *conceiving* instead of merely reflecting and observing.[40t]

---

t The distinction between the passive artist—"the toy of circumstance"— and the active artist, who projects form upon experience by "directing a fluid force against circumstances," remains an important motif in Pound's writings. He recorded the fate of the passive artist in "Hugh Selwyn Mauberley," and found the prototype of the active artist in the figure of Odysseus, who became his principal "searcher after knowledge" in the *Cantos*.

This distinction between the receiving and conceiving artist is similar to that between the phantastikon and the germinal consciousness: if the germinal artist projects gods upon the landscape, the conceptual artist projects geometrical forms upon it. Ancient and contemporary art are thus closely related, and they stand in contrast to the mimetic ideal that prevailed from the Renaissance to the late nineteenth century.

In an illuminating remark on nonmimetic art, Pound recalls how a Vorticist painting transformed his awareness of ordinary London streets:

> I have my new and swift perceptions of forms, of possible form-motifs; I have a double or treble or tenfold set of stimulæ in going from my home to Piccadilly. What was a dull row of houses is become a magazine of forms. There are new ways of seeing them. There are ways of seeing the shape of the sky as it juts down between the houses. The tangle of telegraph wires is conceivable not merely as a repetition of lines; one sees the shapes defined by the different branches of wire. The lumber yards, the sidings of railways cease to be dreary.[41]

A "form-motif" is the basic principle or pattern for organizing the distinctive world of the painting. Once we appropriate the "form-motif," we begin to perceive new configurations in the world about us. Just as the older poets awaken us to the imaginative apprehension of the gods, Vorticist art makes us aware of structural relations we previously failed to discern.

This faith in the transformative power of art is derived from Romantic theories of creative imagination, and it distinguishes Pound from some of his contemporaries, who proposed a more modest art of fancy. For instance, Pound took exception to Gourmont's view of the imagination. According to Gourmont, "to imagine is to associate images and fragments of images; that is not creating. Man cannot create either an atom of matter or an atom of idea." In his copy of *Le Problème du style*, Pound responds to this statement with a marginal note: "it is quite possible, nevertheless, that the imagination does create. I can not remember metal[l]ic architecture—i.e. interior decoration—bronze—from life, etc."[42] Metallic architecture may not be the happiest example, but Pound's position is clear from his remark. Whereas Gourmont's artist merely discovers new associations between sensory particulars, Pound's artist transforms the entire field of perception. An early essay provides some striking illustrations:

> Thus Greek sculpture freed men's minds from the habit of considering the human body merely with regard to its imperfections. The Japanese grotesque frees the mind from the conception of things merely as they *have been* seen. With the art of Beardsley we enter the realm of pure intellect; the beauty of the work is wholly independent of the appearance of the things portrayed. With Rembrandt we are brought to consider the exact nature of things seen, to consider the individual face, not the conventional or type face which we may have learned to expect on canvas. (SP, 360)[u]

Such works of art go beyond the mere association of "images and fragments of images"; they establish new forms of apperception. Through their "resembling unlikeness" (SP, 41) to the ordinary world, these products of imagination provide models that "liberate" the mind from conventional forms of awareness.

II

While Pound's interest in nonmimetic art was inspired by ancient poetry and modern painting, Eliot's was awakened by the theater. In his first discussion of drama, a review of the

---

[u] It should be clear from the allusions to Greek sculpture and to Rembrandt that Pound attacks only the naive mimesis which attempts to mirror conventional reality. He is prepared to praise any work of art that heightens our powers of perception.

Pound/Fenollosa 'Noh' or Accomplishment (1917), Eliot complains that the English stage, unlike the Japanese, is "merely a substitute" for the ordinary world.[43] Over the following years, he continued to attack mimetic drama and proposed an alternative to it. He argues that the dramatist should not represent the familiar world but present a "new world" with a "logic" of its own: ". . . instead of pretending that the stage gesture is a copy of reality, let us adopt a literal untruth, a thorough-going convention, a ritual."[44] By adopting a "thorough-going convention" the dramatist simultaneously detaches us from everyday reality and offers us a new model for arranging it.

Eliot's essay on Ben Jonson (1919) illustrates his position clearly. In this piece, he responds to the traditional charge that Jonson's characters "lack the third dimension, have no life out of the theatrical existence in which they appear" (SW, 117). Eliot readily admits that Jonson's characters lack the human depth of Shakespeare's, but he denies that imaginary beings should behave like actual beings. A work of art should not mirror "the actual world" but display a new world with "a logic of its own":

> We cannot call a man's work superficial when it is the creation of a world; a man cannot be accused of dealing superficially with the world which he himself has created; the superficies *is* the world. Jonson's characters conform to the logic of the emotions of their world. It is a world like Lobatchevsky's; the worlds created by artists like Jonson are like systems of non-Euclidean geometry. They are not fancy, because they have a logic of their own; and this logic illuminates the actual world, because it gives us a new point of view from which to inspect it. (SW, 116-17)

Questioning the preference for lifelike characters and plays that reflect the familiar world, Eliot maintains that "abstraction from actual life is a necessary condition to the creation of the work of art" (SE, 93).

Eliot's allusion to "systems of non-Euclidean geometry" shows that he discerned the correlation between the new theories of knowledge and the development of nonrepresentational art. In his view, dramatic realism is akin to Euclidean geometry; it reflects only the forms of the familiar world. The representational drama that emerged during the Renaissance "ends its course in the desert of exact likeness to the reality which is perceived by the most commonplace mind" (SE, 93). But Jonson's dramas are analogous to non-Euclidean geometries; they anticipate twentieth-century art by presenting an alternative model for organizing sensations. In the presence of such non-Euclidean works of art, we start to wonder about the reality we take for granted. By entering a world "with a logic of its own," we begin to perceive the conventional character of the familiar world and expose ourselves to modes of awareness we have forgotten or never imagined.[v]

At first Eliot's approach to drama seems to contradict his approach to lyric poetry. When he discusses lyric, Eliot describes a passive process through which the poet places himself "at the mercy of impressions."[45] By "surrendering" himself as a "man," or "personality," the poet allows sensory impressions to form "new combinations" in his mind (SW, 52-55). But when he turns to drama, Eliot describes a more active process through which the playwright constructs a "convention," or "fiction," which he projects upon experience: "The strange, the surprising, is of course essential to art; but art has to create a new world, and a new world must have a new structure."[46] Instead of detached receptivity to sensory experience, Eliot now emphasizes the power to create new forms. Classical resignation gives way to Romantic imagination.

However, we should not be misled by Eliot's terminology. The differences notwithstanding, his views of lyric and dra-

---

[v] Eliot achieved this defamiliarization in his own plays by imposing the form of primitive ritual (or the Greek drama that evolved out of ritual) on stories which involve familiar representatives of modern, secular society.

matic creation are virtually the same. The poem in which "impressions and experiences combine in peculiar and unexpected ways" is like the play "with a logic of its own." The first produces "new combinations," the second a "new world." The first works with a succession of metaphors, the second with a single model, but in each case the result is the same. Both the poet and the playwright disrupt the structure of the everyday world and show us new ways of ordering experience. Eliot's attraction to nonmimetic drama is therefore tied closely to his interest in poets such as Donne. Neither the poet nor the playwright *represents* a preexisting reality; both *present* previously undiscerned relations through which to see the world anew.

III

Pound and Eliot portended a momentous but controversial change in literary theory. As painters and poets began to increase the distance between text and ordinary experience, critics began to attend more closely to the intrinsic structure of the text itself. Russian Formalism, in step with new developments in the arts, was one expression of this new tendency. A related development took place in the English-speaking world, where the verbal complexities of Modernist poetry led to the development of a discipline whose object was "the poem in itself." In their famous anthology *Understanding Poetry* (1938), Brooks and Warren maintain that a poem should be regarded as an autonomous entity irreducible to its "content," the historical conditions of its production, or to the "message" we derive from it. The poem is "an organic system of relationships," a complex whole whose sound-patterns, rhythms, imagery, and syntax all contribute to its meaning.[47]

Throughout the twentieth century this new orientation has provoked a good deal of opposition. It has been accused of propagating a pernicious formalism that severs the vital link between art and life. Like many artists themselves, these critics have been attacked for attending to form rather than content. Formalists, it is argued, may have taught us much about literary language, but they gain their insight at the expense of the social, moral, and spiritual dimensions of art. Thus it seems that early twentieth-century developments in the arts have produced a deep rift among literary critics, a rift between those devoted to the formal construction of the text itself and those who demand that the text speak directly to human needs and concerns. While one side celebrates the "pure text" dissociated from common experience, the other side champions the text that minimizes the discontinuity between art and life.

It cannot be denied that certain modern critics have focused exclusively on the formal properties of the text. Indeed, the proliferation of art strikingly discontinuous with common experience demands a special caste to guide the uninitiated through the mysteries of textuality. But Pound, Eliot, and even many so-called formalists never intended to dissociate art from life. For Pound and Eliot, like Brecht after them, it is precisely through its capacity to detach us from ordinary life that art performs its existential function. We value art not for copying the everyday world but for establishing a "resembling unlikeness" to it. A text with a distinctive logic of its own calls into question the conventions that currently govern our existence; it presents us with alternative and perhaps more productive forms of thinking, feeling, and acting.[w]

Critics should therefore be prepared for a twofold endeavor: they must dispassionately examine the logic of the text, and must also reveal the implications of that logic for the world outside the text. In the language of contemporary

[w] Recent developments in Marxist thought have eased the intensity of opposition between formalism and its adversaries. These developments occurred primarily in France, where the convergence of structuralism and Marxism brought about by Althusser and others made it possible to reassess the traditional Marxist hostility to Modernist art and critical formalism. For the effects of this development on literary theory, see Tony Bennett, *Formalism and Marxism* (London: Methuen, 1979).

hermeneutics, criticism ought to involve a dialectical movement between objective "distanciation" and subjective "appropriation": the critic should acknowledge the distance between the world of the text and the everyday world, and at
the same time should help readers appropriate the text to
their own situation. Certain critics emphasize the "otherness"
of the text to the point of dissociating it from life entirely;
others are so eager to "own" the text that they reduce it to
the contours of the familiar world. But by now the controversies over formalism should have taught us that it is possible
to mediate these extreme positions. Interpretation should involve both formal analysis and existential appropriation, examination of the peculiar logic of the text and evaluation of
its human significance.[48]

■

This chapter has extended a particular constellation of ideas
from early twentieth-century philosophy to Modernist poetics. Philosophers and poets of this period shared the same
crucial opposition between abstraction and sensation, the instrumental conventions that determine everyday life and a
deeper realm of immediate experience. This opposition helps
us to clarify problematic features of the new poetics: the os-
cillation between personal expression and impersonal presentation, the apparent inconsistency between the rejection and
the celebration of metaphor, and the dual allegiance to the
recovery of concrete experience and the creation of new abstractions. Moreover, this opposition reveals that individual
articles of the Modernist creed—the emphasis on artistic impersonality, the swift perception of relations, and the autonomy of the text—are closely tied to one another. It is therefore a mistake to consider Modernist/New Critical poetics as
a loose collection of stylistic preferences and critical pro-
nouncements. On the contrary, we should regard it as an
integrated structure whose distinctive elements occupy specific positions within the larger design.

CHAPTER III

Ezra Pound:
Cultural Memory and the
Visionary Imagination

In this chapter and the next, the focus shifts from the articulation of a global structure to the examination of individual writers. While the dynamics of abstraction and experience will continue to guide the investigation, the turn from paradigm to person will bring to light distinctive features of the works of Pound and Eliot. The present chapter, devoted to Ezra Pound, begins with the poet's tendency to think in terms of certain oppositions—form/flux, abstraction/experience, identity/difference, unity/multiplicity—and then to find constructs that hold together the antithetical terms. This attempt to integrate form and flux is typical of Pound's approach to virtually every sphere of human activity, and it helps to explain some of his strengths and weaknesses as a poet. The chapter then turns to a second feature of Pound's work—his habit of creating new poetry by translating or refashioning poetry from the past. Poetic creation, in Pound's view, arises from the interaction between past and present, the recovery of lost forms of expression and the invention of new and distinctively modern forms. As we shall see, these two features of Pound's work are closely related: both manifest a "tensional" relationship that mediates between the desire to recover suppressed experience and the desire to project new forms that reshape the world around us.

Fragments into Unity

The opposition between abstraction and sensation governs Pound's approach to everything from poetry and knowledge to religion and politics. In each of these areas, Pound constantly oscillates between conceptual form and sensory flux, unity and multiplicity, identity and difference. On the one hand, he combats every type of imposed order: he attempts to dissolve fixed ideas and recover the flux of immediate experience; to disrupt established conventions and promote individual diversity; to prevent the state from imposing uniformity on those who constitute it. On the other hand, he associates creativity with the power to project new form: he searches for new ways of organizing experience and new principles for ordering the state. Each of these opposing tendencies had its dangers. The drive against coercive order could produce not merely healthy diversity but sheer chaos. It led to the use of techniques that render sections of the *Cantos* virtually incomprehensible and, in the view of some critics, deprive it of structural coherence. The opposing drive to create new order also led to excesses. Politically, for instance, Pound identified with the will-to-order of a single man, thereby lending support to the coercive order he wished to avoid. In this section I will consider each of these competing tendencies successively, and then turn to Pound's efforts to reconcile them through the use of constructs that establish unity without uniformity, identity without suppression of differences.

I

Pound finds the threat of coercive uniformity in virtually every sphere of human endeavor. Conceptual, linguistic, and social conventions impose a standard pattern of thought and feeling; so do monotheism, the centralized state, and the monopolistic economy. A conceptual abstraction masks the diversity of particulars it connects; the centralized state suppresses differences of opinion. Pound's approach to each of these domains is to encourage unconstrained diversity, or what he calls the "amicable accentuation of difference" (SP, 202).[a]

Pound constantly attacks our propensity to substitute abstractions for concrete sensations. Abstractions—"Damn ideas, anyhow" (LE, 267)—impose uniformity of thought and stifle the varieties of sentient experience. Identifying abstraction with coercive unity and concrete sensation with unobstructed diversity, Pound sought to give poetic voice to many different modes of sentience. This attempt to express various kinds of sensibility linked him to Browning, but Pound tried to avoid the mistakes of his great forerunner, whose metaphysical ideas constricted his otherwise polymorphous imagination. Browning, he claims, "wrote to a theory of the universe, thereby cutting off a fair half of the moods for expression."[1]

The terms of ordinary language also inhibit personal thought and feeling. A language, like a conceptual system, imposes a particular grid upon experience. It has its distinctive *virtù*, making its users "more ready and more unready

---

[a] The following abbreviations are used in this chapter: ABC—*ABC of Reading* (New York: New Directions, 1960); CEP—*Collected Early Poems of Ezra Pound*, ed. Michael John King (New York: New Directions, 1976); GK—*Guide to Kulchur* (New York: New Directions, 1970); L—*The Selected Letters of Ezra Pound, 1907-1941*, ed. D. D. Paige (New York: New Directions, 1971); LE—*Literary Essays of Ezra Pound*, ed. T. S. Eliot (New York: New Directions, 1968); N—*The Classic Noh Theatre of Japan* (New York: New Directions, 1959); P—*Personæ: The Collected Shorter Poems of Ezra Pound* (New York: New Directions, 1971); PD—*Pavannes and Divagations* (New York: New Directions, 1974); SP—*Selected Prose, 1909-1965*, ed. William Cookson (New York: New Directions, 1975); SR—*The Spirit of Romance* (New York: New Directions, 1968). *The Cantos of Ezra Pound* (New York: New Directions, 1972) are cited by a roman numeral, which indicates the number of the canto, followed by an arabic numeral, which indicates the page number in the current edition (e.g., XXIII/109 is Canto XXIII, p. 109). The original "Three Cantos" are cited by the designation Ur-Canto I, II, or III followed by the page number from the version that appeared in *Poetry* magazine, June through August 1917.

for certain communications and registrations" (ABC, 35). But to confine ourselves to one language is to restrict the potential range of experience, since "no single language is CAPABLE of expressing all forms and degrees of human comprehension" (ABC, 34). The only solution to this linguistic provincialism is constant cross-fertilization between different languages. We overcome the constraints of our native tongue by exposing ourselves to the sensitivities of other tongues.

But the constraints of language in general disturbed Pound far less than the specific constraints of English poetic language, which in the first decade of this century imposed a dull uniformity of expression:

> As far as the 'living art' goes, I should like to break up *cliché*, to disintegrate these magnetised groups that stand between the reader of poetry and the drive of it, to escape from lines composed of two very nearly equal sections, each containing a noun and each noun decorously attended by a carefully selected epithet gleaned, apparently, from Shakespeare, Pope, or Horace. For it is not until poetry lives again 'close to the thing' that it will be a vital part of contemporary life.   (SP, 41)

This remark appeared early in 1912, and later that year Pound issued his program for bringing poetry "close to the thing." In order to free English verse from the shackles of a fixed metrical scheme, he proposed the use of "an 'absolute rhythm' . . . which corresponds exactly to the emotion or shade of emotion to be expressed" (LE, 9). At the same time, he sought to liberate verse from the constraints of "symmetrical form": every poem ought to be a precise "rendering of the impulse" and its form should express the contours of the impulse it renders. By means of these principles, which were supported by his own experiments with meter and form, Pound attempted to make English poetic language a more supple instrument for expressing the wide variety of human emotions.

Pound's view of culture also turns on the distinction between unity and multiplicity. Each cultural center projects a distinctive form upon experience; it creates a unique vortex "into which thought may be gathered, in which different ideas may meet, blend, become fecund, and from which they should radiate."[2] But any center stagnates in isolation from others; it establishes fixed forms of thought and drifts into provincialism. Once again, the solution lies in cross-fertilization. Pound claims, for instance, that Renaissance Italy owed its vitality to a healthy exchange between distinct urban centers, and that "France and England have always been at their best when knit closest" (SP, 200). These assertions should not be construed as a plea for a unified world culture. Pound envisions a variety of cultural vortices stimulating one another without blending into homogeneity. It is cultural diversity that exposes us to alternative modes of thought, and it is interaction between different cultures that engenders new modes of thought.

The same emphasis on diversity marks Pound's approach to religion. If intellectual, linguistic, and cultural conventions narrow the individual's range of sentience, monotheism suppresses the variety of emotions that flourish in a polytheistic culture. In Pound's view, monotheism imposes a uniform conception of the divine on all individuals, whereas polytheism encourages each individual to envision the divine as he pleases. Pound associates the former with intellectual abstraction, the latter with concrete sensation. Monotheism replaces "immediate sight" with "verbal formulation" (SP, 59): like an abstract concept, which detaches us from concrete experience, monotheism abstracts the divine from its true source—the individual's immediate experience of natural beauty. Polytheism, by contrast, is tied directly to the individual's contact with nature. The gods arise from the sensuous apprehension of a particular place at a particular time. Pound equated polytheism with unconstrained diversity of experience, and celebrated its tolerant acceptance of "all faith, or the constructive urges of all" (GK, 332).

Pound also posits a sharp opposition between monotheism and Confucianism. Monotheism, he claims, tries to bully people into conformity: "Christianity . . . has reduced itself to one principle: 'Thou shalt attend to thy neighbour's business in preference to thine own' " (PD, 71). Confucianism, on the other hand, cultivates a very different attitude, the tolerant spirit of "fraternal deference" (SP, 193), which Pound illustrates in a passage from the Analects. Here Confucius asks a question and receives a different answer from each of his disciples. Afterwards, one of the disciples, the "potential Xtn convert of the company" (PD, 73), asks the master, "Which had answered correctly?" Confucius replies: "They have all answered correctly, / That is to say, each in his nature" (XIII/ 58). For Pound, this reply expresses an ethical ideal that is alien to monotheistic religions. Unlike Christianity and its counterparts, Confucianism encourages the "amicable accentuation of difference" that prevails in a humane society.

The centralized state is the political equivalent to monotheism, expressing the same "lust after uniformity" (SP, 199). In fact, the state often uses monotheism to guarantee uniformity of thought and feeling. It is no coincidence, for example, that Christianity became the state religion of the Roman empire: "The government must govern by formula. The unknown must be if not formulated at least concealed and treated by formula. . . . Out of a need to administer arises or arose theology" (SP, 56-57). During World War I, Pound directed his attention to the centralized state as it had developed in Germany. In "Provincialism the Enemy" (1917), he argues that the Prussian system reduces individuals to "units" of a system. Like socialism, which fails to provide a genuine alternative, the Prussian system emphasizes "the idea of man as a unit, society as a thing of 'component parts' " (SP, 196). First and foremost, Pound guards the prerogatives of the individual. He issues a libertarian manifesto that simply evades the problem of political organization: "Fundamentally, I do not care 'politically,' I care for civilisation, and I do not care who collects the taxes, or who polices the thoroughfares. Humanity is a collection of individuals, not a *whole* divided into segments or units. The only things that matter are the things which make individual life more interesting" (SP, 199-200). At this point Pound had not yet witnessed the plight of postwar Europe, for which he would soon enough "care 'politically.' " Yet, Pound never sacrificed the individual to the state, or at least he never realized that he had done so. He was deceived by his habit of associating the individual solely with the creative genius—"artists and projective thinkers of all sorts" (SP, 196)—and his belief that Mussolini was one such "projective thinker" led him to identify with the ruler rather than the ruled. But as blind as he may have been, Pound continued to defend the individual against the oppressive power of the state. Despite his infamous association with fascism, many of his political utterances are diametrically opposed to totalitarian ideology.

For Pound, a centralized state is to its individual citizens as an abstract concept is to the particulars it relates: both impose unity at the expense of diversity. We can see this homology between politics and philosophy by comparing two of Pound's mentors, Ernest Fenollosa and Maj. C. H. Douglas, theorist of the Social Credit program. Douglas begins his *Economic Democracy* (1920) with an attack on "Prussianism," which he defines as the "demand to subordinate individuality to the need of some external organization, the exaltation of the State into an authority from which there is no appeal (as if the State had a concrete existence apart from those who operate its functions), the exploitation of 'public opinion' manipulated by a Press owned and controlled from the apex of power."[3] Douglas describes the Prussian state in the same way that Fenollosa describes a conceptual abstraction. The state is homologous to an abstract concept in the traditional "logic of classification": both assume a reality independent of the individual elements that constitute it. The Prussian "pyramid form of control,"[4] which directs individuals from above, is like Fenollosa's conceptual pyramid, which reduces individual particulars at the base to conceptual unity at the apex. Moreover, Douglas and Fenollosa respond to this pyramid form of control in the same fashion. Fenollosa rejects the old logic of classification for a new method that avoids hypostatizing the relations between individual particulars. Similarly, Douglas wishes to replace Prussianism with a system designed to maximize individual freedom and to restore the wealth of the community to those who produce it.

This aversion to abstraction and imposed unity is also evident in the *Cantos*. Like William James, Pound argues that "an abstract or general statement is GOOD if it be ultimately found to correspond with the facts" (ABC, 25). Searching for techniques that ground the abstraction in concrete particulars, he championed "the method of the Luminous Detail" (SP, 21), which would "cash in" the historian's questionable "ideas" for the indisputable facts on which they are based: "The artist seeks out the luminous detail and presents it. He does not comment. . . . Each historian will 'have ideas'—presumably different from other historians—imperfect inductions, varying as the fashions, but the luminous details remain unaltered" (SP, 23). Pound discovered support for this method in the works of Ernest Fenollosa and the naturalist Louis Agassiz. Fenollosa's ideogram taught him to present ideas through the juxtaposition of discrete elements. Agassiz's method of induction taught him to value the painstaking accumulation of observed facts. Both men reinforced his determination to argue his case through the cumulative weight of historical details. By resolving his "tale of the tribe" into a significant "phalanx of particulars" (LXXIV/441), Pound hoped to keep his poem anchored in immediate experience.

This "presentative method," however, suffers from a severe shortcoming. It is often difficult to discern the principle that unifies the "phalanx of particulars." To signify "red" by juxtaposing rose, iron rust, cherry, and flamingo seems relatively unproblematic. But even in this elementary ideogram there is no guarantee that the observer will grasp the intended relation; without other clues to guide interpretation, observers may fail to realize that it is *color* and not some other resemblance that links the objects together. And when each of the constituent elements is itself a complex of traits, as is frequently the case in the *Cantos*, the problems of interpretation begin to multiply. Without prior knowledge of Pound's intentions, it is often difficult, if not impossible, to comprehend the relation between a set of diverse particulars. At their best, Pound's ideograms establish a coherent network of relations, a network whose elements interact to form a whole as rich or even richer than the author originally intended. But often readers are simply overwhelmed by a plethora of details whose unifying principle they cannot identify.[b]

The same aversion to imposed unity affects the overall design of the *Cantos*. The problem of epic unity arose as early as Ur-Canto I (1917), where Pound began his search for an appropriate form:

HANG it all, there can be but one *Sordello*!
But say I want to, say I take your whole bag of tricks,
Let in your quirks and tweeks, and say the thing's an art-
form,
Your *Sordello*, and that the modern world
Needs such a rag-bag to stuff all its thought in;
Say that I dump my catch, shiny and silvery

[b] Michael Bernstein examines the principal weaknesses of Pound's method, both his inductive procedure of accumulating details on the same subject and his ideogrammic procedure of juxtaposing details from disparate subjects. The first, he shows, can be damaged by either an excess or a deficiency of elements: from a great mass of particulars we can discern only the most banal and abstract connections; and from an insufficient number of particulars we may not have enough information to see the relevant connections. Similarly, the ideogram can suffer from twin pitfalls: the text may either give us too little indication of what it signifies or it may indicate what it signifies "without adequately substantiating its own interpretation from the given particulars" (Michael André Bernstein, *The Tale of the Tribe: Ezra Pound and the Modern Verse Epic* [Princeton: Princeton University Press, 1980], pp. 41-48).

As fresh sardines flapping and slipping on the
marginal cobbles?
(Ur-Canto I/113)

Pound starts his epic not with a preconceived structure but
with a multitude of fragments, which he depicts as a catch of
sardines "flapping and slipping on the marginal cobbles." In
earlier ages the epic poet would have aspired to the architec-
tonic design of the *Odyssey* or the *Divine Comedy*. But
Pounds contends that the modern world needs a more open-
ended form—a "rag-bag to stuff all its thought in"—and
Browning's *Sordello* offers one prototype that can accommo-
date the many images that pass through the poet's mind.[c]

Pound refuses to impose a preestablished unity on his epic,
and he abandons both the unified plot of the *Odyssey* and the
"Aquinas-map" (L, 323) of the *Commedia*. He even goes a
step further and relinquishes the "one whole man" (Ur-Canto
I/115) that holds together Wordsworth's *Prelude* and Browning's *Sordello*. Writing in an age without a "set belief" (Ur-
Canto I/115), he was prepared to face uncertainty—"Errors,
i.e. wanderings in search of truth have their rights" (GK,
252)—and to allow his work to exhibit "the defects inherent
in a record of struggle" (GK, 135). Pound was by no means
indifferent to the problem of unity, and he hoped eventually
to bring his many fragments "into some sort of design and
architecture" (L, 180). Nor would the *Cantos* depart entirely
from traditional models: it (they?) would be a Homeric voyage
through many lands and a Dantean articulation of a "hierarchy of values." But more than twenty years after he com-

---

[c] The term "rag-bag" also appears in "Aux Etuves de Wiesbaden," a prose
dialogue based on a letter by a Renaissance humanist, which Pound composed around the time of Ur-Canto I. Here Poggio (Gian Francesco Brac-
ciolini) associates "rag-bag" with unconstrained diversity: "Men have a curious desire for uniformity. . . . They ruin the shape of life for a dogmatic
exterior. What dignity have we over the beasts, save to be once, and to be
irreplaceable! I myself am a rag-bag, a mass of sights and citations, but I will
not beat down life for the sake of model" (PD, 102).

pleted Ur-Canto I, Pound was still uncertain of the overall structure: "As to the *form* of *The Cantos*: All I can say or pray is: *wait* till it's there. I mean wait till I get 'em written and then if it don't show, I will start exegesis. I haven't an Aquinas-map; Aquinas *not* valid now" (L, 323). Pound's aversion to preestablished unity was thus as strong, if not stronger, than his fear of disunity. He elected to live with uncertainty of form, and it meant that his life's work ran the risk of lapsing into chaos.

In various ways, then, Pound campaigns against imposed order. He attempts to resolve the abstract concept into its constituent particulars; to restore the state to the individuals who constitute it; to replace a uniform conception of the divine with an unconstrained diversity of visionary experience. And the same impulse also informs his poetry. It explains his procedure of juxtaposing individual particulars and, at another level, his refusal to employ established principles of epic form. Throughout his works, Pound struggles to invert the traditional hierarchy that privileges unity over multiplicity and conceptual form over concrete sensation.

II

Although he assailed the "lust after uniformity," Pound was not content to remain a miscellaneous "rag-bag." He often equates beauty with order, claiming that art is nothing other than the capacity for "combining things into a whole."[5] He identifies "heaven" with the "form-creator," and "hell" with "exterior formlessness."[6] Hence Pound seems to oscillate between his hostility to imposed order and his desire to project new order. If he employed "many fragments" (Ur-Canto I/ 114) to allay his suspicion of forms with "an insufficient number of parts,"[7] he also wished to combine the fragments into a unified whole.

From the outset of his career Pound equated art with the process of unifying fragments. In "Hilda's Book" (1907), he imagines the artist "gathering fragments that there be no loss."[8] At this time he was also intrigued by the Provençal *dompna soisebuda* (Tuscan *donna ideale*)—the perfect lady formed out of the best features of many—and employs this convention in several poems inspired by Bertran de Born, the Provençal troubadour.[d] In other pieces he collects diverse elements from the past and fuses them into a new unity. For instance, the speaker in "Capilupus Sends Greeting to Grotus" resolves to "make my poem, as I would make my self, / From all the best things, of all good men / And great men that go before me. / Yet above all be myself" (CEP, 267). This process of gathering fragments from the past also explains the title of Pound's famous series in the *New Age*, "I Gather the Limbs of Osiris" (1911-12). The "I" is the Egyptian goddess Isis, who attempts to restore the slain Osiris by collecting the scattered pieces of his body. In this series, which includes translations from Old English ("The Seafarer"), Provençal, and Tuscan poetry, Isis becomes the symbol of Pound's effort to unify disparate elements of the past. Pound never abandoned this early fascination with the gathering of fragments: it anticipates the project of the *Cantos*, which may be defined as an attempt to forge out of the noblest elements of various cultures the image of a new and more constructive culture for our age.

Akin to the process of unifying fragments is the act of projecting form on the sensory flux. Pound constantly celebrates the power of the artist to posit new principles for organizing experience. In the Osiris series he posits the distinction between the "symptomatic" artist, who reflects the prevailing "tendencies and modes of a time" (SP, 25), and the "donative" artist, who projects a new way of organizing the sensory flux. Several years later he was still preaching the same mes-

---

[d] See the preliminary note to "Na Audiart" (P, 8) and the translation of Bertran's "Dompna Pois de me No'us Cal" (P, 105). Bertran is also the subject of the intriguing but perplexing poem "Near Perigord" (P, 151). Here the governing motif is the disintegration of unity into fragments, a motif that underscores the poet's own failure to make sense out of fragments from the past.

sage. Stirred by the nonrepresentational art of Gaudier-Brzeska and Wyndham Lewis, he maintains that the artist can "not only record but create. . . . he can move as a force; he can produce 'order-giving vibrations' " (SP, 376):

> An organisation of forms expresses a confluence of forces. These forces may be the "love of God," the "life-force," emotions, passions, what you will. For example: if you clap a strong magnet beneath a plateful of iron filings, the energies of the magnet will proceed to organise form. It is only by applying a particular and suitable force that you can bring order and vitality and thence beauty into a plate of iron filings, which are otherwise as "ugly" as anything under heaven. The design in the magnetised iron filings expresses a confluence of energy. It is not "meaningless" or "inexpressive."[9]

Like the magnet, which orders the mass of iron filings, the artist brings order to the shapeless mass of sensations. In this image art is at once a process of transforming fragments into unity and a process of imposing form on the chaotic flux.[e]

Pound readily extended the idea of "order-giving vibrations" from the realm of art to those of ethics and politics. Hell is "exterior formlessness," and it is no accident that

[e] The idea of a form-bestowing force, or an "order-giving vibration," also informs Pound's famous definition of the Image (1913): "An 'Image' is that which presents an intellectual and emotional complex in an instant of time. I use the term 'complex' rather in the technical sense employed by the newer psychologists, such as Hart, though we might not agree absolutely in our application" (LE, 4). Pound was struck by the description of a complex in Bernard Hart's *The Psychology of Insanity* (1912). Hart defines a complex as "a system of emotionally toned ideas," a "force" that produces a distinctive manner of organizing experience: "Complexes, then, are causes which determine the behaviour of the conscious stream, and the action which they exert upon consciousness may be regarded as the psychological analogue of the conception of 'force' in physics" ([Cambridge: Cambridge University Press, 1912], p. 62). Thus the complex is more than an association of ideas; it is a force that creates specific patterns of association. Similarly, Pound's Image radiates a force of its own; it produces "that sense of sudden liberation" which occurs when we discover a new way of arranging experience.

Pound consigns to his Inferno those who "set nothing in order" (XXV/118). Heaven, by contrast, is the domain of the "form-creator," and true to his Confucian principles Pound admires the wise leader who transfers the "order within him" into order within his dominions:

> And Kung said, and wrote on the bo leaves:
>   If a man have not order within him
> He can not spread order about him;
> And if a man have not order within him
> His family will not act with due order;
>   And if the prince have not order within him
> He can not put order in his dominions.
> And Kung gave the words "order"
> and "brotherly deference"
> And said nothing of the "life after death."
> (XIII/59)

Statecraft, like art, involves the capacity for bestowing form. As the artist projects an imaginative order upon experience, so the good prince establishes a just political order in his dominions.

But this analogy between the artist and the prince led Pound into trouble. In Canto XIII we have little difficulty reconciling the "order-giving vibrations" of the prince with the best interests of his subjects: order and brotherly deference walk hand in hand. The trouble emerges when the prince takes the form of a tyrant:

> I assert again my own firm belief that the Duce will stand not with despots and lovers of power but with the lovers of
> ORDER
> τὸ καλόν[10]

Here we see the danger of applying the same approach to disparate realms of activity. Pound made the mistake of considering Mussolini a good prince, as did many others in the Twenties. But he compounded his error by considering Mussolini a donative intelligence, a "projective thinker" in the political domain. The notion of the donative mind, which works quite well in the realm of art, is far more problematic in the realm of politics. Unlike the artist, the prince imposes form on the lives of his subjects, and if he is to be a good prince, he must submit his "order-giving vibrations" to constraints from which the creative artist is free. Pound seems to have ignored this elementary distinction. In the case of Mussolini, he identified exclusively with the initiatives of the ruler, and conceiving the fascist state as a work of imagination, he mistook its imposed order for the noncoercive order of art.

In poetry and politics alike, Pound defines creativity as the capacity to bestow new principles of order. This equation between genius and order runs counter to his struggle against fixed principles of order, and it was often difficult to mediate between them. Each of these opposing impulses had its attendant dangers, and oftentimes it produced the condition that the other was meant to overcome. In the *Cantos* the attempt to avoid imposed unity brought Pound to the verge of incoherence, while in the political realm, the desire to create new unity led him to embrace the will-to-order of a single man. As we shall see, Pound was attracted to constructs that mediate between the antinomies of coercive unity and unconstrained diversity. Nevertheless, in many instances he leaped to one extreme or the other, either to the chaos that proceeds from rejection of order, or to an order more reductive and more coercive than anything he left behind.

III

Despite the tendency to embrace one extreme or the other, Pound occasionally achieved a synthesis between form and flux. Here we can see the significance of constructs such as the ideogram and the precise interpretive metaphor, which enabled Pound to mediate between the desire to dissolve coercive forms and the desire to produce new forms. The ideogram is a concept that displays its constituent particulars by synthesizing identity and difference, conceptual unity and sensory multiplicity. It performs the function of abstraction without displacing us from concrete experience. Similarly, the precise interpretive metaphor projects order on experience without collapsing the distinction between the organizing form and the reality to which it gives shape. As we have seen, Pound identified the precise interpretive metaphor with forms that superimpose an image or pattern on the sensory flux: the single-image haiku, which places an imagined object upon a natural one; the geometrical configurations that the Vorticist projects upon experience; the "radiant world" that appears in the presence of the beloved lady; and the visionary experiences of metamorphosis and of the gods. These metaphors present as experiential possibility rather than conceptual certainty a particular way of ordering experience. They maintain a tension between the organizing form and the natural flux it interprets. In this section I will examine one of these metaphors—the gods super-posed on the landscape—and show how it establishes the kind of relationship for which Pound was searching. Then I will turn briefly to the *Cantos* and suggest how the notion of form upon flux sheds light on its problematic structure.

Pound's approach to the gods illustrates his effort to hold together "interpretive" forms and the sensory flux they interpret. Pound maintains that the sense of divine presence arises from the human response to natural beauty; it expresses the kinship between the perceiving subject and the natural object. There is an important difference, however, between the pagan gods and the god of monotheistic religions. The monotheistic god has been detached from the original relationship between humankind and nature. Just as an abstract concept hypostatizes the relationship between individual particulars, the monotheistic god hypostatizes the relationship between perceiving subject and natural object: both the concept and the god become entities that are considered independent of, and ontologically prior to, the things they relate. The gods of

polytheistic culture, by contrast, express the relationship between subject and object without reifying the divine form.
The gods remain tied to the natural landscape from which
they emerge:

> Gods float in the azure air,
> Bright gods and Tuscan, back before dew was shed.
> Light: and the first light, before ever dew was fallen.
> Panisks, and from the oak, dryas,
> And from the apple, mælid,
> Through all the wood, and the leaves are full of voices,
> A-whisper, and the clouds bowe over the lake,
> And there are gods upon them . . .
>
> (III/11)

These visionary deities are more like metaphors than abstract
concepts: unlike the monotheistic god, who transcends man
and nature alike, the divine form remains bound to its constituent terms, the beholder and the world he beholds, and
expresses the relationship between them. Moreover, these
visionary experiences display a tensional relationship between form and flux: we see the divine being together with
the reality it interprets, the organizing form tied to its source
in immediate experience.

This image of divine form super-posed on the natural flux
came to Pound from various sources, both Western and non-
Western. One instance appears in his translation of *Suma
Genji*, a Japanese Noh play he found among Fenollosa's papers. Here the spirit of an ancient hero appears upon the
waters and begins a "blue dance of the sea waves." Genji's
dance is one of the most compelling visionary experiences in
Fenollosa's collection:

> The flower of waves-reflected
> Is on his white garment;
> That pattern covers the sleeve.
> The air is alive with flute-sounds,
> With the song of various pipes

The land is a-quiver
And even the wild sea of Suma

Is filled with resonant quiet.
Moving in clouds and in rain,
The dream overlaps with the real;
There was a light out of heaven,
There was a young man at the dance here;
Surely it was Genji Hikaru,
It was Genji Hikaru in spirit.
                                        (N, 25)

From the Western tradition, Pound especially admired Botticelli's *Birth of Venus*, which depicts the goddess upon the
sea-foam out of which she emerged, and when he made Venus the supreme deity of the *Cantos*, Pound linked her directly to the image of form upon flux. After her brief appearance in Canto I, Venus enters next in a passage adapted from
the Homeric Hymns, where Aphrodite, disguised as the
daughter of an earthly king, seduces Anchises, the father of
Aeneas. Pound supplements the story with a visionary experience of "waves taking form":

"King Otreus, of Phrygia,
"That king is my father."
                        and saw then, as of waves taking form,
As the sea, hard, a glitter of crystal,
And the waves rising but formed, holding their form.
No light reaching through them.
                                        (XXIII/109)

"as the sculptor sees the form in the air . . .
"as glass seen under water,
"King Otreus, my father . . .
and saw the waves taking form as crystal,
notes as facets of air,
and the mind there, before them, moving,
so that notes needed not move.
                                        (XXV/119)

Pound's Venus is an imaginary form that arises from the passionate response to natural beauty. It is therefore no accident that she is associated with the ecstatic vision of "waves taking form": like the goddess herself, this image expresses the creative moment when nature is transfigured by imagination. The vision of waves "rising but formed" manifests the poet's aspiration to project new order in a way that maintains a tensional relationship between the interpretive form and the reality it interprets.

This vision of form upon flux also sheds light on Pound's approach to the structure of the *Cantos*:

> Art very possibly *ought* to be the supreme achievement, the 'accomplished'; but there is the other satisfactory effect, that of a man hurling himself at an indomitable chaos, and yanking and hauling as much of it as possible into some sort of order (or beauty), aware of it both as chaos and as potential. (LE, 396)

The act of "yanking and hauling" recalls Ur-Canto I, where Pound depicts his "many fragments" as a catch of "fresh sardines flapping and slipping on the marginal cobbles." If the modern mind sees reality as "indomitable chaos," modern artists must project order as "potential" rather than actuality, possibility rather than fact. They must find constructs that exhibit simultaneously the potential and the chaos. Pound was aware that he had sacrificed the opportunity to realize "the supreme achievement, the 'accomplished.' " He had given up the symmetries of the *Odyssey* and the *Commedia* for open-ended "wandering in search of truth." He also knew that he was striving for "the other satisfactory effect"—the "yanking and hauling" of chaos into "some sort of order (or beauty)." Caught between his struggle against imposed order and his effort to project new order, Pound may well have thought that the *Cantos* would maintain the tension between potential and chaos, the structure that bestows coherence and the unformulable flux of reality itself.

It remains an open question whether the *Cantos* fully achieves "that other satisfactory effect." Many critics believe that Pound gambled and lost on the likelihood that order would emerge in the process of composition. They feel that because of his aversion to established principles of form, the *Cantos* remained a disconnected series of poetic fragments.[f] Others see Pound erring in the opposite direction: they dwell less on the form of the *Cantos* than its ideology, and view Pound as the exponent of a vicious new dogma. Modern critics are well aware that in a culture that has lost established principles of order, chaos and dogma are the two extremes to which the mind is prey. T. S. Eliot, for instance, is often praised or blamed for turning deliberately to dogma in order to find redemption from the chaos. Pound, for his part, struggled with the polarities of form and flux, and sought to create a productive interaction between them. And while he certainly fell victim to each of the antithetical tendencies within him—the fear of coercive order and the desire to project new order—he was always inspired by the example of constructs like the ideogram and the precise interpretive metaphor, constructs that establish a creative tension between potential and chaos, the interpretive design and the flux it interprets.

The Rites of Remembrance

The search for tensional constructs informs another dimension of Pound's poetics—his habit of fashioning new verse out

[f] According to Yvor Winters, "Mr. Pound proceeds from image to image wholly through the coherence of feeling. . . . the progression from statement to statement is not reasonable: it is the progression either of random conversation or of revery." Associating feeling with chaos and reason with form, Winters contends that "all feeling, if one gives oneself (that is, one's form) up to it, is a way of disintegration; poetic form is by definition a means to arrest the disintegration and order the feeling. Pound, in this view, follows the "way of disintegration" (*In Defense of Reason* [Denver: Alan Swallow, 1947], pp. 57 and 144).

of old. Pound regarded the past as a vast repository of experiences that can expand our horizons in the present. He also saw that it is the task of the modern poet not merely to recover these experiences but to reconstitute them for a new age. The only way to resurrect the past is to "make it new," and Pound labored tirelessly to revitalize dead voices through imaginative translation, adaptation, and new composition. He viewed artistic creativity as a dialectical exchange between tradition and innovation, between the recovery of past experience and the invention of a new voice for modernity. This exchange between past and present manifests a tensional relationship similar to that which informs the ideogram and the precise interpretive metaphor. It involves the same dual emphasis on the restoration of immediate experience and the production of new forms that reinterpret experience. The project of recovering experience from the past is analogous to that of recovering immediate experience in the present: the artist releases us from the limits of our own temporal horizon and restores us to past modes of experience. Similarly, the demand to "make it new" is analogous to the project of producing new forms: the artist frees us from the constraints of tradition by reshaping older works to suit the altered circumstances of modernity. The relationship between past and present is thus an expansion of both Bergson's emphasis on the *recovery* of immediate experience and Nietzsche's emphasis on the *invention* of forms that change the way we order reality.

From one point of view, Pound's approach to historical recollection may be compared to Bergson's approach to personal recollection. According to Bergson, memory is usually restricted to those elements of the past that serve the practical needs of the moment. It is only when we suspend the instrumental mechanisms governing everyday life that we recover full consciousness of our past. We can see this process in the overture to Proust's great novel, when the taste of the *petite madeleine* stirs Marcel's memory and launches his long reexamination of times past. Pound displays a similar approach to memory, although he is concerned with cultural as well as personal recollection. A physical sensation may activate not only personal but also historical remembrance: "The box of scented wood / Recalls cathedrals" (Ur-Canto I/120). The sight of a particular landscape may inspire Pound to recreate the historical moment that endowed it with significance. His visit to Catullus's Sirmio, for instance, revived the visionary presence of the gods that once appeared above the waters of Lake Garda (Ur-Canto I/115-16). Pound approaches the external world as a kind of palimpsest. Beneath the surface of experience lies a world that is laden with valuable presences. While most of us remain oblivious to the traces of the past that surround us, the artist is peculiarly sensitive to the hidden presence of "beauty lost in the years" (N, 27).

From another point of view, Pound's approach to historical recollection may be compared to Nietzsche's. In *Vom Nutzen und Nachteil der Historie fur das Leben* [*Of the Uses and Disadvantages of History for Life*] (1874), Nietzsche posits an inverse correlation between attachment to the past and creative vitality in the present, maintaining that the nineteenth-century obsession with history expresses a peculiarly modern deficiency of being. The study of the past has degenerated into mere nostalgia; the accumulation of historical knowledge has become an end in itself and no longer serves the needs of life in the present. Pound conducts a similar campaign against the abuse of cultural memory. Like Nietzsche, he opposes the dissociation between history and "life." He subordinates memory to imagination, history to art: "Memory," he says, "is one of the least interesting mental attributes. . . . it is indeed purely mechanical. The human addition is the faculty which leaps into memory and snatches up this or that at the moment. The Muses are not memory but the Daughters of Memory."[11] We must overcome our life-denying worship of the past, Pounds declares, and affirm our power to reshape the world around us.

This section begins with Pound's passion for the past, then turns to his Nietzschean critique of this very passion, and finally proceeds to his efforts to strike a balance between them. While he quarried the tradition for valuable modes of experience, Pound, like Nietzsche, recognized the dangers of historical consciousness. He saw that excessive attachment to the past can be as dangerous as ignorance of the past, and his early works record the search for the right relationship between recollection and renewal, between fidelity to tradition and the will to creative innovation.[g]

I

In one of his jeremiads against modern civilization, "Provincialism the Enemy" (1917), Pound attacks not only the regional provincialism that was devastating Europe but also what he calls the "provincialism of time" (SP, 198). He maintains that it is as dangerous for a culture to ignore the past as it is to isolate itself from other cultures in the present. If we forget the historical foundations of our civilization, we lose our sense of cultural identity: "As the present is unknowable we roust amid known fragments of the past 'to get light on it,' to get an inkling of the process which produced what we encounter" (GK, 129). A culture that uses "ideas based on forgotten origins"[12] is like the individual who thinks with abstractions that have lost their grounding in immediate experience. Such a culture uses "only husks and shells of the thoughts that have been already lived over by others" (LE, 371). Moreover, if we neglect alternative forms of awareness

[g] The struggle between recollection and renewal resembles the contemporary debate between Gadamer's hermeneutics and Habermas's "critique of ideologies." Paul Ricoeur summarizes the main issue of this debate: "While hermeneutical philosophy sees in tradition a dimension of historical consciousness, an aspect of participation in cultural heritages and reactivation of them, the critique of ideologies sees in the same tradition the place par excellence of distortions and alienations and opposes to it the regulative idea, which it projects into the future, of communication without frontiers and without constraint" (*Political and Social Essays*, ed. David Stewart and Joseph Bien [Athens: Ohio University Press, 1974], p. 248). See also *Hermeneutics and the Human Sciences*, pp. 63-100.

buried in the past, we lose our ability to assess and renew civilization in the present. Historical recollection makes us aware of both our existing identity and our future possibilities.

From the outset of his career Pound identified his poetry with the revival of dead voices. He quickly discovered predecessors who shared his desire to resurrect lost forms of consciousness. His first published article, "Raphaelite Latin" (1906), applauds those Renaissance poets who returned to ancient poetry and recovered the forgotten sensitivity expressed by the presence of gods in the natural landscape: "The old gods and tutelar deities are no mere machinery for the decoration of poetry, but the very spirits of the trees and meres; and so these men of the rebirth felt them, even as the first Greek singers."[13] A few years later he paid similar tribute to the genius of Ovid, who "raises the dead and dissects their mental processes" (SR, 16). But by far the most important of these precursors was Robert Browning, who taught Pound how a modern poet reanimates the ghosts of the past. Many of his best early poems are, in fact, Browningesque monologues that recreate the spirit of medieval Provençe. Following in the footsteps of these predecessors, Pound wrote about his own work as a kind of journey to the dead. He identified personal creativity with the recreation of voices from the past. In 1908, the unknown poet gazed at the ancient splendors of Venice and described his burgeoning inspiration as a recovery of "old powers" (CEP, 233). Four years later, he looked back on his extraordinary output of the preceding years and imagined himself a triumphant voyager returning from the "tombs" with "strange fashions of music":

> I bring you the spoils, my nation,
> I, who went out in exile,
>   Am returned to thee with gifts.

> I, who have laboured long in the tombs,
>   Am come back therefrom with riches.
>   (CEP, 209)

This motif of the journey to the dead is central to Pound's writings. It appears prominently in his earliest works, and eventually it was given a position of honor at the beginning of the *Cantos*.

Pound, like Browning, was a beneficiary of the historical consciousness that dominated Western thought since the early nineteenth century. He was also indebted to the scholarly tradition that emerged from this new orientation to the past. As a student of Romance languages he learned the philological methods of his day and readily employed them in his creative and critical writings. He was influenced, for example, by the scholarly practice of resolving ancient texts into successive historical layers. Anglo-Saxon scholars maintained that Old English poems often consisted of an original pagan core that was later emended by a Christian redactor, and it has been shown that this approach to literary texts inspired Pound's decision to excise the "Christian" element from his translation of "The Seafarer."[14] The same scholarly practice also accounts for Pound's enduring attraction to the notion of the palimpsest, which he used as a structural principle in the *Cantos*. Pound thus owes his view of history not merely to Browning but to the entire cultural milieu in which Browning participated. From his interest in textual cruces to his conviction that self-understanding proceeds from an understanding of the past, Pound's *œuvre* bears the unmistakable imprint of nineteenth-century historicism.

Pound's approach to the past bears an especially strong resemblance to the project of nineteenth-century hermeneutics, particularly that of Wilhelm Dilthey, the eminent philosopher of history. Like Bergson, Dilthey appeals to the notion of immediate experience, but he is concerned primarily with historical rather than personal recollection. Dilthey associates historical understanding with the recovery of "lived experience" (*Erlebnis*) in the past. He considers history a repository of human experiences, and claims that historical investigation "widens our horizons to include possibilities for human life which can be made accessible only in this way."[15]

Pound assumes a similar position, maintaining that the past reveals experiential possibilities not otherwise available to us. It is the task of the poet to explore earlier forms of thinking and feeling, especially as they are objectified in art. The distinctive visual, auditory, and semantic qualities of literary masterpieces provide us with unique access to forgotten modes of sentience and to the values they manifest.[h]

Like Dilthey, Pound sought to bridge the distance between past and present by recovering the lived experience of the author. He is also akin to Dilthey in his emphasis on the common humanity that enables us to comprehend sensibilities different from our own. Dilthey speaks of "the intimate kinship of all human psychic life"[16] that makes it possible to communicate across the centuries. Pound says the same thing in the more rarified medium he adopted from Neoplatonic philosophy: ". . . the soul of each man is compounded of all the elements of the cosmos of souls" (SP, 28). One of his earliest poems, "Histrion" (1907), celebrates this principle of psychic unity:

No man hath dared to write this thing as yet,
And yet I know, how that the souls of all men great
At times pass through us,

[h] Fredric Jameson labels this approach to the past "existential historicism." He identifies this approach with Dilthey, Croce, Collingwood, Ortega y Gasset, Américo Castro, and with German philologues such as Auerbach, Spitzer, and Panofsky. According to Jameson, existential historicism is "derived from German *Lebensphilosophie*, in which the infinite multiplicity of human symbolic acts is the expression of the infinite potentialities of a nonalienated human nature. The experience of historicity then restores something of this richness to a present in which few enough of those potentialities are practically available to any of us" (Fredric Jameson, "Marxism and Historicism," *New Literary History* 11 [Autumn 1979], 51). Like Pound, Jameson uses Odysseus's journey to the underworld as a symbol for the reawakening of voices from the past. "The historicist act revives the dead and reenacts the essential mystery of the cultural past which, like Tiresias drinking the blood, is momentarily returned to life and warmth and allowed once more to speak its mortal speech and to deliver its long-forgotten message in surroundings unfamiliar to it" (pp. 51-52).

And we are melted into them, and are not
Save reflexions of their souls.
Thus am I Dante for a space and am
One François Villon, ballad-lord and thief
Or am such holy ones I may not write,
Lest blasphemy be writ against my name;
This for an instant and the flame is gone . . .
(CEP, 71)

Despite the differences that separate one soul (or one age) from another, we possess the capacity to identify with any expression of life: "Et omniformis . . . omnis / Intellectus est" ["Every intellect is capable of assuming every shape"] (XXIII/ 107). It is this kinship between ourselves and our predecessors that allows us to transcend our own temporal horizon and participate in an enduring cultural tradition.

For Dilthey, the crux of historical understanding lies in the interaction between our common humanity and the distinctive characteristics of each age. He maintains that hermeneutics "would be impossible if [different] expressions of life were utterly alien," and it would be "unnecessary if there were nothing alien in them."[17] This interplay between unity and diversity also plays a crucial role in Pound's poetics:

The soul of each man is compounded of all the elements of the cosmos of souls, but in each soul there is some one element which predominates, which is in some peculiar and intense way the quality or *virtù* of the individual; in no two souls is this the same. It is by reason of this *virtù* that a given work of art persists. It is by reason of this *virtù* that we have one Catullus, one Villon; by reason of it that no amount of technical cleverness can produce a work having the same charm as the original, not though all progress in art is, in so great degree a progress through imitation. (SP, 28)

Pound's doctrine mediates between identity and difference; it holds together the awareness of a common tradition and a recognition of the distinctive voices that inform it. More importantly, Pound makes a virtue of the ineradicable distance between individual authors. He claims that new art arises through "imitation"—the transformation of the older work that proceeds from the effort to reproduce it. "Works of art beget works of art,"[18] and as a result of the interaction between our shared humanity and unique individuality, we participate in a tradition that both sustains and renews us.

II

Pound was deeply indebted to nineteenth-century historical consciousness, but was also aware of its dangers. He saw that historical consciousness tempts its devotees into an uncritical acceptance of the past; it fosters nostalgic longing for bygone ages and indifference to the challenge of the present. Like many of his generation, Pound resisted any temptation to sanctify tradition. The horrors of the First World War had called into question the validity of the Western heritage, and it made him acutely aware that history is not only a storehouse of valuable experiences but also the scene of oppression and communicative distortion. As a result of the war and its aftermath, Pound went beyond aesthetic identification with "magic moments" of the past and began an investigation of the forces that produced the moral collapse of the West. The aim of this investigation was not the mere recollection of the past but the construction of a new civilization for the future.

If the fascination with remembrance ties Pound to Bergson and Dilthey, the desire to overcome the burden of remembrance ties him to Nietzsche. In *The Uses and Disadvantages of History for Life*, Nietzsche condemns the excesses of nineteenth-century historical culture. He contends that the academic establishment encourages the scholar to detach history from life. The prevailing attitude leads to a passive, retrospective stance that Nietzsche equates with the diminished energies of old age. An excessive preoccupation with history is "a kind of inborn grey-hairedness,"[19] and it saps away the vital impulse to build anew. Historical knowledge is justified solely by its service to "life and action": ". . . only he who constructs the future has a right to judge the past."[20] Nietzsche declares that the retrospective attitude of old age should yield to the constructive attitude of youth. He subordinates memory to imagination, history to art, and celebrates not the mere recovery of the past but the creative power to transform it.

Pound conducts a similar campaign against the excesses of historicism. As a graduate student he had picked up a measure of philological training and observed the conduct of academic research. This experience at the university made a lasting impression: Pound remained indebted to historical scholarship, but in his Inferno we find the professors "sitting on piles of stone books, / obscuring the texts with philology" (XIV/63). For Pound, the professors manifest the danger of historical consciousness, the tendency to divorce the study of the past from the needs of the present. Like Nietzsche, he argues that in the course of developing an efficient system for gathering historical data the university has divorced historical knowledge from "vital values" (SP, 192). The professors cultivate "an ideal of 'scholarship,' not an ideal of humanity"; they stifle the spirit of independent inquiry by compelling students to waste their energies on "some minute particular problem *unconnected* with life" (SP, 191).

The academic approach to literature is also informed by this sterile historicism. According to Pound, the professors are more concerned with the acquisition of historical knowledge than the retrieval of valuable modes of expression. They are methodologically indifferent to artistic value, making no distinction between the masterpiece and the mediocrity, which they consider equally valuable as objects of historical inquiry. Pound responds to the professors by distinguishing sharply between historical and artistic value. Rejecting the "slough of philology," he awaits the day "when it will be possible for the lover of poetry to study poetry—even the poetry of recondite times and places—without burdening himself with the rags of morphology, epigraphy, *privatleben* and the kindred delights of the archaeological or 'scholarly' mind" (SR, 5). Free from these scholarly encumbrances, the study of literature will recover its link to "vital values"; the existing "ideal of scholarship" will give way to an "ideal of humanity."[i]

Pound's quarrel with the professors found its way into the *Cantos*. It is especially prominent in Canto VII, his portrayal of the postwar wasteland, where the professors are the guardians of a moribund tradition. In this canto, Pound gazes at a building with a "sham" ancient façade and imagines the "dry professorial talk" within:

Words like the locust-shells, moved by no inner being;
A dryness calling for death;

Another day, between walls of a sham Mycenian,
"Toc" sphinxes, sham-Memphis columns,
And beneath the jazz a cortex, a stiffness or stillness,
Shell of the older house.
Brown-yellow wood, and the no colour plaster,
Dry professorial talk . . .
now stilling the ill beat music,
House expulsed by this house.

Square even shoulders and the satin skin,
Gone cheeks of the dancing woman,
Still the old dead dry talk, gassed out—

[i] Pound's distinction between historical and artistic value anticipates the battle between historical scholars and literary critics in the Thirties and Forties. Declaring that "all ages are contemporaneous," Pound calls for "a literary scholarship, which will weigh Theocritus and Yeats with one balance, and which will judge dull dead men as inexorably as dull writers of today, and will, with equity, give praise to beauty before referring to an almanack" (SR, 6). We should not misinterpret this remark, which is often considered a kind of New Critical effort to establish an ahistorical criterion for literary value. Like the New Critics, Pound is attempting to shift the focus of literary studies, but does not identify literary quality with any particular set of techniques. Instead, Pound's new scholarship is open to all types of technical accomplishment and to the various forms of lived experience they manifest.

It is ten years gone, makes stiff about her a glass,
A petrefaction of air.
The old room of the tawdry class asserts itself;
The young men, never!
(VII/26)

Pound links the professors to the building they inhabit. He suggests that the same abuse of historical consciousness produced both the scholarly worship of the past and the sham revivalism of nineteenth-century architecture. Just as the professors divorced history from life, architects abandoned the search for a distinctively contemporary style in favor of servile imitation of ancient monuments. Like Nietzsche, Pound identifies this type of historical consciousness with the diminished vitality of old age. The professors' words are "dead," "dry," and "still"; they speak for a culture that cherishes memories of more vigorous times but has lost the capacity for spontaneous action. Taking his indictment a step further, Pound associates professorial talk with "gas" and "shells," and notes the absence of "the young men." The professors are thus implicated in the catastrophe of the Great War, which carried off the young men of Pound's generation. The young men themselves are linked to the "dancing woman . . . ten years gone," who recalls the short-lived cultural renascence disrupted by the war. In this canto Pound sets up a sharp contrast between vitality and caducity, the creative youth who have been casually sacrificed and the old professors whose "dead dry talk" has shamefully survived the debacle. The professors therefore represent more than a dry-as-dust approach to literature; they symbolize the death-in-life of a stagnant culture that remains fixated on the past and indifferent to new initiatives.

Pound, like Nietzsche, disdained passive acceptance of tradition and demanded a more active exchange between past and present. The professors attempt to eliminate the tension between old and new by identifying with the author in his original milieu. Pound, on the other hand, makes productive use of the tension between past and present. He is often less concerned with a text's original meaning than its potential for instigating new thought. This dialectical exchange informs his work as a translator and critic, for which the professors frequently condemned him. His translations, such as "Homage to Sextus Propertius," sacrifice faithful reproduction for creative interpretation. His criticism follows a similar pattern: authorial intention is less important than the reader's imagination, the original meaning subordinate to constructive thought in the present. In his earliest essays, for instance, he praises a group of Renaissance poets for creatively (mis)translating their Latin forebears. In Silver Age verse, the gods had become "stale, a matter of course, a belief beginning to die." But for the Renaissance Latinists who encountered them, these deities possessed the vitality they had for "the first Greek singers," expressing "a world of elusive beauty, new found . . . and their wonder was dew-fresh upon them, even as it always is to whoso truly cares to find it."[21] For Pound, the significance of the Renaissance Latinists lies in their retrieval of a valuable form of awareness, which was lost to the Latin poets themselves. While scholars might object that these Renaissance poets misread their predecessors, Pound maintains that fidelity to authorial intention is far less important than the recovery of an "eternal state of mind."

Pound also reacts to the pedagogues by adopting a more critical approach to the past. Once again, his attitude is similar to that of Nietzsche, whose aim is not to participate in the tradition but to examine it from an independent point of view. The life of any culture is an expression of an underlying set of values, and Nietzsche measures these values against what he claims are the highest values. From this suprahistorical vantage point he declares that the Western tradition expresses a debased form of life, and that the Platonic-Christian ethos has disfigured the supreme values so successfully that we now abhor them. In response to this inversion of the highest values, Nietzsche calls for a radical break with the prevailing tradition. Turning for his model to the pre-Socratic culture of the Greeks, he seeks to unmask the life-denying values of the dominant ethos and to inspire new reverence for the tradition it suppressed.

Pound, too, regards the thoughts, actions, and institutions of a culture as an expression of its underlying "direction of the will." He assesses a tradition (or any one of its phases) in terms of "the relative importance of the various moral, intellectual, and material values" (SP, 320).[j] Like Nietzsche, Pound detaches himself from prevailing Western values and measures them against his own hierarchy of values. At the bottom of this hierarchy are the "infernal" values: self-aggrandizement in the form of indifference to communal welfare or intolerance of differences; the disorder of the passions that leads to violence or perversion; wholesale exploitation of nature's resources. At the top are the "paradisal" values: the Confucian concern for communal harmony and brotherly deference; the refinement of the passions expressed in Provençal and Tuscan verse; the reverence for nature's beauty and fecundity manifest in the visionary experience of the gods.[k] These paradisal values express an "eternal state of mind" that flourished occasionally in the past and ought to prevail in the future. Thus, Pound judges history from a suprahistorical point of view. His "tale of the tribe" is designed to limn out

[j] Consider Pound's comment on a sentence by Burckhardt: ". . . when in Burckhardt we come upon a passage: 'In this year the Venetians refused to make war upon the Milanese because they held that any war between buyer and seller must prove profitable to neither,' we come upon a portent, the old order changes, one conception of war and of the State begins to decline. The Middle Ages imperceptibly give ground to the Renaissance. A ruler owning a State and wishing to enlarge his possessions, could under one régime, in a manner opposed to sound economy, make war; but commercial sense is sapping this régime" (SP, 22). Here the change from the Middle Ages to the Renaissance is essentially a change in the "direction of the will," a shift in fundamental values that will manifest itself in every aspect of the culture.

[k] Aphrodite, the goddess of love, fertility, and beauty, is the purest expression of paradisal values. She represents the "direction of the will" that regards both nature and humanity as objects of love rather than exploitation.

the moral possibilities of man and to identify the highest expressions of human life.

From the vantage point of his own "hierarchy of values," Pound views the Western heritage not as a harmonious process of cumulative development, but as a perpetual struggle between the prevailing ideology and its potential rivals. All too often the course of Western history has been determined by a morally pernicious but powerful group that suppresses a superior form of awareness. Pound contends that the medieval Church and the modern usurocracy alike have attempted to eliminate alternatives that threaten their dominion. Moreover, in its drive to achieve ideological hegemony, the dominant group controls the historical record; it shapes the interpretation of events in a way that discredits the opposition and legitimates its own authority. The modern "seeker after knowledge" must therefore view the past with a critical eye; he must delve beneath official history and search for traces of alternative values that have been ideologically distorted and physically suppressed.

Pound devotes many cantos to these lost forms of awareness. The Malatesta Cantos, for example, show how a corrupt papacy discredited initiatives that threatened its ideology. Pound knew that the received view of Sigismundo Malatesta was originally promulgated by his enemy, Pope Pius II, and at the beginning of Canto VIII he sets up his own muse in opposition to the pope's official truth:

> These fragments you have shelved (shored).
> "Slut!" "Bitch!" Truth and Calliope
> Slanging each other sous les lauriers . . .
>
> (VIII/28)

Pound's "fragments," which are historical documents that reveal the true character of Malatesta, have been "shelved" by the pope, whose slanderous account has been accepted for centuries. Following the lead of a few twentieth-century historians, Pound reopens the case and presents documents that bear witness to a "live man" struggling against the destructive current of his age. The poet associates Malatesta with a short-lived polytheistic revival, the pope with a coercive monotheism intolerant of other forms of expression, and together they exemplify the recurrent struggle between creative individuals and oppressive institutions. Pound knew that the victory has usually gone to the pope and his kind, and that it is the privilege of the victors to write the history of the struggle. Hence Calliope must have a long memory and keen vision to unmask what Truth has kept safely disguised.

Pound's historicism, then, has more in common with Nietzsche than with those whom Nietzsche attacked. Shaken by the Great War and its aftermath, which convinced him of the moral bankruptcy of the West, Pound subordinates recollection to renewal, identification with the past to construction of the future: "Quite simply," he says, "I want a new civilization."[22] Pound's ultimate aim is to instigate a change in the "direction of the will": if the thoughts, actions, and institutions of a culture express an underlying system of values, then a change in the condition of mind will alter the course of history. The *Cantos* were thus designed to challenge the corrupted values of Western civilization and to inspire reverence for the highest values—the "eternal state of mind"—which will lay the groundwork for a new and more humane society.

III

Pound was critical of historical consciousness but refused to abandon it. Instead, he attempted to establish a tensional relationship between tradition and innovation. It is evident from his early works that he was struggling with a series of interrelated oppositions—memory/imagination, impersonal recollection/personal expression, fidelity to tradition/creative innovation—and that he had considerable difficulty resolving the conflict between them. The conflict became acute in the Ur-Cantos (1917), where he employed a model that made it impossible to reconcile historical veracity and artistic expression. Pound eventually overcame his problems and discarded the Ur-Cantos, but the early poetry offers a revealing record of his efforts to find the right relations between competing points of view.

In his early poems Pound often seems uncertain of his orientation to the past. His verse suggests that he was attempting to mediate between Mnemosyne and the Muses, between faithful restoration and creative transformation of the past. At certain times, he imagines himself fully possessed by his precursors; his own thoughts are purely "reflexions of their souls" (CEP, 71). At other times, however, he regards the ghosts of the past as extensions of himself—"crescent images of *me*" (CEP, 36). Pound was seeking a voice that bridges the distinction between cultural memory and creative imagination, effacement of the self before the historical object and free expression of the self in response to it. But in his early works he had not yet found the solution, and we find him oscillating erratically between alternative positions.

This conflict between memory and imagination reaches its climax in Ur-Canto I. Near the outset of the poem, Pound considers the relationship between history and art in Browning's *Sordello*. Browning, he notes, takes liberties with historical fact: ". . . And half your dates are out, you mix your eras; / For that great font Sordello sat beside— / 'Tis an immortal passage, but the font?— / Is some two centuries outside the picture" (Ur-Canto I/114). Pound is evidently disturbed enough to make an issue of this misrepresentation of the past, but he is ready to affirm Browning's higher purpose. The misplaced font and the other historical inaccuracies pose no substantial problem:

Does it matter?
           Not in the least. Ghosts move about me
Patched with histories. You had your business:
To set out so much thought, so much emotion;
To paint, more real than any dead Sordello,
The half or third of your intensest life
And call that third *Sordello*;
And you'll say, "No, not your life,

He never showed himself."
Is't worth the evasion, what were the use
Of setting figures up and breathing life upon them,
Were it not *our* life, your life, my life, extended?
I walk Verona. (I am here in England.)
I see Can Grande. (Can see whom you will.)
(Ur-Canto I/114-15)

Pound claims that we should assess Browning's poem not as
a statement of fact but as an expression of "so much thought,
so much emotion." The historical Sordello should be regarded merely as the instigation for the imaginative *Sordello*,
which is a mask for "the half or third of your intensest life."
Personal expression takes priority over impersonal recollection.

However, near the end of Ur-Canto I, the issues raised by
Sordello emerge once again. After "breathing life" upon his
own ghosts from the past, Pound still wonders whether the
visions inspired by history are merely a "sweet lie":

What have I of this life,
    Or even of Guido?
    Sweet lie!—Was I there truly?
Did I knew Or San Michele?
    Let's believe it. . . .
        *   *   *
"But we forget not."
        No, take it all for lies.
I have but smelt this life, a whiff of it—
The box of scented wood
Recalls cathedrals. And shall I claim;
Confuse my own phantastikon,
Or say the filmy shell that circumscribes me
Contains the actual sun;
            confuse the thing I see
With actual gods behind me?
            Are they gods behind me?
                (Ur-Canto I/120)

Such Prufrockian self-doubt is uncharacteristic of Pound, and it indicates his uncertainty over the relationship between history and art. Pound has been trapped in his own net: he has privileged subject over object, imagination over memory, but now seems disturbed by the thought that his subjective experience lacks an objective foundation. In other words, after he reduces history to a mere stimulus for thought, Pound begins to fear that the visions arising from his encounter with the past are merely solipsistic extensions of the self.

In the final passage of Ur-Canto I, Pound attempts to dispel his doubts for the last time:

> Are they gods behind me?
> How many worlds we have! If Botticelli
> Brings her ashore on that great cockle-shell—
> His Venus (Simonetta?)
> And Spring and Aufidus fill all the air
> With their clear-outlined blossoms?
> World enough. Behold, I say, she comes
> "Apparelled like the spring, Graces her subjects,"
> (That's from *Pericles*).
> Oh, we have worlds enough, and brave *décors*,
> And from these like we guess a soul for man
> And build him full of aery populations.
> Mantegna a sterner line, and the new world about us:
> Barred lights, great flares, new form, Picasso or Lewis.
> If for a year man write to paint, and not to music—
> O Casella!
>
> (Ur-Canto I/120-21)[1]

---

[1] "O Casella!": In *Purgatorio* II, Dante listens to Casella, who once set Dante's poems to music and now sings one of his canzoni. As Dante becomes entranced by the music, Cato rebukes him for delaying his ascent of the purgatorial mount. The poet must leave behind his friend and his own lyric poetry to pursue his epic purpose. Similarly, the opening words of Ur-Canto II, "Leave Casella," indicate that Pound must also turn from music to painting, from his youthful lyrics to the epic canvas before him. See Ronald Bush, *The Genesis of Ezra Pound's Cantos* (Princeton: Princeton University Press, 1976), p. 141.

For several years Pound had been discussing the possibility of a long Imagist or Vorticist poem, and here he appeals to the new worlds of nonrepresentational art—the visionary art of Botticelli and the geometrical art of Picasso and Lewis. Just as the painter transforms ordinary reality into a visionary world, so the epic poet transforms his various historical fragments into a new imaginative unity. Pound was attempting to construct an epic poem on Vorticist foundations, and the relationship between imagination and history that informs Ur-Canto I issues from the Vorticist principle that gives priority to creative invention over passive representation.

It is this very principle, however, that led Pound into trouble. Vorticist aesthetics is far better suited to painting and sculpture than to epic poetry, and the attempt to transplant it from the visual to the historical realm caused significant difficulties. Pound was impressed by Botticelli's transformation of the historical Simonetta into the goddess of love, and by Picasso's ability to turn an ordinary landscape into a brilliant configuration of forms. But he had difficulty imagining how the epic poet transforms historical materials into imaginative order without distorting the facts of the past. By adopting Vorticist aesthetics as his model, Pound had begun his epic in such a way that imaginative order could be purchased only at the price of historical veracity. The attempt to create a Vorticist epic produced an intolerable dissociation between history and imagination, and Pound's awareness of this dissociation may well have influenced his decision to scuttle Ur-Canto I.

In 1925 Pound finally replaced Ur-Canto I with a new opening—a translation of Odysseus's voyage to the underworld—which presents a more tenable relationship between past and present. It is well known that he did not translate Homer's original Greek but a Renaissance Latin version by Andreas Divus Justinopolitanus. Pound associated Divus with the Renaissance revival of classical antiquity, and he created a "subject-rhyme" (L, 210) between Odysseus's physical voyage to the dead and the translator's literary voyage to the past. Divus assumes epic status as another "live man" who brings back wisdom from the shades. Moreover, Pound places himself in the line of Odysseus and Divus and embarks on his own journey to the dead. He explores the potentials of Old English verse, using heavy alliteration, consonantal stops, midline caesuras, and Germanic monosyllables to revive forgotten powers of the English tongue:

And then went down to the ship,
Set keel to breakers, forth on the godly sea, and
We set up mast and sail on that swart ship,
Bore sheep aboard her, and our bodies also
Heavy with weeping, and winds from sternward
Bore us out onward with bellying canvas,
Circe's this craft, the trim-coifed goddess.
Then sat we amidships, wind jamming the tiller,
Thus with stretched sail, we went over sea till day's end.

(I/3)

In the act of translation, Pound finds the proper relationship between tradition and innovation. Translation is not a slavish reproduction of the older work but a creative process that transforms it. While the translation reveals new "shades and glamours inherent in the original text," the original inspires new forms of expression in the present. The entire process involves an exchange, or "overchange," between recollection and invention: ". . . is not a new beauty created, an old beauty doubled when the overchange is well done?" (LE, 235). The artist is a translator who transforms identification with the dead into new creation for the living. New art arises from the interaction between past and present, between the older form of expression and the attempt to "make it new" in the present.

Pound thus resolves the conflict between historical consciousness and its antithesis by positing a tensional relation between recollection and innovation. In the same way that he creates tensional constructs such as the ideogram and the interpretive metaphor, he establishes a productive interaction between past and present. If the ideogram and the interpretive metaphor hold together immediate experience and the forms that organize it, Pound's approach to tradition holds together memory and imagination, the recovery of past experience and the invention of forms that reorder the present.

CHAPTER IV

Incarnate Words: Eliot's Early Career

The opposition between "surfaces" and "depths" is central to the works of T. S. Eliot. In his readings of turn-of-the-century philosophy, psychology, and ethnology, Eliot encountered this opposition in various forms. Bradley's immediate experience dovetailed with Jung's substratum of archetypal symbols and Frazer's substratum of ritual behavior: all expressed the same distinction between the surface forms of everyday life and the hidden depths that ordinarily elude us. This distinction is evident in the early poetry, where Eliot places highly conventional personae in contexts that evoke a deeper reality of which they are unaware. It is also a feature of the literary criticism, in which art is considered a principal means of recovering the "deeper, unnamed feelings . . . to which we rarely penetrate." Poetry, he states, "may help to break up the conventional modes of perception and valuation which are perpetually forming, and make people see the world afresh, or some new part of it. It may make us from time to time a little more aware of the deeper, unnamed feelings which form the substratum of our being, to which we rarely penetrate; for our lives are mostly a constant evasion of ourselves, and an evasion of the visible and sensible world."[1] This remark is characteristic of Eliot's outlook: the coalescence of philosophy, depth psychology, and ritual anthropology underlies his association between poetry and the hidden depths "which form the substratum of our being."

This chapter explores one aspect of the relationship between surfaces and depths in Eliot's work—his use of Bradley's distinction between abstraction and immediate experience. My argument in the first section is that Eliot's doctoral dissertation on Bradley is crucial to an understanding of his literary criticism. In his essays of the Teens and Twenties, Eliot approaches literary issues in terms of the division of immediate experience into subjective and objective realms. Employing the same arguments that appear in the thesis, he discerns in his literary predecessors a pernicious dissociation between internal emotion and external objects, as well as a bifurcation between thought and feeling, intellect and sensation. The second section turns to Eliot's poetry and shows that the subject/object dialectic also illuminates some of the most prominent features of the early verse. I will focus on the notion of the "half-object," which is Eliot's term for the way we apprehend both others and ourselves as subjects and as objects simultaneously. This notion will reveal how Eliot's personae take account of other persons and will help to explain the peculiar process through which these personae become detached observers of their own thoughts and actions.

From Philosopher to Critic

In April 1916 Eliot completed his doctoral dissertation, "Experience and the Objects of Knowledge in the Philosophy of F. H. Bradley," and mailed it from England to his advisors at Harvard. At that time, Eliot intended to sail to America to defend his thesis, and knew that he was being considered for an instructorship in Harvard's philosophy department. But only a few months later he informed his professors that he had decided to remain in England and pursue a literary career. It was at this time that the young poet, age twenty-seven, began to write reviews for several newspapers and periodicals. Soon he was reviewing actively for the *Egoist*, *Athenæum*, and eventually the *Times Literary Supplement*. Within a few years the transformation from philosopher to critic was complete, and Eliot was publishing the essays that would establish his reputation as the preeminent critic of his generation.

When he decided to change careers, Eliot had been studying philosophy for nearly a decade, and his philosophical training influenced his approach to literary issues.[2] Since the publication of his thesis in 1964, there have been various attempts to relate his philosophy to his literary criticism, but most of them suffer from the flaw of identifying Eliot's thinking too closely with Bradley's. Either they fail to look beyond Bradley to the larger intellectual framework of the period, or they neglect the distinctive characteristics of Eliot's dissertation, which is not a mere précis of Bradley's philosophy. The two mistakes are interrelated: the failure to go beyond Bradley leads to the failure to discern Eliot's own position, which is deeply indebted to Bradley but makes use of other philosophers as well. In this section I will examine the dialectical strategy of Eliot's thesis, and show how Eliot continued to employ this strategy in his literary essays. By approaching Eliot from the vantage point of his early philosophical writings, we will recover a fundamental but neglected dimension of his literary criticism. When restored their original context, the familiar touchstones of Eliot's early essays—the "objective correlative," the "dissociation of sensibility," and the "impersonal theory of poetry"—will alter their accepted meanings and regain their lost significance.

I

Eliot's thesis begins with a discussion of Bradley's "immediate experience," or "feeling." Eliot warns us at the outset that these terms are misleading: both "immediate experience" and "feeling" suggest events in the mind of a subject distinguishable from the world of external objects. For Bradley, however, these terms refer not to a subjective state, but rather to a point that precedes the distinction between subject and object, internal consciousness and external thing:

> We have, or seem to have at the start a 'confusion' of feeling, out of which subject and object emerge. We stand before a beautiful painting, and if we are sufficiently carried away, our feeling is a whole which is not, in a sense, *our* feeling, since the painting, which is an object independent of us, is quite as truly a constituent as our consciousness or our soul. The feeling is neither here nor anywhere: the painting is in the room and my 'feelings' about the picture are in my 'mind.' If this whole of feeling were complete and satisfactory it would not expand into object, and subject with feelings about the object; there would, in fact, be no consciousness. (KE, 20)[a]

Immediate experience is not strictly speaking a state of consciousness, as it is for Bergson and James. In immediate experience, consciousness is still one with its objects; both the "I" who perceives and the "world" which is perceived are indistinguishable aspects of the original "whole of feeling."

According to Bradley, immediate experience is an unstable whole, and it divides inevitably into subjective and objective realms. But Bradley makes it clear that this division between subject and object is always an arbitrary one. Although we inevitably distinguish between mental and physical worlds, there is no fixed point at which we naturally and inevitably mark the boundary between them. The dividing line, as Eliot puts it, "is always a question for partial and practical interests to decide" (KE, 21). From one point of view, everything may be considered subjectively as *my* experience; from another

[a] The following abbreviations are used in this chapter: CP—*Collected Poems, 1909-1962* (New York: Harcourt Brace, 1963); KE—*Knowledge and Experience in the Philosophy of F. H. Bradley* (New York: Farrar, Straus, 1964); SE—*Selected Essays* (New York: Harcourt Brace, 1964); and SW—*The Sacred Wood: Essays on Poetry and Criticism* (London: Methuen, 1960).

point of view, everything may be considered objectively as the experienced *world* external to myself. Idealists gravitate to the first alternative and realists to the second, but there is "no *absolute* point of view" (KE, 22) from which to judge between them: "We have no right, except in the most provisional way, to speak of *my* experience, since the I is a construction out of experience, an abstraction from it; and the *thats*, the browns and hards and flats, are equally ideal constructions from experience, as ideal as atoms" (KE, 19). As this passage indicates, neither the subjective "I" nor the objective "real world" has a substantial identity. The identities of each are established solely in relation to one another, and transient interests and values determine the point at which we designate the boundary between them.

After he shows that there is no absolute distinction between subject and object, Eliot demonstrates that there is no absolute distinction between the real and the ideal, that which is immediately given and that which is introduced by the mind (ch. 2). He then devotes the middle portion of the thesis (chs. 3-5) to sciences that rely on a fixed distinction between subject and object, ideal and real. In chapter 3 he discusses the psychologist, who assumes that he can isolate consciousness from its objects, and make the former into the object of an independent science. In chapters 4 and 5 he considers the epistemologist, who commits the error "of assuming that there is a real world outside of our knowledge and asking how we may know it" (KE, 109). The psychologist is like the philosophical idealist: he grants priority to the subjective side of experience. The epistemologist, on the other hand, is like the philosophical realist: he grants priority to the objective side of experience. The first pair begins with consciousness and shows how it constitutes our knowledge of the external world. The second pair starts with the external world and asks how it becomes reflected in consciousness. Eliot distances himself from both groups, asserting that the position of each is ultimately indefensible. While each pair elevates one side of experience and makes the other dependent upon it, Eliot denies "that objects are dependent upon consciousness, or consciousness upon objects" (KE, 29-30). Neither the subjective nor the objective aspect of experience should be privileged over the other.

Having shown that there is no absolute boundary between subject and object, Eliot responds to the psychologist and the epistemologist (as well as the idealist and realist) by demonstrating that the domains of each may be reduced entirely to the terms of the other: "Consciousness, we shall find, is reducible to relations between objects, and objects we shall find to be reducible to relations between different states of consciousness; and neither point of view is more nearly ultimate than the other" (KE, 30). In other words, Eliot attacks the psychologist by assuming the standpoint of the epistemologist, and then attacks the epistemologist by assuming the standpoint of the psychologist. Similarly, he becomes a realist when criticizing the idealist, an idealist when criticizing the realist. Claiming that neither side is entirely right, he curbs the excesses of one by adopting the position of the other.

Eliot's dialectic would be of little interest if it did not anticipate the strategy of his early literary criticism. In his critical prose of the late Teens and early Twenties, Eliot analyzes literature in terms of subject/object relations. He assails the excessive subjectivity of the poet who expresses emotion with no definite object, or makes his work a vehicle for personal expression. At the same time, he criticizes the excessive objectivity of the artist who simply mirrors the existing "real world" instead of "intensify[ing] the world to his emotions" (SW, 102). It is significant that Eliot responds to each of these excesses in the same way that he does in his thesis. Just as he declares that consciousness "is reducible to relations between objects" (KE, 30), he maintains that an author's subjective life—his emotions and his personality—may be transmuted into its "objective correlative" (SW, 100). And just as he contends that objective reality is "reducible to relations between different states of consciousness," he asserts that the

INCARNATE WORDS · 161

artist may transform the "real world" of ordinary life into a "new world," a world that arises from his emotions and personal sensations. The boundary between subject and object, emotions and things, is more fluid than we ordinarily assume. Hence the subjective may be objectified, and the objective transformed by that which we ordinarily relegate to mere subjectivity.

Eliot considered the nineteenth century especially prone to subjectivist and objectivist extremes. He derived this attitude in part from his Harvard mentor, Irving Babbitt, whose division of nineteenth-century culture into extremes of emotional and scientific naturalism merges easily into Bradley's dialectic. Like Babbitt, Eliot identifies Romanticism not simply with excessive subjectivity, but with the bifurcation of experience into subjectivist and objectivist extremes:

> Romanticism stands for *excess* in any direction. It splits up into two directions: escape from the world of fact, and devotion to brute fact. The two great currents of the nineteenth century—vague emotionality and the apotheosis of science (realism) alike spring from Rousseau.[3]

Eliot struggled against both of these currents, the "vague emotionality" of Romantic poetry and the "devotion to brute fact" in fiction and drama. His early critical essays may be regarded as an attempt to overcome these antithetical extremes of nineteenth-century culture.

Eliot did not confine this dialectical analysis to the nineteenth century. He began to examine earlier literature in much the same way, claiming that the bifurcation of experience into subjective and objective extremes began not with Romanticism but with the "dissociation of sensibility" that occurred in the seventeenth century. By examining his critical prose in light of this dialectical approach, we can clarify the meaning of "objective correlative," "dissociation of sensibility," and the other key terms of his literary essays. Following the sequence he uses in the dissertation, I will first consider

Eliot's critique of reified subjectivity and then turn to his less familiar critique of reified objectivity.[b]

II

In his dissertation, Eliot argues his case against the psychologist by claiming that we can make no absolute distinction between consciousness and its objects: ". . . in an act of apprehension is there a part which is strictly mental and a part which is strictly external? and even if the distinction can be made, can it be made sharply enough to give us a class of objects which can form a separate science, psychology?" (KE, 58). The psychologist assumes that he can isolate "mental content," or consciousness, from the objects external to it. But Eliot argues that once we subtract the object from the mental content (or references from meanings), the psychologist has nothing left to study.[c] Taking a stance that owes less to Bradley than to realists such as Meinong and Russell, Eliot contends that the mind is "nothing more than the system of objects which appears before it." We cannot examine the mind without its objects, since "the 'mind' simply *is* its world . . . this particular set of terms and relations."[4]

Reified subjectivity characterizes not only the psychologist

[b] My choice of Lukács's term "reification" is not accidental. Both Eliot (via Bradley) and Lukács (via Marx) employ a dialectic that derives ultimately from Hegel. Eliot sees immediate experience dividing into a fixed opposition between subjective and objective realms. Similarly, Lukács sees bourgeois thought "reifying" into an unmediated antinomy between the passive, contemplative subject and the presumably unchanging reality he seeks to understand. See "Reification and the Consciousness of the Proletariat," in *History and Class Consciousness: Studies in Marxist Dialectics*, trans. Rodney Livingstone (Cambridge, Mass.: MIT Press, 1971), pp. 83-222.

[c] One interesting qualification. Eliot admits that we can turn subjective life into a special kind of object, a "half-object." Later in the chapter we will see that the "half-object" is a notion of considerable importance in Eliot's writings. Since it deals with the problem of apprehending our own internal state or that of another person, it sheds light on the social dynamics of the early poetry.

but also the philosophical idealist and the Romantic poet. All three rose to the fore in the nineteenth century, which produced various manifestations of the tendency to elevate subject over object: the spectacular development of psychology as an independent science; a philosophical movement that emphasized the constitutive role of the mind in determining our knowledge of external reality; and a poetry devoted at times explicitly to the outpouring of subjective life. Eliot has the same response to each of these developments. In his thesis he shows the psychologist and idealist that consciousness is reducible to its objects, and in his literary essays he offers two similar correctives to the Romantic poet, each of which involves a turn toward the objective side of experience: 1) he offsets the "vague emotionality" of late Romantic poetry by claiming that subjective emotion may be transmuted into its "objective correlative"; and 2) he counteracts the Romantic emphasis on personal expression by proposing a new "impersonal theory of poetry" for the twentieth century.

Emotions and objects. Eliot is especially harsh on one subjectivist affliction of the nineteenth century—the use of vague language to express an emotional state. In a well-known essay, he attacks Swinburne's habit of expressing emotion with words detached from objective reference:

. . . he uses the most general word, because his emotion is never particular, never in direct line of vision, never focused; it is emotion reinforced, not by intensification, but by expansion.

There lived a singer in France of old
    By the tideless dolorous midland sea.
In a land of sand and ruin and gold
    There shone one woman, and none but she.

You see that Provence is the merest point of diffusion here. Swinburne defines the place by the most general word, which has for him its own value. "Gold," "ruin," "dolorous": it is not merely the sound that he wants, but the vague associations of idea that the words give him. He has not his eye on a particular place, as—

> Li ruscelletti che dei verdi colli
> Del Casentin discendon giuso in Arno . . .

It is, in fact, the word that gives him the thrill, not the object. (SW, 147-48)

Maintaining a reserved admiration for Swinburne's ability to "dwell so exclusively and consistently among words" (SW, 150), Eliot asserts that "language in a healthy state presents the object, is so close to the object that the two are identified" (SW, 149). All emotions, he believes, can and should be rendered precisely through their correlative objects.[d]

Most of us are familiar with Eliot's critique of "vague emotionality" in late nineteenth-century poetry. But less well known is the fact that Eliot attacks nineteenth-century philosophy for the very same defect. In "The Perfect Critic," published the same year as the Swinburne piece, Eliot claims that philosophers since Hegel have ceased "to deal with objects which [they] believed to be of the same exactness as the mathematician's" (SW, 9). Just as Swinburne expresses emotion with no precise object, Hegelian idealism has aggravated "the tendency of words to become indefinite emotions" (SW, 9). Unlike Aristotle, who "looked solely and steadfastly at the object" (SW, 11), Hegel became "the most prodigious exponent of emotional systematization, dealing with his emotions as if they were definite objects which had aroused those emotions" (SW, 9). As a result of this aspiration to make language express the priority of emotions over objects, mind over ex-

---

[d] See also "Andrew Marvell" (SE, 251-63), where Eliot compares the "mistiness" of William Morris to Marvell's "bright, hard precision," arguing that "this precision is not due to the fact that Marvell is concerned with cruder or simpler or more carnal emotions. The emotion of Morris is not more refined or more spiritual; it is merely more vague: if anyone doubts whether the more refined or spiritual emotion can be precise, he should study the treatment of the varieties of discarnate emotion in the *Paradiso*" (p. 258).

ternal reality, philosophy like poetry succumbed to a pernicious "verbalism" that dissociates words from precise objects.[e]

In response to verbalism and vague emotionality, Eliot suggests that emotion should be presented through its objective correlative. Hints of this idea can be found in Bradley and other idealists of the period. While most philosophical idealists grant priority to subject over object, Bradley (like his associate Bernard Bosanquet) espouses a version of idealism which asserts that the subjective can never be detached entirely from the objective. In his critique of the psychologist, Eliot rehearses Bradley's argument that purely subjective emotion or pleasure is merely an abstraction and "in reality is always partially objective: the emotion is really part of the object, and is ultimately just as objective" (KE, 80). The wording of Eliot's next remark—"when the object, or complex of objects, is recalled, the pleasure is recalled in the same way" (KE, 80)—anticipates the famous literary dictum that would appear several years later:

> The only way of expressing emotion in the form of art is by finding an "objective correlative"; in other words, a set of objects, a situation, a chain of events which shall be the formula of that *particular* emotion; such that when the external facts, which must terminate in sensory experience, are given, the emotion is immediately evoked. (SW, 100)

Here Eliot transfers one of Bradley's ideas from philosophy to literature. Just as he shows the psychologist that there is no pure subjectivity by pointing to the objective aspect of all subjective phenomena, Eliot responds to the subjectivism of nineteenth-century poets by arguing that emotions should be

[e] We should not forget, however, that Hegel is the original source of the dialectical philosophy that Eliot received from Bradley. To be sure, there are significant differences between Hegel and Bradley, but the latter often asserted that his own work added little to what Hegel had already done.

transmuted into the objects from which they have been detached.

But Bradley is not the only source for the objective correlative. Eliot derived aspects of this notion (and probably the expression itself) from another group of philosophers usually considered opponents rather than allies of Bradley—the "new realists," who included Moore and Russell in England and Meinong and Husserl on the Continent. Bradley emphasized "the unity and continuity of feeling and objectivity" (KE, 115), and taught Eliot that subjective phenomena are always partially objective. But the "new realism" encouraged Eliot to go a step further and consider mental life primarily in terms of the objects to which it is directed. Meinong's theory of objects is especially prominent in Eliot's student essays and in his doctoral dissertation.[5] One of Eliot's classmates records that in May 1914 Eliot read a paper on Meinong to Josiah Royce's seminar, and in the discussion that followed, he argued that emotion is as external as any other object of perception: "In my theory there is something outside—e.g., beauty is outside, and distressed world, etc."[6] Eliot argues the same point in chapter 3 of his thesis, where he shows that consciousness is reducible to the objects that appear before it. All subjective phenomena—emotions, sensations, fantasies, and the like—are directed to objects. Thus, from his exposure to Meinong and other turn-of-the-century realists, Eliot was acquainted with the idea that subjective life may be presented through its objective correlates.

The "new realism" may have supplied Eliot not only with the concept of the objective correlative, but also with the expression itself. Eliot probably got the words not from Meinong but from Brentano's other distinguished student, Edmund Husserl. For years scholars have known that the terms "*objektiv*" and "*Korrelat*" appear frequently in Husserl's *Logische Untersuchungen* [*Logical Investigations*] (1900), and that Husserl occasionally put the two together to form the expression, "*objektive Korrelat*."[7] But the connection with Eliot was not pursued, first because there was no evidence that Eliot was familiar with Husserl, and second, because there seemed to be little similarity in the use to which they put the expression.[8] However, recently discovered evidence from Eliot's own hand shows that he was reading Husserl in 1914.[9] Furthermore, Husserl's argument that intentionality is the distinctive feature of consciousness—"consciousness is consciousness *of* something"—is precisely what Eliot had learned from Meinong. Although there is no sign that Eliot was strongly influenced by Husserl, he may well have taken the words "objective correlative" from *Logical Investigations*, particularly since he used the expression to do for literature what Husserl was doing for philosophy. Turn-of-the-century realists were reacting against the excessive subjectivism of nineteenth-century philosophy; they were redirecting the study of consciousness from internal sensations to intentional objects. Eliot was well acquainted with this change in philosophy. In his thesis he undermines the assumptions of the psychologist by reducing consciousness to its objects, and later used the same strategy in his critique of nineteenth-century poetry. Eliot thus owes a considerable debt to early twentieth-century realism. From this new philosophical movement he probably derived the term "objective correlative" and with it a new way of thinking about literary expression.[f]

In his literary essays, Eliot shows that the process of transmuting emotions into objects is no simple matter. For example, in "Reflections on Contemporary Poetry" (1917) he focuses on the difficulties of two groups of poets, one British, the other American. The Georgian poets, he claims, dwell on

[f] We should remember that Eliot adopts the realist's position only to criticize the idealist. Afterwards, he turns around and assumes the idealist's stance to assault the realist. In chapter 3 of his thesis he reduces consciousness to its objects; in chapters 4-5 he reduces objects to states of consciousness. In other words, he uses the standpoint of each side to correct the excesses of the other, but ultimately rejects the premises of both: "That objects are dependent upon consciousness, or consciousness upon objects, we most resolutely deny" (KE, 29-30).

trivial objects. These followers of Wordsworth attend to the external object "for its own sake, not because of association with passions specifically human," and therefore fail to rise above the commonplace.[10] Their American counterparts (whom Eliot does not name) have the related problem of fixing upon the incidental features of an object. Influenced by Russian novelists such as Dostoevski, these poets exhibit the "curious trick of fastening upon accidental properties of a critical situation, and letting these in turn fasten upon the attention to such an extent as to replace the emotion which gave them their importance." British and American alike are now committed to the presentation of objects, but they fail to make the object a correlative of significant emotion.

In the same article, Eliot praises John Donne for his ability to find appropriate objects. He cites several lines in which "the feeling and the material symbol preserve exactly their proper proportions":

> When my grave is broke up again . . .
> And he that digs it, spies
> A bracelet of bright hair about the bone

Eliot then states that lesser poets would have erred in one of two directions: one group would have become absorbed in the hair as a material object and forgotten the emotional association that originally made it significant; the other would have yielded to the temptation to "endow the hair with ghostly or moralistic meaning." In other words, Eliot suggests that objects may slide toward pure reference or pure meaning, toward excessive objectivity on one side or excessive subjectivity on the other. The superior poet maintains an equilibrium between these extremes and in this respect corresponds, in Eliot's view, to the novelist who steers between "photographic" realism and its opposite, the "arid pièce à thèse" (see below). The use of objects is therefore most effective when the poet strikes the right balance between reference and meaning.

Personality and impersonality. Eliot linked vague emotionality to another subjectivist excess of the nineteenth century—the attempt to make the work of art an expression of authorial "personality." He often accuses his immediate predecessors of first dividing experience rigidly into subjective and objective domains, and then projecting their reified subjectivity, or personality, upon the world of external objects.[11] This Romantic tendency to project personality upon the external world leads ultimately to solipsism. It led one of Eliot's "imperfect critics," George Wyndham, to replace the real world around him with a "fairyland" spun out of his own personality:

What is permanent and good in Romanticism is curiosity . . . a curiosity which recognizes that any life, if accurately and profoundly penetrated, is interesting and always strange. Romanticism is a short cut to the strangeness without the reality, and it leads its disciples only back upon themselves. George Wyndham had curiosity, but he employed it romantically, not to penetrate the real world, but to complete the varied features of the world he made for himself. (SW, 31-32)

The Romantic detaches personality from external reality and then fails to regain contact with that reality. An unbridgeable gulf between subject and object prevents him from ever getting fully outside himself.[g]

[g] Whereas the Romantic projects his personality upon the object, the Classicist apprehends the object directly. Eliot compares Wyndham's Romanticism to Leonardo da Vinci's Classicism: Wyndham created a fairyland out of his emotions, but Leonardo had a mind that "went out and became a part of things" (SW, 27). The distinction between Romantic and Classical is similar to the distinction between idealism and realism. Wyndham is akin to Hegel, who treated his emotions "as if they were definite objects which had aroused those emotions." If Wyndham turns the world into a fairyland, Hegelianism transforms reality into a drama of evolving consciousness. Leonardo, by contrast, is akin to Aristotle, who "looked solely and steadfastly at the object." According to Eliot, "the romantic is deficient or undeveloped in his ability to distinguish between fact and fancy, whereas the classicist, or adult mind,

As in the case of vague emotionality, Eliot responds dialectically to the cult of personality. If the objective correlative is the cure for the former, the "impersonal theory of poetry" is the antidote to the latter. The *locus classicus* of the impersonal theory is "Tradition and the Individual Talent" (1919):

> The point of view which I am struggling to attack is perhaps related to the metaphysical theory of the substantial unity of the soul: for my meaning is, that the poet has, not a "personality" to express, but a particular medium, which is only a medium and not a personality, in which impressions and experiences combine in peculiar and unexpected ways. Impressions and experiences which are important for the man may take no place in the poetry, and those which become important in the poetry may play quite a negligible part in the man, the personality. (SW, 56)[h]

Here Eliot describes a process of "depersonalization" through which the poet surrenders himself "to something which is more valuable" (SW, 52-53). By sacrificing his personality, the artist dissolves the existing split between subjective and objective worlds, and becomes a medium through which

---

is thoroughly realist—without illusions, without day-dreams, without hope, without bitterness, and with an abundant resignation" ("The Function of Criticism," *Criterion* 2 [Oct. 1923], 39). The cult of personality, Romanticism, and idealism are thus part of a single syndrome, and they stand in opposition to impersonality, Classicism, and realism.

[h] Notice that Eliot compares personality to the idea of "the substantial unity of the soul." For Eliot, terms such as "personality," "self," and "soul" reify the subjective side of experience. In his thesis, he recalls Bradley's argument that the soul is an indefensible abstraction, and in the same way that he reduces consciousness to its objects, Eliot resolves the soul into the events and impressions of which it appears to be independent: ". . . the soul is not something definite to which phenomena can be attached all on the same plane, but varies with the meaning which each phenomenon has for it. . . . the soul exists only in the events which occur to it; so that the soul is, in fact, the whole world of its experience at any moment" (KE, 79). In "Tradition and the Individual Talent," he performs the same operation on the notion of personality.

"impressions and experiences combine in peculiar and unexpected ways" (SW, 56). As a result of his "continual extinction
of personality," he produces a work of art that expresses not
"personal emotion" but a "new art emotion" (SW, 57), which
"has its life in the poem and not in the history of the poet"
(SW, 59). The focus of critical attention has shifted from the
personality of the author to the objective structure of the text
itself.

In his dissertation, Eliot provides an interesting formulation of this shift from author to text:

> We may mean the character as a presentation to the au-
> thor's mind; *but a figure in fiction may and often does*
> *have an existence for us distinct from what is merely our*
> *interpretation of what the author 'had in mind.'* Fre-
> quently we feel more confidence in our own interpreta-
> tion of the character than in any account of the genesis
> and meaning which the author may give himself. This is
> not always mere accident; *no really 'vital' character in*
> *fiction is altogether a conscious construction of the au-*
> *thor.* On the contrary, it may be a sort of parasitic
> growth upon the author's personality, developing by in-
> ternal necessity as much as by external addition. So that
> we come to feel that the point of view from which the
> author criticizes is not wholly internal to the point of
> view from which he created the character.   (italics mine;
> KE, 124)

Anticipating future developments in literary theory, Eliot
maintains that a work of art is irreducible to the author's
"consciousness," "emotions," "personality," or any other
terms that designate a subjective state. Since a work arises
not from the author's personality but from "internal necessity," the meaning of a text is to be found not in the author's
psyche but in the logic of the "world" he produces. Imaginative constructs are not "peculiarly subject-matter for psychology" (KE, 76); they are "bound by as logical necessity as
any connections to be found anywhere" (KE, 75), and may be

studied independently of the author's psyche.[12] We understand the artwork not by searching for the subjective life of the author, but by analyzing the structure of the world he has made.

Eliot was participating in a major change in literary theory, as critics began to turn their attention from the subjective life of the author to the intrinsic design of the text. Signs of this transformation appear not only in Eliot's essays, which anticipate the New Criticism, but also in Russian Formalism, which is the antecedent to contemporary structuralism. A similar change has also been observed in the career of Wilhelm Dilthey.[13] For many years Dilthey followed the lead of his great predecessor, Friedrich Schleiermacher, who equated the interpretive process with the recovery of the author's subjective life. But around the turn of the century Dilthey shifted his focus from psychological identification with the writer to the immanent meaning of the text. His writings reveal no sudden conversion, only a gradual shift in emphasis, but this shift marks one of the crucial changes from nineteenth- to twentieth-century poetics.

Dilthey's works also reveal the link between changes in the arts and contemporaneous changes in philosophy. It is significant that his own shift from author to text was encouraged by the publication of Husserl's *Logical Investigations* (also the probable source for Eliot's "objective correlative").[14] Husserl relentlessly attacked the subjectivism of nineteenth-century philosophy. He identified meaning not with a subjective state or with ideas in the mind, but with the objects to which consciousness is directed. Dilthey similarly shifted his emphasis from the authorial subject to the textual object. In other words, the philosophical turn from consciousness to its objects, from the psychological to the logical, corresponds to a shift in textual theory from psychic identification with the author to the study of the text as an autonomous entity.

Eliot's early works bear witness to the same intellectual transformation. It was primarily Meinong who trained Eliot to think of consciousness in terms of its objects, but Meinong led Eliot in the same direction that Dilthey was led by Husserl. Thus, Eliot's emphasis upon the objective and the impersonal expresses not a mere idiosyncracy but a significant change in philosophy and the arts, a change from subject to object that signals the passage from the nineteenth century to the twentieth.

III

Most of us are acquainted with Eliot's critique of subjectivism, even if we are unfamiliar with its philosophical foundations. But there is another aspect of Eliot's essays that is generally overlooked—his highly developed if less conspicuous critique of objectivism. Eliot's concern with reified objectivity is readily evident in his approach to literary "realism," but it is also the basis for several key terms in the early criticism, including the "dissociation of sensibility." Proceeding from his philosophical to his literary works, I will explore this significant but neglected dimension of his critical theory.

In chapter 4 of his thesis, Eliot turns from the psychologist to the epistemologist, who assumes "that there is one consistent real world . . . and that it is our business to find it" (KE, 136). Having denied that we can dissociate consciousness, or "mental content," from its objects, Eliot now denies that we can dissociate the objective "real world" from the subjects who perceive it. And having shown the psychologist that consciousness is reducible to its objects, he shows the epistemologist that external objects are "reducible to relations between different states of consciousness" (KE, 30). In short, after assuming the stance of the realist to refute the psychologist and the idealist, Eliot takes the position of the idealist to challenge the epistemologist and the realist.

Eliot contends that we reify the objective side of experience as readily as the subjective. We assume the existence of a consistent "real world" external to ourselves, and fail to realize that this world has been constituted by a community of subjects. Eliot claims that the real world is a construct that emerges in the process of social interaction: "We come to interpret our own experience as the attention to a world of objects, as we feel obscurely an identity between the experiences of other centres and our own. And it is this identity which gradually shapes itself into the external world. . . . Thus in adjusting our behaviour to that of others and in cooperating with them we come to intend an identical world" (KE, 143). In the course of social exchange, the immediate experience of each finite center divides into the subjective realm internal to itself and the objective reality it shares with others. Unaware that collective interests have determined the dividing-line between subjective and objective realms, we treat the former merely "as the debris of our own slight structure" (KE, 118) and consider the latter an objective real world independent of ourselves.

The same critique of objectivism appears in Eliot's literary criticism. It is most apparent in his attack on art that simply mirrors the everyday world. Eliot repeatedly expresses dissatisfaction with literary realism, which "ends its course in the desert of exact likeness to the reality which is perceived by the most commonplace mind" (SE, 93). If late nineteenth-century poets like Swinburne and Morris "escape from the real world" into "vague emotionality," realism manifests the objectivist extreme of "devotion to brute fact." Eliot maintains that art should not mirror the familiar world but "create a new world," a world with a coherence of its own that in turn "illuminates the actual world" (SW, 117). In a revealing phrase, Eliot maintains that the artist must "intensify the world to his emotions" (SW, 102); that is to say, the artist must draw upon the subjective side of experience in order to transform the familiar world into the new world of art. If reified subjectivity is offset by turning to the impersonal and objective, reified objectivity is overcome by exploiting the creative potential of subjective impressions and emotions.

In his thesis Eliot shows that the construction of an authentic fictional world is no easy matter. It requires that the artist strike the right balance between subjective "meaning" and objective "reference":

> Can we, in reading a novel, simply assume the characters and the situations? On the contrary, I seem to find that we either accept them as real . . . or consider them as *meanings*, as a criticism of reality from the author's point of view. Actually, I think that if we did not vacillate between these two extremes (one of which alone would give the 'photographic' novel and the other the arid 'pièce à thèse') a novel would mean very little to us. . . . If the character in fiction is an imaginary object, it must be by virtue of something more than its being imaginary, i.e. merely intending to be a reality which it is not. It must be, as I said, contrasted with this reality; to be contrasted it must be more than a pure reference; it must have in fact another aspect in which it has a reality of its own distinct from its reference. The fiction is thus more than a fiction: it is a *real* fiction.   (KE, 123-24)

While "photographic" realism goes astray by presenting a world no different from everyday reality, the "pièce à thèse" errs by presenting no distinctive world at all, merely a "criticism of reality from the author's point of view." The successful novel avoids either extreme, maintaining a desirable tension between "reference" and "meaning." In this respect it has something in common with the poetry of Donne, whose "bracelet of bright hair about the bone" avoids the temptation to fixate on the realistic details of the object as well as the opposing temptation to overload the object "with ghostly or moralistic meaning."

Eliot's critique of objectivism extends beyond his analysis of literary realism to other aspects of his critical essays. In his thesis he exposes not only the assumption that there is a single real world, but also the assumption that it is the task of the intellect to represent that world. Similarly, in his criticism he assails the artist whose intellect has become a faculty detached from his personal feelings and devoted primarily to objective knowledge of the outer world. Such a split between intellect and feeling informs several recurrent distinctions in Eliot's essays: the "dissociated" versus the "unified" sensibility; "intellect" versus "intelligence"; and "ideas" versus "points of view." These distinctions are familiar to readers of Eliot's criticism, but their meanings are more precise than they seem. All are part of his critique of reified objectivity.

Dissociated and unified sensibility. In "The Metaphysical Poets" (1923), Eliot maintains that English verse since the seventeenth century displays a widening rift between intellect and sensation, thought and feeling. He uses the notion of a historical "dissociation of sensibility" to explain the difference between Metaphysical and high Victorian poetry:

> The difference is not a simple difference of degree between poets. It is something which had happened to the mind of England between the time of Donne or Lord Herbert of Cherbury and the time of Tennyson and Browning; it is the difference between the intellectual poet and the reflective poet. Tennyson and Browning are poets, and they think; but they do not feel their thought as immediately as the odour of a rose. A thought to Donne was an experience; it modified his sensibility. . . . In the seventeenth century a dissociation of sensibility set in, from which we have never recovered. (SE, 247)[i]

The thoughts and feelings of the Metaphysicals were in harmony, but their successors "thought and felt by fits, unbalanced" (SE, 248). Certain poets have relied too heavily on emotion, others on intellectual abstraction. If Swinburne expresses emotion with no precise object, Tennyson uses ab-

---

[i] In this case "intellectual" is the positive term, "reflective" the negative term. Elsewhere, "intelligence" becomes the positive term, "intellect" the negative.

stract concepts that have no foundation in concrete sensation. He manifests a tendency to "substitute the definition for the experience, and then experience the definition" (KE, 167). A third group of poets displays both vices. In Laforgue, for instance, whom Eliot otherwise applauded, "there are unassimilated fragments of metaphysics and, on the other hand, of sentiments floating about."[15] The "dissociation of sensibility" thus involves a bifurcation of experience into subjective and objective domains. Whatever its merits as a historical hypothesis, this notion expresses Eliot's tendency to analyze literary works in terms of subject/object relations.[j]

Intellect and intelligence. The dissociated sensibility may possess "intellect," but the unified sensibility has "intelligence." Carlyle is typical of many high Victorians who have "intellect without intelligence."[16] Here intellect denotes a state in which mind is divorced from body, thoughts from feelings. Intelligence, on the other hand, overcomes these divisions: it involves "the discernment of exactly what, and how much, we feel in any given situation."[17] Eliot is demanding not the abdication of intellect but rather the unification of intellect and feeling. "Men ripen best," he maintains, "through experiences which are at once sensuous and intellectual; certainly many men will admit that their keenest ideas have come to them with the quality of a sense-perception; and that their keenest sensuous experience has been 'as if the body thought.' "[18] Intelligence is this union of the sensuous and the intellectual, the union to which Eliot refers in expressions such as the "direct sensuous apprehension of

[j] The "dissociation of sensibility" corresponds both chronologically and thematically to the mind/body dualism of Western philosophy from Descartes to the early twentieth century. While Eliot makes no explicit connection between Cartesian dualism and the "dissociation of sensibility," his knowledge of the history of philosophy may well have influenced his understanding of the history of literature.

thought" (SE, 246), "thinking with our feelings," and "the senses thinking."[19k]

By reintegrating intellect and sensation, the artist overcomes the prevailing division between subjective and objective worlds. Donne's capacity for "direct sensuous apprehension of thought" allowed him to replace the conventional world with the new world, or "new wholes," that appear in his poems:

A thought to Donne was an experience; it modified his sensibility. When a poet's mind is perfectly equipped for its work, it is constantly amalgamating disparate experience; the ordinary man's experience is chaotic, irregular, fragmentary. The latter falls in love, or reads Spinoza, and these two experiences have nothing to do with each other, or with the noise of the typewriter or the smell of cooking; in the mind of the poet these experiences are always forming new wholes. (SE, 247)

The ability to "think with the feelings" entails an exchange between subjective and objective sides of experience. The intellect is released from its attachment to the existing "real world," and its objectifying power is directed to personal sensations and feelings usually consigned to mere subjectivity. The subjective is objectified by the intellect, and the objective real world, now suffused by personal emotions and sensations, is replaced by the new world of the poem itself. Like the dramatist, who produces a new world through his ability "to intensify the world to his emotions," the poet creates "new wholes" by overcoming the dissociation between feeling and thought, the subjective and the objective aspects of his sensibility.

[k] While Eliot is indebted to Bradley's emphasis on the original unity of intellect and sensation, thought and feeling, we should not overlook his debt to Remy de Gourmont, who influenced the language of *The Sacred Wood* and other early essays. According to Gourmont, "the real problem of style is a question of physiology. . . . We write, as we feel, as we think, with our entire body" (*Selected Writings*, p. 109).

Ideas and points of view. Eliot associates the "intellect" with "ideas" and the "intelligence" with "points of view." The writer who has ideas rather than a point of view is like the one who possesses intellect without intelligence. Edwardian England, for instance, has become infested with ideas that replace genuine thought and feeling: ". ∴ . ideas run wild and pasture on the emotions; instead of thinking with our feelings (a very different thing) we corrupt our feelings with ideas; we produce the public, the political, the emotional idea, evading sensation and thought."[20] Eliot was not insulting Henry James, but offering him the supreme compliment, when he wrote that "James's critical genius comes out most tellingly in his mastery over, his baffling escape from, Ideas; a mastery and an escape which are perhaps the last test of a superior intelligence. He had a mind so fine that no idea could violate it."

Eliot is prepared to accept ideas in literature, but only if the writer achieves a "recreation of thought into feeling" (SE, 246). He criticizes Goethe for failing to sacrifice his philosophy to his art, which he made into a platform for his ideas: "[Goethe] embodies a philosophy. A creation of art should not do that: he should *replace* the philosophy. Goethe has not, that is to say, sacrificed or consecrated his thought to make the drama; the drama is still a means" (SW, 66). Yet Eliot condones the use of Thomistic philosophy in Dante's *Commedia,* since the "philosophic idea . . . has become almost a physical modification" (SW, 162-63). This process of transmuting idea into sensation is the reverse of the process of transmuting emotions into their objective correlative. In one case, the artist offsets excessive subjectivity by turning to the objective side of experience; in the other, he overcomes excessive objectivity by returning to subjective feelings and sensations.

Eliot extols the writer who possesses a "point of view" rather than "ideas." Henry James has no ideas but presents a point of view, a distinctive "world of thought and feeling."[21]

Similarly, Eliot compares the ideas of Kipling and Swinburne to the point of view of Conrad and others:

> If we deprecate any philosophical complications, we may be allowed to call Swinburne's Liberty and Mr. Kipling's Empire "ideas." They are at least abstract, and not material which emotions can feed long upon. . . . Swinburne and Mr. Kipling have these and such concepts; some poets, like Shakespeare or Dante or Villon, and some novelists, like Mr. Conrad, have, in contrast to ideas or concepts, points of view, or "worlds"—what are incorrectly called "philosophies." . . . Mr. Conrad has no ideas, but he has a point of view, a "world"; it can hardly be defined, but it pervades his work and is unmistakable.[22]

Eliot never explicitly defines the expression "point of view," but its meaning is clear from its use in conjunction with other terms. The terms "unified sensibility," "intelligence," and "point of view" are virtually synonymous, at times interchangeable. All refer to a distinctive manner of apprehending and arranging experience, and all point to the same reintegration of thought and feeling expressed in the new world of the text.

A "point of view," however, may refer not only to an individual sensibility but to any coherent principle for ordering experience. A particular meter or form may express a unique point of view, a "precise way of thinking and feeling." Or an entire generation may share a point of view, as was the case in Elizabethan England, where artists possessed a distinctive "framework," which "imposed itself on everything that came to it" (SW, 62-63). A scientific discipline and a cultural tradition are also points of view. A science, like the "framework" of an age, provides not a transparent mirror of reality but a specific principle for arranging experience, a principle embodied in the kind of world, or system of objects and relations, it posits. Any particular science imposes a form which is in a sense prior to "any of the facts that are referred to that science":

Facts are not merely found in the world and laid together like bricks, but every fact has in a sense its place prepared for it before it arrives, and without the implication of a system in which it belongs the fact is not a fact at all. . . . There is a sense, then, in which any science— natural or social—is *a priori*: in that it satisfies the needs of a particular point of view, a point of view which may be said to be more original than any of the facts that are referred to that science. The development of a science would thus be rather organic than mechanical; there is a fitness of the various facts for each other. . . . Thus the character of a science, like the character of a man, may be said both to be already present at the moment of conception, and on the other hand to develop at every moment into something new and unforeseen. (KE, 60-61)

Eliot's emphasis on the a priori character of a science, the overall coherence of its individual facts, and its capacity to alter over the course of time—all anticipate his celebrated essay on tradition, published several years later.

A tradition, like a science, is "organic" rather than "mechanical"; it is an ideal order which endures over time yet is capable of developing into "something new and unforeseen":

. . . what happens when a new work of art is created is something that happens simultaneously to all the works of art which preceded it. The existing monuments form an ideal order among themselves, which is modified by the introduction of the new (the really new) work of art among them. The existing order is complete before the new work arrives; for order to persist after the supervention of novelty, the *whole* existing order must be, if ever so slightly, altered; and so the relations, proportions, values of each work of art toward the whole are readjusted; and this is conformity between the old and the new. (SW, 49-50)

Like the scientist, who submits himself to a special discipline, the artist surrenders his personality "to something which is more valuable," and "it is in this depersonalization that art may be said to approach the condition of science" (SW, 52-53). Neither a science nor a tradition, however, represents an objective order purely external to ourselves. Although they demand that the individual surrender his own personality, each provides a special point of view that makes possible the creation of something genuinely new.

The notion of a "point of view" can be somewhat confusing, particularly when Eliot uses it with reference not to an individual but to a literary form or tradition. Applied to an individual it is virtually synonymous with the terms "unified sensibility" and "intelligence," and refers to the artist's distinctive mode of apprehending experience. Instead of possessing "ideas" about the accepted "real world," the artist assumes a definite "point of view" that is expressed in the distinctive world of the text. But the application of this notion to a literary form or tradition is more complicated, and its relationship to a critique of objectivism more obscure. At first glance the adoption of a form or the acceptance of a tradition seems to involve a shift from subject to object: the author surrenders his own subjectivity to an objective standard external to himself. Yet Eliot is opposed to the view that reifies form or tradition into a purely objective order that stifles subjective expression. He maintains, for example, that the acceptance of formal constraints does not eradicate but transfigures the subjective side of experience: the artist gives up "personal emotion" but only in exchange for the "new art emotion" embodied in the work. Hence, by approaching them not simply as external standards to which one conforms but as points of view that one adopts, Eliot counteracts what he regarded as the reified objectivism of Romantic attitudes toward form and tradition.

In sum, Eliot complements his well-known critique of excessive subjectivity with a highly developed if less obvious critique of the opposing vice. The latter is most evident in his approach to literary realism, but it also appears in his distinctions between dissociated and unified sensibility, intellect and intelligence, idea and point of view. Following the strategy of his dissertation, Eliot opposes the artistic reification of either side of experience. He considers the description of objects severed from emotion to be as damaging as the expression of emotion detached from objects. Both defects arise, he maintains, from the same bifurcation of experience into subjective and objective extremes, a bifurcation that accounts for his insistence on the union of emotion and object and the wedding of intellect and sensation.

IV

Why has Eliot's attack on reified subjectivity received so much attention while its counterpart has gone virtually unrecognized? There are several reasons for the oversight. First, Eliot placed far greater emphasis on the critique of subjectivity; like others of his generation, he reacted against what was regarded as the subjectivism of nineteenth-century culture. His indictment of the psychologist, the philosophical idealist, and the Romantic poet were all part of the same effort to redress imbalances of the previous century. Second, Eliot's dissertation was not published until 1964, and without the thesis it is difficult to discern the connection between terms like "idea" and "point of view" and a concern with reified objectivity. But once we grasp the entire dialectical strategy, the key terms of Eliot's early essays move into clearer focus. Shopworn expressions such as "objective correlative" and "dissociation of sensibility" recover not only their original meaning but also some of their lost vitality.

Eliot's Observer/Agents: Self and Other as "Half-Objects"

In his thesis Eliot uses the subject/object dialectic to examine how individuals perceive other persons. He maintains that we apprehend others from an internal as well as an external point of view; we are aware of them not merely as objects but as subjects like ourselves. In a similar manner, Eliot claims that we may apprehend ourselves in part from an external point of view, which makes it possible to turn our own subjective life into a "kind of object" (KE, 22): "To say that one part of the mind suffers and another part reflects upon the suffering is perhaps to talk in fictions. But we know that those highly-organized beings who are able to objectify their passions, and as passive spectators to contemplate their joys and torments, are also those who suffer and enjoy the most keenly" (KE, 23). The apprehension of self and other is thus a complex affair: we perceive both ourselves and other persons neither as subjects nor as objects exclusively, but rather, to use Eliot's term, as "half-objects."

The "half-object" is one expression of Eliot's enduring interest in the process of social interaction. The self-conscious personae of his early poems constantly agonize over their encounters with other persons. They are suspended between their external apprehension of others, whom they know directly through observable behavior alone, and their internal apprehension of others as active centers of consciousness. These personae also experience a subject/object split within themselves. They are at once detached observers and conventional agents, spectators of their own participation in the social world. This division of the self into observer and agent is also a prominent feature of Eliot's critical essays, where he maintains that the artist must separate "the man who suffers" and "the mind which creates" (SW, 54): "The artist is part of him a drifter, at the mercy of impressions, and another part of him allows this to happen for the sake of making use of the unhappy creature."[23] Thus the "half-object" appears not only in the philosophical but also in the literary writings, and by examining Eliot's abiding interest in this notion, we can illuminate some of the most significant features of his early works.

I

In chapter 3 of his thesis, Eliot uses the term "half-object" to account for the problematic relationship between the psychologist and the mental phenomena he investigates. The term first appears during a discussion of will, in which Eliot considers how the psychologist studies subjective life:

> From a purely external point of view there is no will; and to find will in any phenomenon requires a certain empathy; we observe a man's actions and place ourselves partly but not wholly in his position; or we act, and place ourselves partly in the position of an outsider. And this doubleness of aspect is in fact the justification for the use of the term. Another person, and in its degree another *thing*, is not for us simply an object; there is always, I believe, a felt continuity between the object and oneself. The only error lies in regarding this community as due to the common possession of a character which belongs to both subject and object as such, and belongs to each independently. This character is then treated as a thing. (KE, 81)

The psychologist does not have direct access to the mental state of another individual. He studies the mental life of another by moving beyond external observation and placing himself "partly but not wholly" in the other person's position. For instance, from "a purely external point of view," the psychologist has no immediate awareness of another person's hallucination. Nonetheless, he may attend to the hallucination as a half-object—" i.e., we intend something which from our point of view is wholly inexistent" (KE, 115). Eliot maintains that the study of mental life necessarily proceeds through this kind of indirection. Unlike the natural scientist, who examines "objects," the psychologist always examines "half-objects." Such half-objects arise from the conflict between two points of view: the external or objective point of view, through which the psychologist observes the external behavior of another, and the internal or subjective point of view, through which he identifies with the other as a subject like himself. Since a half-object is constituted by the act of perceiving another as an object and simultaneously identifying with him as a subject, it "belongs to a place half-way between object and subject" (KE, 81). The half-object depends "upon our apprehending two points of view at once, and pursuing neither" (KE, 160).

In his thesis Eliot also employs the half-object to describe how individuals apprehend one another in social life. He speculates that it is our perception of one another as half-objects which transforms the original "worlds" of separate finite centers into the shared "real world" (KE, 142-43). At first we apprehend other finite centers only as "recognized resistances and felt divergences," but slowly we develop a feeling of "identity between the experiences of other centres and our own." By gradually adjusting our point of view to that of others, Eliot concludes, "we come to intend an identical world."

Eliot seems ambivalent about the socializing process. Although our ability to identify with other finite centers is an essential part of human development, the language Eliot employs to describe social interaction abounds in images of pain and conflict. The initial recognition of others as half-objects ruptures the original unity of immediate experience: "It is only in social behaviour, in the conflict and readjustment of finite centres, that feelings and things are torn apart" (KE, 24-25). In addition, the valuable process of developing from a mere "finite centre" into a conscious "soul" involves "the painful task of unifying (to a greater or lesser extent) jarring and incompatible [worlds]" (KE, 147). Socialization also threatens the integrity of the individual. As disparate points of view coalesce into an "identical world," the individual loses his unique point of view and becomes absorbed into conventional reality:

"The majority not only have no language to express anything save generalized man; they are for the most part unaware of themselves as anything but generalized men. They are first of all government officials, or pillars of the church, or trade unionists, or poets, or unemployed; this cataloguing is not only satisfactory to other people for practical purposes, it is sufficient to themselves for their 'life of the spirit.' Many are not quite real at any moment. When Wolstrip married, I am sure he said to himself: 'Now I am consummating the union of two of the best families in Philadelphia.' "[24]

Thus, while he acknowledges that social interaction leads to personal growth and mutual cooperation, Eliot reveals his anguish over the socializing process, which destroys our original world and compels us to enter an impoverished "real world."

The same anguish is expressed in the interpersonal conflicts of the early poetry. Eliot's personae struggle with all the difficulties of adapting themselves to the disturbing presence of others. They are caught in the "internal-external point of view" (KE, 162) of the half-object, oscillating painfully between the internal point of view, which leads to sympathetic identification with another subject, and the external point of view, which leads to the apprehension of the other as a mere object. The half-object, then, expresses Eliot's preoccupation with the way we take account of others, a process he explores both in his dissertation and in his poetry. By using the notion of the half-object to examine his verse, we can develop a phenomenology of intersubjective life in Eliot's early poetry, a phenomenology that lays out the various ways his personae apprehend other persons.[1]

[1] We should avoid the misconception that Eliot first formulated the "half-object" and then dramatized it in his poetry. Long before he wrote his dissertation, Eliot had composed "Prufrock," "Portrait of a Lady," and several other poems that exhibit the internal-external point of view of the half-object. But even though it does not antedate all of the poetry, the half-object provides us with a means of analyzing recurrent features of Eliot's verse that have been recognized but insufficiently examined.

II

Eliot's early poems can be analyzed in terms of the stance the observer takes toward other persons. At one extreme, the observer perceives others as mere objects. In many of Eliot's street scenes, other persons appear not as whole individuals but as parts of bodies:

> The morning comes to consciousness
> Of faint stale smells of beer
> From the sawdust-trampled street
> With all its muddy feet that press
> To early coffee-stands.

> With the other masquerades
> That time resumes,
> One thinks of all the hands
> That are raising dingy shades
> In a thousand furnished rooms.
>   (CP, 13)

"Consciousness" may refer to the "morning" or to the observer, but in either case the word is set in relief against the observer's purely external perspective upon the scene before him. He apprehends not other centers of consciousness, but "feet that press / To early coffee-stands" and "hands that are raising dingy shades." Human activities are reduced to empty "masquerades / That time resumes." In this poem, as in others, the source of the observer's alienation from others as subjects is uncertain. It is difficult to know whether his perception arises from the internal impoverishment of those he observes or from the failure of his own sympathetic imagination. In some cases, the observer tries but fails to discern subjective life behind the external gesture:

> So the hand of the child, automatic,
> Slipped out and pocketed a toy that was running along the
>   quay,

I could see nothing behind that child's eye.
                                        (CP, 17)

But in other cases the observer seems to have made his decision in advance:

Unreal City,
Under the brown fog of a winter dawn,
A crowd flowed over London Bridge, so many,
I had not thought death had undone so many.
                                        (CP, 55)

Here the spectator expresses a feeling of loss; he recognizes the damned as those who no longer possess an internal life distinguishable from their external role. But the observer himself seems more disposed to the external than the internal point of view; that is, he is more inclined to pass judgment upon the crowd than to identify with any of the individuals in it. Whatever the source of the observer's stance in these poems, we find the same tendency to apprehend others as mere objects rather than fully human subjects.

This reduction of others to objects is quite common in Eliot's early poetry, but it represents only one position, and an extreme one, along a broad spectrum. At the other end of the spectrum, Eliot envisions an ecstatic state of total identification between two subjects. Eliot finds this state in the love scenes of *Romeo and Juliet*, where all externality dissolves and Shakespeare "shows his lovers melting into incoherent unconsciousness of their isolated selves, shows the human soul in the process of forgetting itself" (SW, 83). Such moments of transfiguration, however, are virtually absent from the bleak world of Eliot's own early verse: One questionable approximation appears in "The Waste Land":

'You gave me hyacinths first a year ago;
'They called me the hyacinth girl.'
—Yet when we came back, late, from the hyacinth garden,
Your arms full, and your hair wet, I could not

Speak, and my eyes failed, I was neither
Living nor dead, and I knew nothing,
Looking into the heart of light, the silence.
Oed' und leer das Meer.
(CP, 54)

Even here the experience is recalled from a subsequent state
of loss, as the line from Wagner's *Tristan and Isolde* suggests.
The moment is rendered primarily in negative terms—loss of
voice, sight, consciousness—that convey no sense of rapture.
We find not two lovers "melting into incoherent unconsciousness of their isolated selves," but one person gazing ambigu-
ously "into the heart of light, the silence." Such divine moments "in and out of time" (CP, 199) are more the province
of Eliot's later poetry, and there they have little to do with
relations between one individual and another. In his early
poetry, the state of total communion between two subjects is
never realized in actual human encounters. We are aware of
it primarily through its absence, more as repeatedly frus-
trated possibility than achieved reality.

Most of Eliot's human encounters take place between the
extremes of pure identification and pure alienation. His personae usually apprehend others as half-objects, and struggle
with the conflict between internal and external points of view.
They are caught between their perception of others as subjects like themselves and as objects reducible to their external
gestures. These personae sense a vast rift between the internal and external self, and therefore remain unsure of other
persons, whom they know directly through external behavior
alone. This uncertainty often causes them to waver between
the desire to become involved and the desire to remain detached, between the wish "to force the moment to its crisis"
and the compulsion to adhere to protective social rituals.

Eliot's brief prose poem, "Hysteria," portrays the conflict
between the feelings that draw us to another person and the
defensive reaction that protects us from those feelings. As the
observer and his lady wait to be seated, the narrator finds

himself gazing at a girl and "becoming involved in her laughter and being part of it, until her teeth were only accidental stars with a talent for squad-drill" (CP, 24). The observer undergoes, after a fashion, a moment of transport akin to that of the hyacinth girl: "I was drawn in by short gasps, inhaled at each momentary recovery, lost finally in the dark caverns of her throat, bruised by the ripple of unseen muscles." The observer conveys his growing involvement by leading us from the external description of "short gasps" to the imaginative apprehension of "the ripple of unseen muscles." Then a break occurs in the poem, and we pass from the internal to the external point of view, from intense involvement with another to the world of conventional interaction: A waiter spreads a cloth over a table and announces: " 'If the lady and gentleman wish to take their tea in the garden, if the lady and gentleman wish to take their tea in the garden. . . .' " Does the waiter repeat himself, or does the repetition occur in the disconcerted mind of the observer? In either case, the observer now tries to regain his self-possession: "I decided that if the shaking of her breasts could be stopped, some of the fragments of the afternoon might be collected, and I concentrated my attention with careful subtlety to this end." Here at the end of the poem the observer attempts to pull himself back from the abyss and to regain his composure. The poem as a whole reveals some of the characteristic tensions of Eliot's early verse: it dramatizes the conflict between internal and external points of view, which is expressed in the sexual conflict between our attraction to another and our need to defend ourselves from feelings that disturb our "self-possession."

Eliot's male personae often protect themselves from threatening feelings by adhering to social conventions. The young man in "Portrait of a Lady" uses his polite smile to ward off the lady's pleas for intimacy:

'Ah, my friend, you do not know, you do not know
What life is, you who hold it in your hands';

(Slowly twisting the lilac stalks)
'You let it flow from you, you let it flow,
And youth is cruel, and has no more remorse
And smiles at situations which it cannot see.'
I smile, of course,
And go on drinking tea.
(CP, 9)

The lady repeatedly asks the young man to identify with her as a subject: " 'I am always sure that you understand / My feelings, always sure that you feel, / Sure that across the gulf you reach your hand' " (CP, 10). But the narrator, for his part, refuses to give her any sign of his own inner state. Trying to maintain a strictly external point of view, he takes refuge in social decorum. Nevertheless, each successive encounter poses a greater threat to his self-possession:

'Perhaps you can write to me.'
My self-possession flares up for a second;
This is as I had reckoned.
'I have been wondering frequently of late
(But our beginnings never know our ends!)
Why we have not developed into friends.'
I feel like one who smiles, and turning shall remark
Suddenly, his expression in a glass.
My self-possession gutters; we are really in the dark.
(CP, 11)

The narrator still resists the lady. But as his "self-possession gutters," he begins to sense a split between his own internal and external self. "I smile" has now become "I feel like one who smiles," and he imagines himself surprised by the sight of his own public expression in a glass. By the end of the poem, when he wonders how he would respond to news of her death, it is clear that part of him has lapsed into confusion:

Doubtful, for a while
Not knowing what to feel or if I understand

Or whether wise or foolish, tardy or too soon . . .
Would she not have the advantage, after all?
(CP, 12)

The young man has tried to maintain an external rather than an internal point of view. To identify with the lady as a subject would require that he acknowledge feelings which either he does not have or does not wish to have. But as she gradually wears away his defenses, the young man becomes aware of a subject/object split within himself. The man no longer has full control over his mask. At the end he is still scarcely cognizant of feelings for the lady herself, but he senses that she has disturbed his cherished self-possession.

A variant of "Portrait of a Lady" appears in "The Waste Land," where the persona seems to have no feelings for the other and resists her efforts to awaken them:

'My nerves are bad to-night. Yes, bad. Stay with me.
'Speak to me. Why do you never speak. Speak.
  'What are you thinking of? What thinking? What?
'I never know what you are thinking. Think.

I think we are in rats' alley
Where the dead men lost their bones.
(CP, 57)

The desperation of one party is answered by the inert self-possession of the other, the plea for sympathy by a shift to external ritual:

"What shall I do now? What shall I do?
"I shall rush out as I am, and walk the street
"With my hair down, so. What shall we do tomorrow?
"What shall we ever do?"

                    The hot water at ten.
And if it rains, the closed carriage at four.
And we shall play a game of chess:

> The ivory men make company between us
> Pressing lidless eyes and waiting for a knock upon the
>   door.[25]

These lines are often thought to display the poet's sense of a fatal chasm between our inner lives and the social conventions through which we are compelled to interact. Yet here, as in "Portrait," the persona's calculated adherence to social ritual expresses not an inevitable rift between internal feeling and external action but rather a compulsive strategy for distancing oneself from another person.

The problem of approaching others as half-objects is especially prominent in "The Love Song of J. Alfred Prufrock." Here the observer oscillates between the external and the internal points of view. At certain moments, Prufrock views other persons exclusively as objects; the ladies appear as conventional creatures whose formulaic behavior constitutes their entire being. Like the observers in other poems, he sees parts of bodies rather than whole persons: "And I have known the arms already, known them all— / Arms that are braceleted and white and bare. . . . Arms that lie along a table, or wrap about a shawl" (CP, 5). When he assumes this stance, Prufrock remains cool and detached. But when he moves to the internal point of view and apprehends others as perceiving subjects, Prufrock loses his equanimity. He grows disconcerted as he imagines other persons observing him from a purely external point of view:

> And I have known the eyes already, known them all—
> The eyes that fix you in a formulated phrase,
> And when I am formulated, sprawling on a pin,
> When I am pinned and wriggling on the wall,
> Then how should I begin
> To spit out all the butt-ends of my days and ways?
>   (CP, 5)

The act of identifying with another as a center of experience like oneself often leads to the recognition of a spiritual bond between two persons. However, when Prufrock places himself in the other person's position, he only becomes more aware of himself as an object in the conventional world perceived by the other person:

(They will say: 'How his hair is growing thin!')
My morning coat, my collar mounting firmly to the chin,
My necktie rich and modest, but asserted by a simple pin—
(They will say: 'But how his arms and legs are thin!') . . .

(CP, 4)

Prufrock is also haunted by the sense of an insuperable distance between himself as a private center of consciousness and as a social agent—"It is impossible to say just what I mean!" He assumes that one's external behavior inevitably misrepresents the inner life, and conceives his entry into social life as a drowning of his own consciousness in a sea of "human voices." He imagines, therefore, that when others take account of him, they are looking solely at the public agent rather than the private subject. Ironically, his own internal life is consumed by the effort "to prepare a face to meet the faces that you meet." His consciousness consists of little more than his nervous, though often humorous, recognition that we are alienated from ourselves in the social world.

The conflict between internal and external points of view in "Prufrock" also accounts for the reader's difficulty in identifying the relationship between persona and auditor. As readers we are uncertain whether we are overhearing the persona's stream of consciousness or hearing him present himself to another. Beginning with the epigraph, Eliot confounds any clear distinction between private and public, lyric and dramatic voices:

S'io credessi che mia risposta fosse
a persona che mai tornasse al mondo,
questa fiamma staria senze più scosse.
Ma per ciò che giammai di questo fondo
non tornò vivo alcun, s'i'odo il vero,
senza tema d'infamia ti rispondo.

[If I thought that my answer were to one who might ever
return to the world, this flame would shake no more; but
since from this depth none ever returned alive, if what
I hear is true, I answer you without fear of infamy.][26]

Guido da Montefeltro, consigned to the eighth circle of Hell
for fraudulent counsel, is himself the victim of deception. He
reveals his identity to Dante, but only because he believes
that his auditor is a permanent inhabitant of the underworld.
What appears to be a private confession to one of the dead
turns out to be a public disclosure to the world of the living.
Thus, by blurring the boundary between private and public
utterance, the epigraph sets the stage for the rest of the
poem, which hovers between internal and external voices.

Prufrock's monologue opens with the speaker addressing
what seems to be an external auditor:

> Let us go then, you and I,
> When the evening is spread out against the sky . . .

But between the first stanza and the last there is only a single
hint that a listener is present (the reference to "you and me"
on line 78), and the poem appears to drift into a private revery. Then in the last three lines the persona suddenly shifts
from "I" to "we": "We have lingered in the chambers of the
sea / By sea-girls wreathed with seaweed red and brown / Till
human voices wake us, and we drown." Readers of the poem
debate the meaning of these pronominal shifts. Some claim
that the presence of an auditor after the first stanza is so slight
that we should assume that Prufrock has been addressing
himself from the beginning: the "you and I" of the opening
lines and the "we" of the conclusion express the persona's
own divided sensibility. Other readers, following one of
Eliot's remarks, maintain that we must assume the presence
of a definite auditor.[27] It is difficult to decide between these
options: the poem seems to leave us suspended between an
internal point of view, through which we overhear a lyric self-
disclosure, and an external point of view, through which we

listen to a speaker's dramatic presentation of himself to another. In other words, the poem may be so constructed that
we apprehend the persona neither as a subject nor as an object but as a half-object. And this tension between internal
and external points of view corresponds to the struggle within
the persona himself—the conflict between the desire to maintain a distinct internal identity and the inability to do so in
the presence of others.

III

In his thesis, Eliot associates the half-object not only with our
perception of others but also with our self-perception: ". . .
we observe a man's actions and place ourselves partly but not
wholly in his position; or we act, and place ourselves partly
in the position of an outsider" (KE, 81). In the first case, we
move from the observation of another as an object to partial
identification with him as a subject; in the second case, we
move from the experience of ourselves as subjects to an external point of view that allows us to observe our own
thoughts and actions as objects. Eliot regards this self-detachment as either an active or a passive process: "To say that one
part of the mind suffers and another part reflects upon the
suffering is perhaps to talk in fictions. But we know that those
highly-organized beings who are able *to objectify* their passions, and as passive spectators *to contemplate* their joys and
torments, are also those who suffer and enjoy the most
keenly" (italics mine; KE, 23). Here, as in his early essays,
Eliot applauds the dual capacity to dramatize one's emotions
and to observe one's performance from a detached point of
view. Eliot's own personae, however, exhibit only the passive
side of this process. Unable "to objectify their passions," they
are merely "passive spectators" of their own highly conventional behavior. They are detached enough to observe their
actions, but seem incapable of changing them.

Eliot's interest in self-objectification figures prominently in
an early essay, " 'Rhetoric' and Poetic Drama" (1920), origi-

nally a review of the dramatist Edmond Rostand. In this piece, Eliot focuses on moments during a play when a character "*sees himself* in a dramatic light." He selects several examples from Shakespeare:

OTHELLO.   And say, besides,—that in Aleppo once . . .
CORIOLANUS. If you have writ your annals true, 'tis there,
            That like an eagle in a dovecote, I
            Fluttered your Volscians in Corioli.
            Alone I did it. Boy!
TIMON.   Come not to me again; but say to Athens,
            Timon hath made his everlasting mansion
            Upon the beachèd verge of the salt flood . . .
                                                      (SW, 81)

Eliot notes that dramatists in the "realistic" theater rarely endow their characters with such self-awareness "for fear, perhaps, of their appearing less real." Then, echoing the words of his dissertation, he claims that this self-awareness is very much part of real life; we possess this form of consciousness in "those situations in actual life which we enjoy consciously and keenly" (SW, 83). In the desert of modern realistic drama, Rostand's characters are unique in their ability "to objectify their passions" and "as passive spectators" to observe themselves in action. Associating this flair for self-dramatization with the possession of a sense of humor—"for when anyone is conscious of himself as acting, something like a sense of humour is present" (SW, 83)—Eliot maintains that characters like Cyrano de Bergerac derive their uncommon vitality from this ability to objectify their emotions.

Significantly, Eliot qualifies his praise for Rostand's characters. Despite their talent for self-dramatization, which distinguishes them from characters in the realistic theater, Rostand's figures "often fail of any other existence than this in which they are aware of their own rôle."[28] Eliot compares the love scenes in *Cyrano* to those in *Romeo and Juliet*, and asserts that "the profounder dramatist shows his lovers melting into incoherent unconsciousness of their isolated selves, shows the human soul in the process of forgetting itself" (SW, 83). In effect, he is situating Rostand's characters between the characters of realistic drama, who are fully absorbed into the everyday world, and those like Shakespeare's lovers, who momentarily transcend conventional reality entirely. Cyrano and his counterparts occupy a broad middle ground between these two poles, the ground of those who are neither fully absorbed into the ordinary world nor fully detached from it. These characters, who include the observer/agents of Eliot's early poetry, apprehend themselves as half-objects; they are detached enough from their participation in social life to stand back and observe the roles they perform.

In "Hamlet and His Problems," composed the same year as " 'Rhetoric' and Poetic Drama," Eliot again examines the relationship between emotion and action. Whereas Cyrano depicts "the expression of the emotion" (SW, 84), Hamlet exhibits the failure to objectify emotion: "Hamlet (the man) is dominated by an emotion which is inexpressible, because it is in *excess* of the facts as they appear. . . . Hamlet is up against the difficulty that his disgust is occasioned by his mother, but that his mother is not an adequate equivalent for it; his disgust envelops and exceeds her" (SW, 101). Hamlet's antics express neither madness nor mere dissimulation; they are rather "a form of emotional relief" (SW, 102) from feelings that have no adequate object and cannot be objectified in action. Hence, the emotion "which he cannot understand . . . cannot objectify" remains "to poison life and obstruct action" (SW, 101). The protagonist is caught between his disturbance with the world as it exists and his failure to locate and eradicate the disease that plagues it.

The self-conscious personae of Eliot's poetry are akin both to Cyrano and to Hamlet. Like Cyrano, they are partially detached observers of the social roles they perform. These personae also share Cyrano's limitations, since they "often fail of any other existence than this in which they are aware of their own rôle." But there is an important difference: Cyrano

takes conscious delight in the objectification of his feelings;
Eliot's personae, on the other hand, merely observe themselves performing social rituals in situations from which they
feel estranged. Like Hamlet, they are unable to alter the
world as they find it. Incapable of objectifying their emotions,
these observer/agents remain passive spectators to their own
conventional behavior. They possess self-awareness, but this
awareness either fails to produce any action at all or it leads,
as Eliot saw in Hamlet, to merely antic behavior.

Eliot's personae are most often men who observe themselves posturing on the social stage. They act and simultaneously display an ironic detachment from their actions. For
instance, the speaker in "Conversation Galante" is partially
estranged from the romantic role he is expected to play and
ends up striking a ridiculous pose:

> I observe: 'Our sentimental friend the moon!
> Or possibly (fantastic, I confess)
> It may be Prester John's balloon
> Or an old battered lantern hung aloft
> To light poor travellers to their distress.'
> She then: 'How you digress!'
> (CP, 25)

In this early Laforguean experiment, Eliot places his hero in
a romantic situation and then undermines the romantic element. The speaker's behavior, like Hamlet's, is a cross between his designated role and personal resistance to it.[m]

In "Conversation Galante," the spectator at least coaches

---

[m] In "La Figlia che Piange," the speaker seems to be directing an event
external to himself and simultaneously acting in it. The pronominal shifts of
the second stanza suggest that he is both a spectator who relishes "a gesture
and a pose" and a participant in an emotional drama: "So I would have had
him leave, / So I would have had her stand and grieve, / So he would have
left / As the soul leaves the body torn and bruised, / As the mind deserts the
body it has used. / I should find / Some way incomparably light and deft, /
Some way we both should understand, / Simple and faithless as a smile and
shake of the hand" (CP, 26). In this last gesture, the external action is dissociated entirely from the internal feeling it is meant to signify.

the participant, whose behavior expresses his estrangement from the situation. But in "Prufrock" the spectator offers no assistance to the participant. Prufrock is a partially detached observer, but he adheres fastidiously to social convention. Conscious of the banality of his actions, he is unable to modify them. His self-awareness never rallies him "to force the moment to its crisis." As he observes himself in the role he is incapable of altering, his capacity for self-detachment produces nothing more than a bit of self-compromising humor:

No! I am not Prince Hamlet, nor was meant to be;
Am an attendant lord, one that will do
To swell a progress, start a scene or two,
Advise the prince; no doubt, an easy tool,
Deferential, glad to be of use,
Politic, cautious, and meticulous;
Full of high sentence, but a bit obtuse;
At times, indeed, almost ridiculous—
Almost, at times, the Fool.
(CP, 7)[n]

Prufrock inhabits the modern inferno where mere knowledge of one's condition does nothing to relieve it. The persona as perceiving subject is totally estranged from his own external actions.

The same split between spectator and participant appears in "The Waste Land," but without the humor that relieves "Prufrock." In Section III, "The Fire Sermon," Eliot depicts Tiresias, the prophet doomed to foresee the future he cannot change, as an observer/agent of the modern scene. As Tiresias watches "the young man carbuncular" mechanically seduce the typist, the text indicates that he is not merely a detached observer:

[n] Recall Eliot's remark in " 'Rhetoric' and Poetic Drama": ". . . for when anyone is conscious of himself as acting, something like a sense of humour is present."

(And I Tiresias have foresuffered all
Enacted on this same divan or bed;
I who have sat by Thebes below the wall
And walked among the lowest of the dead.)
(CP, 62)

Earlier in the scene, Tiresias says that he has "foretold" the outcome; now he uses the word "foresuffered," which suggests not only clairvoyance but resigned participation in the sorry affair. And in the notes that follow the poem, Eliot claims that Tiresias is the observer/agent of the poem as a whole:

> Tiresias, although a mere spectator and not indeed a 'character,' is yet the most important personage in the poem, uniting all the rest. Just as the one-eyed merchant, seller of currants, melts into the Phoenician Sailor, and the latter is not wholly distinct from Ferdinand Prince of Naples, so all the women are one woman, and the two sexes meet in Tiresias. What Tiresias *sees*, in fact, is the substance of the poem.   (CP, 72)

As the impotent observer who must "foresuffer all," Tiresias is akin to Eliot's other observer/agents, who are spectators to their own participation in the rituals of a debased civilization.

Thus, Eliot's fascination with observer/agents appears throughout his early works. His dissertation describes the process of self-objectification conceptually, and provides us with the terms for analyzing it elsewhere. The literary criticism exhibits several types of observer/agent, exposing us to figures like Cyrano who can objectify their passions and those like Hamlet who cannot. The poetry is closely tied to the criticism, but displays only one recurrent type of observer/agent—the persona who observes his own behavior but cannot direct it. This persona displays a severe rift between inner and outer worlds, between the subject who perceives and the agent who performs. Incapable of objectifying his subjective life, he remains alienated from his own external actions, a passive spectator who suffers the indignity of participating in a culture he despises but cannot transform.

IV

The observer/agent relationship also plays a major part in Eliot's theory of artistic creation. Like Eliot's personae, who are spectators of their own actions, Eliot's artist is a detached observer of his own mental activity. He must separate the "man who suffers" from the "mind which creates" (SW, 54): "The artist is part of him a drifter, at the mercy of impressions, and another part of him allows this to happen for the sake of making use of the unhappy creature." Eliot describes this process in both active and passive terms. At times he treats artistic creation as an active process of self-objectification; at other times, he treats it as a passive process of self-detachment. We should not be misled by this variation in terms: in the criticism, unlike the poetry, self-objectification and self-detachment are two sides of the same coin. Those who "objectify their passions" are also those who can "as passive spectators . . . contemplate their joys and torments" (KE, 23). Both self-objectification and self-detachment involve the same ability to turn one's subjective life into an object, that is, to assume the standpoint of the half-object. Let us examine each of these descriptions in turn.

In "Hamlet and His Problems," Eliot discusses art as a process of self-objectification. The artist expresses his emotions, Eliot declares, by presenting their objective correlative—"a set of objects, a situation, a chain of events which shall be the formula of that *particular* emotion" (SW, 100). In the case of *Hamlet*, however, this process has not taken place. Eliot maintains that Hamlet and Shakespeare have the same problem—an inability to find an object adequate to their emotions. Hamlet's failure to objectify his emotions is continuous with Shakespeare's failure to make the play an expression of his emotion:

. . . Hamlet's bafflement at the absence of objective
equivalent to his feelings is a prolongation of the bafflement of his creator in the face of his artistic problem.
. . . In the character Hamlet it is the buffoonery of an
emotion which can find no outlet in action; in the dramatist it is the buffoonery of an emotion which he cannot
express in art.   (SW, 101-102)

If Hamlet cannot act to transform the world around him,
Shakespeare cannot transform his materials into the dramatic
world that objectifies his internal state. But the superior artist, like Shakespeare in his other plays, is more akin to Cyrano than to Hamlet. Like Cyrano, who can objectify his passions, the artist has the ability "to intensify the world to his
emotions." The artist "objectifies his passions" by transforming the everyday world into the new world of art.

The process described in "Hamlet and His Problems" is
more the exception than the rule. For the most part, Eliot
describes the artist's endeavor in passive terms as a process
of self-detachment. From this perspective the artist is a "passive spectator" of his own "joys and torments." He does not
express emotion or personality, but detaches himself from
them: "the more perfect the artist, the more completely separate in him will be the man who suffers and the mind which
creates; the more perfectly will the mind digest and transmute the passions which are its material" (SW, 54). Using
terms that anticipate his conversion to Christianity, Eliot describes this process of self-detachment as a "sacrifice" or "extinction" of the self: ". . . the creation of a work of art is like
some other forms of creation, a painful and unpleasant business; it is a sacrifice of the man to the work, it is a kind of
death."[29] As a result of this "continual extinction of personality" (SW, 53), the artist's mind becomes "a more finely per-
fected medium in which special, or very varied, feelings are
at liberty to enter into new combinations" (SW, 53-54). The
process of self-disengagement allows the artist to bring forth
the new combinations or the new world embodied in the text.

Eliot's two accounts of artistic creation are really versions
of the same thing. Whether he describes the process in terms
of self-objectification or self-detachment, Eliot is referring to
the same observer/agent relationship that appears elsewhere
in his writings. The artist possesses the capacity to assume
the standpoint of the half-object, an ability that brings into
being the new work of art.

V

Eliot's account of the creative process suggests that there is a
connection between his view of the artist and the poetic personae he actually created. Both the artist and the personae
are observer/agents; they have the same capacity to stand
back and observe their own thoughts and actions. But there
is a difference in the nature and the degree of this self-detachment. In his critical essays, Eliot describes the artist in
terms of a total detachment, or "death," of the personality, a
"death" that makes possible the creation of a new world. In
his poetry, on the other hand, Eliot creates personae who are
only partially detached from, and cannot transform, their own
external behavior. Their self-awareness produces no change
in the world around them. Like Prufrock, these observer/
agents possess certain characteristics of the artist. They display the ironic detachment and the "wit"—"a recognition,
implicit in the expression of every experience, of other kinds
of experience which are possible" (SE, 262)—which distinguish them from mere creatures of convention. But their partial detachment offers little more than painful awareness of
their deplorable condition. Neither absorbed fully into the
temporal order nor entirely detached from it, they remain
acquiescent participants in a society from which they are estranged. Gerontion, for instance, desires release from the
wheel of time, but his self-awareness brings him despair
rather than deliverance. He can sustain no more than a fleeting vision of "Christ the tiger" (CP, 29), and finishes the
poem in the same dejected state in which he began. While

the artist objectifies his emotions into a new world, Eliot's personae are reduced to mere disaffection with the old world. They are sufficiently detached to observe its ruined state, but recognition does not lead them to redemption.[o]

This comparison between Eliot the critic and Eliot the poet may also tell us something about Eliot the man. If the personae are in any way representative of their creator, we may view the early poetry as an expression of Eliot's desire to gain detachment from the "man who suffers." The recurrent portraits of personal struggle and cultural void, along with the intimations of a reality that transcends ordinary life, attest to the persistent longing for release and transformation. In his criticism, Eliot imagines the artist achieving this release and transformation: the artist surrenders himself as a man, and passes through a kind of death that leads to a new creation. But the vocation of art did not meet the spiritual needs of the man himself: Eliot's critical vocabulary—"sacrifice," "surrender," "death"—expresses needs that only religious commitment could satisfy. Prior to his conversion, it is not his criticism but his poetic personae who reflect Eliot's actual condition.[p] Eliot's personae are detached enough to recognize the depravity of the temporal order, but nonetheless find themselves inextricably bound to it. Like Gerontion, they sit

[o] "The Death of Saint Narcissus" is one of the most striking expressions of the fear that there may be no deliverance from the burden of temporal life. The protagonist separates himself from the everyday world and becomes "a dancer before God," but he never succeeds in mortifying the desires of the flesh. His successive metamorphoses into a tree, a fish, and then a girl do more to heighten than to purge his sensual nature. The protagonist's flesh is in love even with the arrows designed for its mortification, and in the end the long ritual of transformation leaves him "green, dry and stained / With the shadow in his mouth" (Poems Written in Early Youth [London: Faber & Faber, 1967], pp. 34-35).

[p] In other words, the criticism presents an ideal that is not fulfilled in the poetry. Eliot may have been aware of such a relationship between his criticism and his poetry. In 1933 he stated "that in one's prose reflexions one may be legitimately occupied with ideals, whereas in the writing of verse one can only deal with actuality" (After Strange Gods: A Primer of Modern Heresy [London: Faber & Faber, 1934], p. 28).

and wait without hope of redemption. Thus, the early poetry manifests the personal need for deliverance that is only partially relieved through the depersonalizing ritual of art. It exhibits the capacity for partial detachment, a capacity that turned passion into poetry but failed to redeem the man.

However, the early verse displays certain signs of the death and transformation ascribed to the artist, and these signs anticipate the changes in the course of Eliot's own life. In his essays, Eliot states that the sacrifice of the man to the work makes possible the creation of a new world, or a "simplification of current life into something rich and strange."[30] The tag "rich and strange," which Eliot uses repeatedly, comes from Ariel's song in Act I of *The Tempest*. Here the Spirit of the Air tells Prince Ferdinand of his father's death and metamorphosis:

> Full fathom five thy father lies;
> Of his bones are coral made;
> Those are pearls that were his eyes:
> Nothing of him that doth fade
> But doth suffer a sea-change
> Into something rich and strange.
> Sea-nymphs hourly ring his knell.
>   (I.ii.399-405)

Eliot uses this song as a leitmotif in "The Waste Land," where it first appears in the Tarot deck of Madame Sosostris:

> Here, said she,
> Is your card, the drowned Phoenician Sailor,
> (Those are pearls that were his eyes. Look!)
>   (CP, 54)

In Section IV, "Death by Water," the Phoenician sailor returns in the form of the drowned Phlebas, whose sea-change is presented at an important point in the poem. Phlebas's death by water marks the release from the earthly inferno of Sections I-III and anticipates the expression of hope and renewal (however qualified it may be) in "What the Thunder

Said." Though it predates his conversion, the poem dramatizes the process of death and spiritual rebirth that is expressed more directly in the Christian poetry of the late
Twenties. The voices in the "Ariel Poems" and "Ash Wednes-
day" have passed through the death of the old self. Like
Eliot's Magi, they speak as Christian pilgrims who have re-
nounced the fires of earthly desire for the fires of spiritual
purgation. But prior to his conversion, Eliot could not affirm
the transcendent reality that offered him the one possibility
of death and renewal. Therefore, like the Sibyl in the epigraph to "The Waste Land," who longs for the death that is
denied to her, he remained imprisoned in the temporal order
from which he wished to be delivered. The early personae,
who are disaffected with the conventional world but remain
trapped within it, reveal the plight of Eliot the man. Until
the season of faith arrived, the poetry manifested the conflict
between the desire for release from earthly despair and the
inability to affirm the only possible source of redemption.

CONCLUSION
The New Criticism and Beyond

Throughout this book I have explored the modern tendency to think in terms of "surfaces" and "depths," focusing particularly on the opposition between conceptual abstraction and concrete sensation. These terms have been used to conduct an investigation that might be extended well beyond the limits of this study. They inform the works of many writers of the early twentieth century, and Chapters III and IV merely suggest the kind of work to be done with Yeats, Stevens, and Williams, as well as the novelists of the period. In many respects these terms are still central to the human sciences, philosophy, and literature of our own day. It is a short leap from Saussure to Levi-Strauss, or from Nietzsche to Derrida, and when the current controversy passes, it will be easier to trace the line from Modernist to post-structuralist poetics. In these concluding pages I will look briefly beyond the early twentieth century, and consider the relationship of Modernist poetics to some subsequent developments in literary theory. The primary focus is Anglo-American New Criticism, the direct descendant of Modernism, but I will turn briefly at the end to more recent developments on the Continent, suggesting how we might begin to explore the affiliations between the two traditions.

From the Twenties to the Fifties Modernist poetics rose to ascendancy in the English-speaking world. It was aided by the development of New Criticism, which acclimated readers to the perplexing verse of Eliot and his contemporaries, and eventually revolutionized the study of literature. Inspired by the new poetry and by the criticism of Eliot, Richards, and Empson, New Criticism gained momentum during the Thirties, when the prevailing tradition of historical scholarship came under attack from many quarters. It was associated with a group of Southern writers—John Crowe Ransom, Allen Tate, Cleanth Brooks, Robert Penn Warren—and more loosely with Yvor Winters, R. P. Blackmur, and several others. The Southern New Critics were especially successful promoters of the new movement, and by the early Fifties they had transformed New Criticism into a new orthodoxy.

New Criticism was inspired by Modernism, and it turns on the same crucial distinction between instrumental abstraction and immediate experience. It should not surprise us, then, to find the New Critics employing the same set of argumentative strategies as Hulme, Pound, and Eliot. Like their predecessors, the New Critics emphasize both the recovery of immediate experience and the construction of forms that reorder experience. They, too, argue that poetry should maintain a tensional relationship between form and flux. The ideal New Critical poem, like Pound's ideogram and Eliot's "new wholes," holds together rational coherence and experiential complexity, the unity of conceptual form and the diversity of sensory particulars.

The appeal to immediate experience is especially crucial to the Southern New Critics. Ransom and his colleagues opposed the mentality produced by scientific (i.e., Northern) technology, and expressed the abstraction/experience dichotomy in terms of a distinction between scientific discourse, which is abstract and reductive, and poetic discourse, which is concrete and inclusive. Ransom, for instance, asserts that poetry must penetrate beneath instrumental abstractions to the reality of immediate experience "dense with its cross-relations and its interpenetrations of content":

I suggest that the differentia of poetry as discourse is an ontological one. It treats an order of existence, a grade of objectivity, which cannot be treated in scientific discourse. . . . We live in a world which must be distinguished from the world, or the worlds, for there are many of them, which we treat in our scientific discourses. They are its reduced, emasculated, and docile versions. Poetry intends to recover the denser and more refractory original world which we know loosely through our perceptions and memories. By this supposition it is a kind of knowledge which is radically or ontologically distinct.[1]

Ransom in effect reiterates Bergson's distinction between the abstract, quantitative knowledge of science and the concrete, qualitative knowledge of poetry, which brings us back to immediate experience.

However, the New Critics readily shift from this Bergsonian stance to its opposite, identifying poetry not with the experiential flux but with the intelligible forms that order it. Indeed, their emphasis on rational control over the sensory stream seems even more insistent than that of Pound and Eliot. Surveying more than two decades of literary innovation, some of the New Critics were appalled by the excesses of Modernist experimentation, which seemed to sacrifice logical clarity for experiential immediacy. Winters and Blackmur were especially concerned with this indifference to principles of order. In *Primitivism and Decadence* (1937), Winters condemns the fallacy of "expressive" form—the attempt to present the sensory stream directly by abandoning the mediation of the rational intellect. It is characteristic of modern poets, Winters asserts, "to express a state of uncertainty by uncertainty of expression; whereas the sound procedure would be to make a lucid and controlled statement regarding the condition of uncertainty, a procedure, however, which would require that the poet understand the nature of uncertainty, not that he be uncertain."[2] Similarly, in *The Double Agent* (1935) and *The Expense of Greatness* (1940), Blackmur argues that the modern artist should order his immediate impressions into intelligible form:

> Form, we might say, is the only sanity—the only principle of balanced response—possible to art: as lyric form will make the right nonsense into poetry; and to force your material—which is to say to condense, to elaborate, to foreshorten and give perspective and direction—into your chosen form so as to express it primarily by actualizing it—that is the minimum of your rational responsibility.[3]

For Blackmur as for Winters, form is closely allied to reason: it is the poet's "rational responsibility" to impose coherent principles of order on the otherwise chaotic flux of sensations.

This insistence on rational control notwithstanding, New Critics such as Blackmur position themselves between the extremes of form and flux. Blackmur urges the poet to resist not only the lapse into sensory chaos but also the lure of reductive ideologies. Other New Critics adopt the same position. Ransom wants to combine the logical "structure" of rational argument with the felt "texture" of concrete experience. Tate wishes to balance the "extensive" comprehension of the intellect and the "intensive" power of direct intuition. Winters, in a similar manner, seeks to unify thought and feeling, rational "denotation" and emotional "connotation." The ideal for all these critics is poetry that establishes order without violating our sense of experiential complexity. The New Critics, like Pound and Eliot before them, envision a tensional relationship between identity and difference, the stability of conceptual form and the free play of the sensory flux.

■

It has been years since anyone regarded Modernism as truly modern or New Criticism as really new. "The Waste Land" has receded into the postwar gloom of the Twenties, and John Donne has returned to the company of mere mortals. Signs of change began to appear in the late Fifties. Robert Lowell published his *Life Studies* in 1959, and his turn from the style of Ransom and Tate to a poetry of direct self-disclosure was a portent of things to come. A similar change was taking place in the academy, where interest in Romanticism started to revive and scholars began to challenge the Classicism of Eliot and the New Critics. At the same time critics grew tired of paradox and ambiguity, and began to look for new sources of inspiration, first from critics such as Northrop Frye and then from a succession of Continental sources, which provided new strategies for reading and awakened interest in disciplines once considered marginal to literary study. After several decades of dramatic change, New Criticism now seems as quaint as the tradition it replaced. In books with titles such as *After the New Criticism* it has become a point zero from which to measure the gains of the last twenty-five years. Many now look back upon their New Critical heritage as a kind of provincial embarrassment, a reminder of the humble origins they have left behind.

Nevertheless, there is a widespread suspicion, common to advocates and adversaries alike, that the new modes of criticism bear an unmistakable resemblance to the old. This suspicion is well-founded, and at least one reason for the continuity between past and present is that Modernist/New Critical poetics is related more closely than is ordinarily assumed to Nietzsche, Saussure, and other sources of contemporary theory. As we have seen, Modernist views of abstraction and experience proceed from the same inversion of Platonism that engaged Bergson and Nietzsche in the late nineteenth century and attracts post-structuralist critics today. Modernist poetics also anticipates the contemporary "decentering of the subject," which derives from the common turn-of-the-century assumption that ordinary consciousness is structured by forces of which it is unaware. In addition, we have seen that the Modernist emphasis on the "swift perception of relations" is tied to Nietzsche's approach to literal and figurative language, which plays an important role in post-structuralist criticism. In this respect as well as others, Modernist and New Critical poetics prepared the way for more recent developments in literary theory.

To be sure, the continuities between old and new should not be overstressed. While they address similar problems, Modernism and post-structuralism respond with different answers. The differences, however, are not as great as they may seem, and they are akin to those that distinguish James and Nietzsche (see Chapter I). The Modernists, like James, are less extreme in their challenge to the traditional hierarchy that privileges rational form over sensory flux. Their strategy is to employ constructs that hold together identity and difference, conceptual unity and sensory multiplicity. Like James, they hold that invention is tied to discovery: a new form projects a coherent system of relations that may disclose new aspects of reality itself. In response to the same issue, post-structuralism assumes the more radical posture of Nietzsche. It does not merely challenge but deliberately subverts the hierarchy that grants priority to form over flux. Instead of maintaining tensional relationships between opposing terms—abstraction/sensation, unity/multiplicity, identity/difference—it resolves the traditionally privileged term into a special case of the subordinate term. In other words, Modernist identity-in-difference yields to the free play of difference. The text that embodies a unified system of relations gives way to the "absolutely plural text," which is irreducible to a determinate network of relations and suggests ever new ways of ordering its various elements.[4] Interpretation no longer involves the unification of discordant or opposing elements but rather the "teasing out of warring forces of signification within the text itself."[5] Here again we find the long shadow of Nietzsche, whose vision of the cosmic flux as a ceaseless play of differences set the stage for contemporary criticism.

These differences between old and new are not to be minimized, and their implications for critical practice are significant. But the very terms that distinguish these two traditions suggest the affiliations between them. These terms are often identified with post-structuralism but rarely with Modernism and New Criticism; that is to say, we have failed to appreciate the conceptual foundations of the Anglo-American tradition, which is deeply involved with philosophical issues that are generally considered the exclusive province of the Continental tradition. Paradoxically, the failure to grasp this dimension of the Anglo-American heritage can be attributed in part to New Criticism itself, which aggravated the development of highly specialized and relatively isolated disciplines in English-speaking universities. The New Critics maintained that a poem is irreducible to the viewpoint of history, philosophy, or any other extrinsic discipline, and in their effort to preserve the integrity of the text, they encouraged the study of literary texts in isolation from their surrounding contexts. While students learned how to cope with ambiguity, paradox, and other complex features of Modernist verse, they were not encouraged to investigate the intellectual milieu in which these features rose to the fore. It has been the principal aim of this study to restore Modernist/New Critical poetics to this intellectual milieu, and thereby to discover why our poet-critics came to write and read the way they did. If, in addition, this essay has suggested that the tradition we are leaving behind should be treated as seriously as the tradition we are now assimilating, and that the two overlap in their assumptions and interests, then the other aim of this book would also be achieved.

NOTES

Introduction

1. T. S. Eliot, *The Use of Poetry and the Use of Criticism: Studies in the Relation of Criticism to Poetry in England* (London: Faber & Faber, 1964), p. 155.

Chapter I. *"This Invented World": Abstraction and Experience at the Turn of the Century*

1. William James, *The Meaning of Truth* (Cambridge, Mass.: Harvard University Press, 1975), p. 40.
2. Henri Bergson, *An Introduction to Metaphysics*, trans. T. E. Hulme (Indianapolis: Bobbs-Merrill, 1949), pp. 56-59.
3. Henri Poincaré, *Science and Hypothesis*, trans. W. J. Greenstreet (1905; rpt. New York: Dover, 1952), p. 50.
4. Ibid., p. 48.
5. William James, "The Sentiment of Rationality," in *Collected Essays and Reviews* (1920; rpt. New York: Russell & Russell, 1969), pp. 86-87.
6. Ernst Cassirer, *'Substance and Function' and 'Einstein's Theory of Relativity,'* trans. William Curtis Swabey and Marie Collins Swabey (1923; rpt. New York: Dover, 1953), p. 166.
7. Alfred North Whitehead, *Science and the Modern World* (New York: Macmillan, 1925), p. 75.
8. *Time and Free Will: An Essay on the Immediate Data of Consciousness*, trans. F. L. Pogson (1910; rpt. New York: Harper & Row, 1960), pp. 129-30. Page numbers for subsequent references appear in the text.
9. James published his critique of associationism five years prior to Bergson's. See "On Some Omissions of Introspective Psychology," *Mind*, o.s. 9 (1884), 1-26, parts of which were incorporated into

The Principles of Psychology (1890). Bergson claimed that he had not read James's article before he published *Time and Free Will* in 1889.

10. William James, *The Principles of Psychology* (Cambridge, Mass.: Harvard University Press, 1983), p. 233.

11. From another piece on memory, "The Soul and the Body," in *Mind-Energy*, trans. H. Wildon Carr (New York: Henry Holt, 1920), p. 71.

12. *An Introduction to Metaphysics*, pp. 38-39.

13. Ibid., p. 51.

14. F. H. Bradley, *Collected Essays*, 2 vols. (1935; rpt. Westport, Conn.: Greenwood Press, 1970), 1:209.

15. *Appearance and Reality: A Metaphysical Essay*, 2nd ed. (London: Oxford University Press, 1969), p. 141. Page numbers for subsequent references appear in the text.

16. *The Meaning of Truth*, p. 3.

17. *Essays on Truth and Reality* (Oxford: Clarendon Press, 1914), p. 123.

18. Friedrich Nietzsche, *The Will to Power*, trans. Walter Kaufmann and R. J. Hollingdale (New York: Vintage, 1968), p. 307. Page numbers for subsequent references appear in the text.

19. *The Gay Science*, trans. Walter Kaufmann (New York: Vintage, 1974), p. 242; *Beyond Good and Evil: Prelude to a Philosophy of the Future*, trans. Walter Kaufmann (New York: Vintage, 1966), pp. 136 and 205; *The Will to Power*, p. 326.

20. *The Letters of William James*, ed. Henry James, 2 vols. (Boston: Atlantic Monthly Press, 1920), 1:147-48.

21. See Vernon Lee, *Vital Lies: Studies of Some Varieties of Recent Obscurantism*, 2 vols. (London: John Lane, 1912), which begins with an attack on James's "will to believe" as a summons to believe a "vital lie." The author took the expression "vital lie" from Ibsen's *The Wild Duck*:

> RELLING: I'm fostering the vital lie in him.
> GREGERS: Vital lie? Is that what you said?
> RELLING: Yes—I said vital lie—for illusion,
>   you know, is *the* stimulating principle.

22. *The Meaning of Truth*, p. 6.

23. *The Will to Believe and Other Essays in Popular Philosophy* (Cambridge, Mass.: Harvard University Press, 1979), p. 84.

24. See *The Principles of Psychology*, pp. 916ff.

Chapter II. Elements of the New Poetics

1. Pound attended Hulme's lectures and his Tuesday night salon, where he was introduced to A. R. Orage, editor of the *New Age*, for which he began writing in November 1911. In October 1912, he appended five of Hulme's poems, "The Complete Poetical Works of T. E. Hulme," to his own *Ripostes*. But years later, after Hulme had posthumously acquired considerable fame, Pound declared that Hulme's impact on the Modernist movement was highly overestimated. See "This Hulme Business," *Townsman* 2 (Jan. 1939), 15, reprinted in Hugh Kenner, *The Poetry of Ezra Pound* (Norfolk, Conn.: New Directions, 1951), app. 1, pp. 307-309. Most scholars now share the view that Pound expresses in the *Townsman*.

2. Henri Bergson, "The Soul and the Body," in *Mind-Energy*, pp. 56-57.

3. On Nietzsche's influence upon Hulme and other members of Orage's circle, see David S. Thatcher, *Nietzsche in England, 1890-1914: The Growth of a Reputation* (Toronto: University of Toronto Press, 1970), ch. 8. Hulme's distinction between "visual" and "counter" language is also similar to Gourmont's distinction between the "visual" and the "emotive" mind (see pp. 83-84).

4. Remy de Gourmont, *Selected Writings*, trans. Glenn S. Burne (Ann Arbor: University of Michigan Press, 1966), p. 115.

5. Henri Bergson, "The Perception of Change," in *An Introduction to Metaphysics: The Creative Mind*, trans. Mabelle L. Andison (Totowa, N.J.: Littlefield, Adams, 1965), p. 136. This book is a translation of *Le Pensée et le mouvant* (1934), a collection of Bergson's essays. The translator's title comes from one of the essays, "An Introduction to Metaphysics," which was translated by T. E. Hulme and published as a separate volume. See Chapter I, notes 2, 12, and 13.

6. I. A. Richards, *Practical Criticism: A Study of Literary Judgment* (New York: Harcourt Brace, 1956), pp. 231-32.

7. *Italics mine.* I. A. Richards, *Principles of Literary Criticism* (New York: Harcourt Brace, 1961), pp. 251-52.

8. "The Approach to Paris . . . V," *New Age*, n.s. 13 (2 Oct. 1913), 662.

9. Ibid.

10. "Breviora," *Little Review* 5 (Oct. 1918), 23.

11. Maurice Merleau-Ponty, *Phenomenology of Perception*, trans. Colin Smith (London: Routledge & Kegan Paul, 1962), pp. vii and xviii.

12. *Gaudier-Brzeska: A Memoir* (New York: New Directions, 1974), p. 89.

13. From Pound's translations of Guido's "Sonetto VII." See David Anderson, *Pound's Cavalcanti: An Edition of the Translations, Notes, and Essays* (Princeton: Princeton University Press, 1983), p. 46.

14. "Eeldrop and Appleplex . . . II," *Little Review* 4 (Sept. 1917), 19.

15. "Studies in Contemporary Criticism," *Egoist* 5 (Oct. 1918), 114.

16. *Philosophy and Truth: Selections from Nietzsche's Notebooks of the Early 1870's*, ed. and trans. Daniel Breazeale (Atlantic Highlands, N.J.: Humanities Press, 1979), p. 83. Compare Nietzsche's approach to the generic concept with that of Ernst Cassirer (*Substance and Function*, ch. 1).

17. Ibid., p. 85.

18. Ibid., pp. 84 and 86.

19. Ibid., pp. 88-89.

20. See, for example, *The New Nietzsche: Contemporary Styles of Interpretation*, ed. David B. Allison (New York: Delta, 1977), which includes pieces by Heidegger, Derrida, Deleuze, and others who have revived interest in Nietzsche.

21. See "The Perfect Critic" (SW, 1-16), especially pp. 13-14. Eliot also acknowledges Gourmont's influence in his 1928 Preface to *The Sacred Wood* (SW, viii).

22. Gourmont, *Selected Writings*, pp. 167-68.

23. *L'Idéalisme* (Paris: Mercure de France, 1893), p. 24.

24. Ibid., p. 53.

25. On historical semantics see Michel Bréal, *Semantics: Studies in the Science of Meaning*, trans. Mrs. Henry Cust (1900; rpt. New York: Dover, 1964).

26. *Le Problème du style*, 6th ed. (Paris: Mercure de France, 1907), p. 93. My translation. Burne's *Selected Writings* includes only a fraction of Gourmont's book.

27. *Esthétique de la langue française* (Paris: Mercure de France, 1955), p. 197.

28. *Selected Writings*, p. 115.

29. Ibid., pp. 137-38.

30. Ibid., pp. 11-12.
31. *The Selected Letters of Ezra Pound, 1907-1941*, ed. D. D. Paige (New York: New Directions, 1971), p. 61.
32. *ABC of Reading* (New York: New Directions, 1960), pp. 21-22.
33. *The Cantos of Ezra Pound* (New York: New Directions, 1972), p. 13.
34. Guy Davenport, *Cities on Hills: A Study of I-XXX of Ezra Pound's "Cantos"* (Ann Arbor: UMI Research Press, 1983), pp. 127-31.
35. From one of Pound's footnotes to his edition of *The Chinese Written Character*, p. 23.
36. *Gaudier-Brzeska*, pp. 88-89.
37. "Pastiche. The Regional . . . XV," *New Age*, n.s. 25 (30 Oct. 1919), 448; *ABC of Reading*, p. 84.
38. See Black, *Models and Metaphors*, especially ch. 3, "Metaphor," and ch. 13, "Models and Archetypes."
39. *Substance and Function*, p. 322.
40. *Gaudier-Brzeska*, p. 89.
41. "Affirmations . . . II. Vorticism," *New Age*, n.s. 16 (14 Jan. 1915), 278.
42. Cited in Richard Sieburth, *Instigations: Ezra Pound and Remy de Gourmont* (Cambridge, Mass.: Harvard University Press, 1978), p. 63.
43. "The Noh and the Image," *Egoist* 4 (Aug. 1917), 103.
44. "Dramatis Personae," *Criterion* 1 (Apr. 1923), 305.
45. "Eeldrop and Appleplex . . . II," *Little Review* 4 (Sept. 1917), 19.
46. "London Letter," *Dial* 71 (Aug. 1921), 216.
47. Cleanth Brooks and Robert Penn Warren, *Understanding Poetry* (New York: Henry Holt, 1938), pp. iv and ix.
48. See Paul Ricoeur, *Hermeneutics and the Human Sciences: Essays on Language, Action and Interpretation*, ed. John B. Thompson (Cambridge: Cambridge University Press, 1981), pp. 182-93.

Chapter III. Ezra Pound: Cultural Memory and the Visionary Imagination

1. "Swinburne versus Biographers," *Poetry* 11 (Mar. 1918), 327.
2. "The Revolt of Intelligence . . . IX," *New Age*, n.s. 26 (11 Mar. 1920), 301.

3. C. H. Douglas, *Economic Democracy* (New York: Harcourt Brace, 1920), pp. 10-11.
4. Ibid., p. 16.
5. *Ezra Pound and Music: The Complete Criticism*, ed. R. Murray Schafer (New York: New Directions, 1977), p. 98.
6. Pound's Postscript to *The Natural Philosophy of Love*, by Remy de Gourmont, trans. Ezra Pound (New York: Collier, 1961), pp. 149-58.
7. "Pastiche. The Regional . . . XIV," *New Age*, n.s. 25 (23 Oct. 1919), 432.
8. *End to Torment: A Memoir of Ezra Pound by H.D.*, ed. Norman Holmes Pearson and Michael King (New York: New Directions, 1979), p. 71.
9. "Affirmations . . . II. Vorticism," *New Age*, n.s. 16 (14 Jan. 1915), 277.
10. *Jefferson and/or Mussolini* (New York: Liveright, 1970), p. 128.
11. *Ezra Pound and Music*, p. 130.
12. "From the Editor of 'The Exile,' " *Poetry* 30 (June 1927), 175.
13. "Raphaelite Latin," *Book News Monthly* 25 (Sept. 1906), 33.
14. See Fred Robinson, " 'The Might of the North': Pound's Anglo-Saxon Studies and 'The Seafarer,' " *Yale Review* 71 (Jan. 1982), 199-224.
15. Wilhelm Dilthey, *Descriptive Psychology and Historical Understanding*, trans. Richard M. Zaner and Kenneth L. Heiges (The Hague: Martinus Nijhoff, 1977), pp. 134-35.
16. Ibid., p. 80.
17. Ibid., p. 143.
18. "Status Rerum," *Poetry* 1 (Jan. 1913), 125.
19. Friedrich Nietzsche, *Untimely Meditations*, trans. R. J. Hollingdale (Cambridge: Cambridge University Press, 1983), p. 101.
20. Ibid., p. 94.
21. "Raphaelite Latin," *Book News Monthly* 25 (Sept. 1906), 33; "M. Antonius Flamininus and John Keats: A Kinship in Genius," *Book News Monthly* 26 (Feb. 1908), 447.
22. "Desideria," *Exile* 3 (Spring 1928), 108.

Chapter IV. Incarnate Words: Eliot's Early Career

1. *The Use of Poetry and the Use of Criticism*, p. 155.
2. On Eliot's career as a philosopher, see *Knowledge and Experience*

in the Philosophy of F. H. Bradley (New York: Farrar, Straus, 1964), which contains his doctoral dissertation of 1916 as well as two articles published during the same year in the *Monist*. Additional material may be found in Eliot's early reviews for the *Monist* and other philosophical journals, and in a collection of his student essays at the Houghton Library. There is also some valuable information in Harry T. Costello, *Josiah Royce's Seminar, 1913-1914: As Recorded in the Notebooks of Harry T. Costello*, ed. Grover Smith (New Brunswick, N.J.: Rutgers University Press, 1963).

3. From a syllabus that Eliot prepared for a university extension course in 1916. See Ronald Schuchard, "T. S. Eliot as an Extension Lecturer, 1916-1919," *Review of English Studies*, n.s. 25 (May 1974), 165.

4. Quoted from some unpublished essays on the theory of objects, probably written at Oxford. These essays are part of a collection of Eliot's student papers at the Houghton Library.

5. It was Bertrand Russell who introduced Meinong's works to the English-speaking world. See his "Meinong's Theory of Complexes and Assumptions," *Mind*, n.s. 13 (1904), 204-19, 336-54, 509-24. Roderick Chisholm traces the resurgence of realism in a collection that shows the affinities of the Austrian school of Brentano, Meinong, and Husserl to the Anglo-American movement launched by Moore and Russell. See *Realism and the Background of Phenomenology*, ed. Roderick Chisholm (Glencoe, Ill.: Free Press, 1960).

6. Costello, *Josiah Royce's Seminar*, p. 176.

7. Edmund Husserl, *Logische Untersuchungen*, 2 vols., 2nd ed. (Tübingen: Max Niemeyer, 1980), 2: pt. 1, 25. For the English version, see *Logical Investigations*, trans. J. N. Findlay, 2 vols. (London: Routledge & Kegan Paul, 1970), 1:271. Findlay uses the English expression "objective correlate" for several related German expressions that refer to the intentional object.

8. John M. Steadman wrote to *Notes and Queries* in 1958 that Eliot may have found the expression "objective correlative" in Husserl's works. But he went on to say that Husserl and Eliot have nothing in common. See "Eliot and Husserl: The Origin of the 'Objective Correlative,' " *Notes and Queries*, n.s. 5 (June 1958), 261-62. For one of the few attempts to link Husserl and Eliot, see Jitendra Kumar, "Consciousness and Its Correlates: Eliot and Husserl,"

Philosophy and Phenomenological Research 28 (Mar. 1968), 332-52.

9. In October 1914, Eliot wrote to the chairman of the Harvard philosophy department, James Haughton Woods, "I have been plugging away at Husserl, and find it terribly hard, but very interesting; and I like very much what I think I understand of it." The letter is part of a private collection on deposit in Special Collections at the Regenstein Library of the University of Chicago.

10. "Reflections on Contemporary Poetry . . . I," *Egoist* 4 (Sept. 1917), 118.

11. Eliot finds this tendency not only in the poetry of the nineteenth century but also in certain works of fiction. The novels of Balzac, for instance, display an "atmosphere thrown upon reality direct from the personality of the writer." See "Beyle and Balzac," *Athenæum* 4648 (30 May 1919), 392.

12. Here Eliot is elaborating Bradley's argument that imaginary ideas are not "free floating" but always qualify a real world. See Bradley's "On Floating Ideas and the Imaginary," in *Essays on Truth and Reality*, pp. 28-64.

13. See Ricoeur, *Hermeneutics and the Human Sciences*, pp. 43-62 and 145-64. Michael Ermarth, who has examined many of Dilthey's unpublished writings, supports Ricoeur's interpretation. See his *Wilhelm Dilthey: The Critique of Historical Reason* (Chicago: University of Chicago Press, 1978), pp. 255-56.

14. Both Ricoeur and Ermarth see Husserl as an important influence on Dilthey. Nevertheless, they maintain that Dilthey's thinking changed gradually, and signs of change had begun to appear before he read Husserl.

15. "Observations," *Egoist* 5 (May 1918), 70.

16. "Contemporary English Prose," *Vanity Fair* 20 (July 1923), 51.

17. "Reflections on Contemporary Poetry . . . III," *Egoist* 4 (Nov. 1917), 151.

18. "A Sceptical Patrician," *Athenæum* 4647 (23 May 1919), 362.

19. "In Memory of Henry James," *Egoist* 5 (Jan. 1918), 2.

20. Ibid.

21. "A Prediction in Regard to Three English Authors," *Vanity Fair* 21 (Feb. 1924), 29.

22. "Kipling Redivivus," *Athenæum* 4645 (9 May 1919), 298.

23. "Eeldrop and Appleplex . . . II," *Little Review* 4 (Sept. 1917), 19.

24. "Eeldrop and Appleplex . . . I," *Little Review* 4 (May 1917), 10.
25. Quoted from Eliot's draft, which includes the line, "The ivory men make company between us." See *"The Waste Land": A Facsimile and Transcript of the Original Drafts*, ed. Valerie Eliot (New York: Harcourt Brace, 1971), p. 13 and Mrs. Eliot's note, p. 126.
26. The translation is by Charles S. Singleton, *The Divine Comedy: Inferno*, 2 vols. (Princeton: Princeton University Press, 1970), 1:287.
27. Many years later Eliot wrote to Kristian Smidt, in response to the latter's inquiry, "I am prepared to assert that the 'you' in THE LOVE SONG is merely some friend or companion, presumably of the male sex, whom the speaker is at that moment addressing, and that it has no emotional content whatever." From Kristian Smidt, *Poetry and Belief in the Work of T. S. Eliot* (London: Routledge & Kegan Paul, 1961), p. 85. Nevertheless, we should remember Eliot's warning that the writer as an interpreter of his own work is in no better position than the reader.
28. Quoted from the original version of this essay, "Whether Rostand Had Something About Him," *Athenæum* 4656 (25 July 1919), 665.
29. "Artists and Men of Genius," *Athenæum* 4704 (25 June 1920), 842.
30. "London Letter," *Dial* 71 (Aug. 1921), 214.

Conclusion. The New Criticism and Beyond

1. John Crowe Ransom, *The New Criticism* (Norfolk, Conn.: New Directions, 1941), pp. 73 and 281.
2. Winters, *In Defense of Reason*, p. 87.
3. R. P. Blackmur, *The Expense of Greatness* (New York: Arrow Editions, 1940), p. 190.
4. Barthes, *S/Z*, pp. 3-16. As Barthes himself indicates, the idea of the "absolutely plural text" is derived from Nietzsche's vision of a sensory flux irreducible to determinate order and open to an endless series of new interpretations.
5. Barbara Johnson, *The Critical Difference: Essays in the Contemporary Rhetoric of Reading* (Baltimore: The Johns Hopkins University Press, 1980), p. 5.

INDEX

abstraction/experience in philosophy and poetics, 5-8, 10, 12-21, 44-49, 50-51, 113, 209-212, 213-14. *See also* entries for abstraction/experience under Bergson, Bradley, Eliot, James, Nietzsche, Pound; conscious/unconscious; form/flux; hypostasis; identity/difference; Platonism; surfaces/depths

abstraction in art: and Modernist poetics, 50-51, 60-62, 102-113; as related to formalism, 104-105, 111-12. *See also* entries for abstraction in art under Eliot, Hulme, Pound; Cubism, Vorticism

Agassiz, Louis, 121

Althusser, Louis, 112n

ambiguity, as poetic technique, *see* Modernist poetry and poetics, techniques of

Anderson, David, 219 n.13

Aristotle, 73, 80, 164, 169n

Auerbach, Erich, 139n

autonomy of the text in Modernist and New Critical poetics, 3, 51, 71-72, 104, 111-13, 171-73, 215. *See also* Eliot, critique of subjectivism in; personality and impersonality

Avenarius, Richard, 18

Babbitt, Irving, 161

Balzac, Honoré de, 223 n. 11

Barthes, Roland, 102-103n, 224 n. 4

Beardsley, Aubrey, 108

Bennett, Tony, 112n

Bergson, Henri, 21-31; abstraction/experience (*durée réelle*) in, 5-6, 7, 14, 19-20, 21-31, 32, 36-37, 45-48, 52-56, 61, 63, 158; on art, 29, 30-31, 48, 52-56, 61, 64, 211; on associationist psychology, 24-27, 216-17 n. 9; and Bradley, James, Nietzsche, 7, 21, 24, 26, 27n, 32, 35, 36-38, 45-48, 63, 158; and Dilthey, 27n, 138, on *élan vital*, 30n, 37-38; and French voluntarism, 18, 41; and Freud, 6, 21; and inversion of Platonism, 8, 29-30, 37-38, 213; and Kant, 7-8, 14; on language, 20, 21, 22, 28-29, 30, 54-57; on memory, 24, 28, 134; and Modernist/New Critical poetics, 3, 9, 30-31, 46-49, 50, 52-57, 61, 62, 64, 72, 134, 138, 211, 213; space/time in, 23-24, 26-27, 55-56, 61; vital/mechanical processes in, 23, 26-27, 30n, 36, 37-38, 45

Bernstein, Michael André, 122n

Black, Max, 60n, 220 n. 38

Blackmur, R. P., 210, 211-12

Bloom, Harold, 72n

Bolyai, Farkas, 15

Bosanquet, Bernard, 165

Botticelli, 131, 151-52

228 · INDEX

60, 62, 218 n. 1
—on images and Imagism, 66, 92-
95, 103, 126n, 152
—memory/imagination, tradition/in-
novation in, 69n, 114, 133-54;
Canto I, 152-53; compared to
Bergson on recollection, 134;
compared to Dilthey's hermeneutics, 138-40, 141; compared to
Nietzsche's critique of historicism, 134, 135-36, 141-48; ideogrammic method, 91-92, 121;
mediated by translation, adaptation, and imitation, 114, 125,
133-34, 140-41, 145, 152-53; the
palimpsest, 90-91, 135, 138; relation to Browning, 137, 138, 149-
50; response to historicism, 135-
36, 138, 142-45; Ur-Cantos, 148-
52
—on metaphor (explanatory, interpretative, ornamental), 44, 59-60,
73-75, 85-86, 90n, 92-95, 100-
101, 128-34, 153-54
—personal expression/impersonal
presentation in, 46-47, 62-63, 65-
69, 73, 148-52
—and poetic tradition: Browning,
116, 122-23, 137, 138, 149-50;
Catullus, 91, 135, 140; Dante,
74, 92, 123-24, 132, 140, 151n;
English poetry, 66, 117, 125,
138, 153; Greek poetry, 68, 91,
93, 105-106, 123, 131-32, 137,
145, 152-53; Ovid, 137; Provençal
and Tuscan poetry, 68, 92-93,
125, 146; Renaissance poetry,
137, 140, 145, 152-53
—visionary forms in: abstract art,
66, 93, 105-108, 126, 129, 151-
52; donative, germinal, or conceiving mind, 105-107, 125-28;
the gods, 68, 93-94, 106, 118,
124, 129-32, 135, 137, 146 and n,

150; haiku, 67-68, 93, 129; interpretive metaphor, 90n, 92-95,
128-32, 133; myth and metamorphosis, 93, 129, 131-32, 146n
Works
—*ABC of Reading*, 88, 94, 106,
116-17, 121
—*Cantos*: aims and motifs of,
106n, 125, 131-32, 138, 148;
structure of, 115, 122-24, 128,
129, 132-33, 138, 152; techniques in, 91-92, 115, 121-22;
Ur-Cantos, 122-23, 124, 132,
135, 148-52; Canto I, 131,
139n, 152-53; Canto III, 130;
Canto IV, 91; Canto VII, 143-
44; Cantos VIII-XI (Malatesta),
147-48; Canto XIII, 119, 127;
Canto XIV, 142; Canto XXIII,
131-32, 140; Canto XXV, 127,
131-32; Canto LXXIV, 121
—*Collected Early Poems*: "Capilupus Sends Greeting to Grotus," 125; "Epilogue," 137;
"Histrion," 139-40, 149; "Plo-
tinus," 149; "San Vio. June,"
137
—*Ezra Pound and Music*, 124,
135
—*Gaudier-Brzeska*, 67, 93, 106
—*Guide to Kulchur*, 118, 123,
136
—"Hilda's Book," 124-25
—*Jefferson and/or Mussolini*, 127
—*Letters*, 86, 123, 124, 152
—*Literary Essays*: "Cavalcanti,"
68, 92; "Dr. Williams' Posi-
tion," 132; "Lionel Johnson,"
66; "Notes on Elizabethan
Classicists," 153; "The Prose
Tradition in Verse," 136; "A
Retrospect," 117, 126n; "The
Serious Artist," 66, 67; "Trans-
lators of Greek: Early Transla-

Library of Congress Cataloging in Publication Data

Schwartz, Sanford, 1948-
  The matrix of modernism.

  Includes index.
  1. American poetry—20th century—History and
criticism.   2. Modernism (Literature)   3. Pound,
Ezra, 1885-1972—Criticism and interpretation.
4. Eliot, T. S. (Thomas Stearns), 1888-1965—
Criticism and interpretation.   5. English poetry—
20th century—History and criticism.   6. Philosophy,
Modern—20th century.   7. Philosophy in literature.
I. Title.
PS324.S38   1985   811'.52'091   85-42702
ISBN 0-691-06651-5 (alk. paper)

Sanford Schwartz is Associate Professor of English at the
University of Chicago.